HIT-GIRL
IN COLOMBIA

MARK MILLAR
WRITER

RICARDO LOPEZ ORTIZ
ARTIST

SUNNY GHO
COLORIST

AMY REEDER
COVERS

RACHAEL FULTON
EDITOR

MELINA MIKULIC
LETTERING, DESIGN AND PRODUCTION

HIT-GIRL and KICK-ASS created by MARK MILLAR and JOHN ROMITA JR

IMAGE COMICS, INC.

Robert Kirkman — Chief Operating Officer
Erik Larsen — Chief Financial Officer
Todd McFarlane — President
Marc Silvestri — Chief Executive Officer
Jim Valentino — Vice President

Eric Stephenson — Publisher / Chief Creative Officer
Corey Hart — Director of Sales
Jeff Boison — Director of Publishing Planning & Book Trade Sales
Chris Ross — Director of Digital Sales
Jeff Stang — Director of Specialty Sales
Kat Salazar — Director of PR & Marketing
Drew Gill — Art Director
Heather Doornink — Production Director
Nicole Lapalme — Controller

IMAGECOMICS.COM

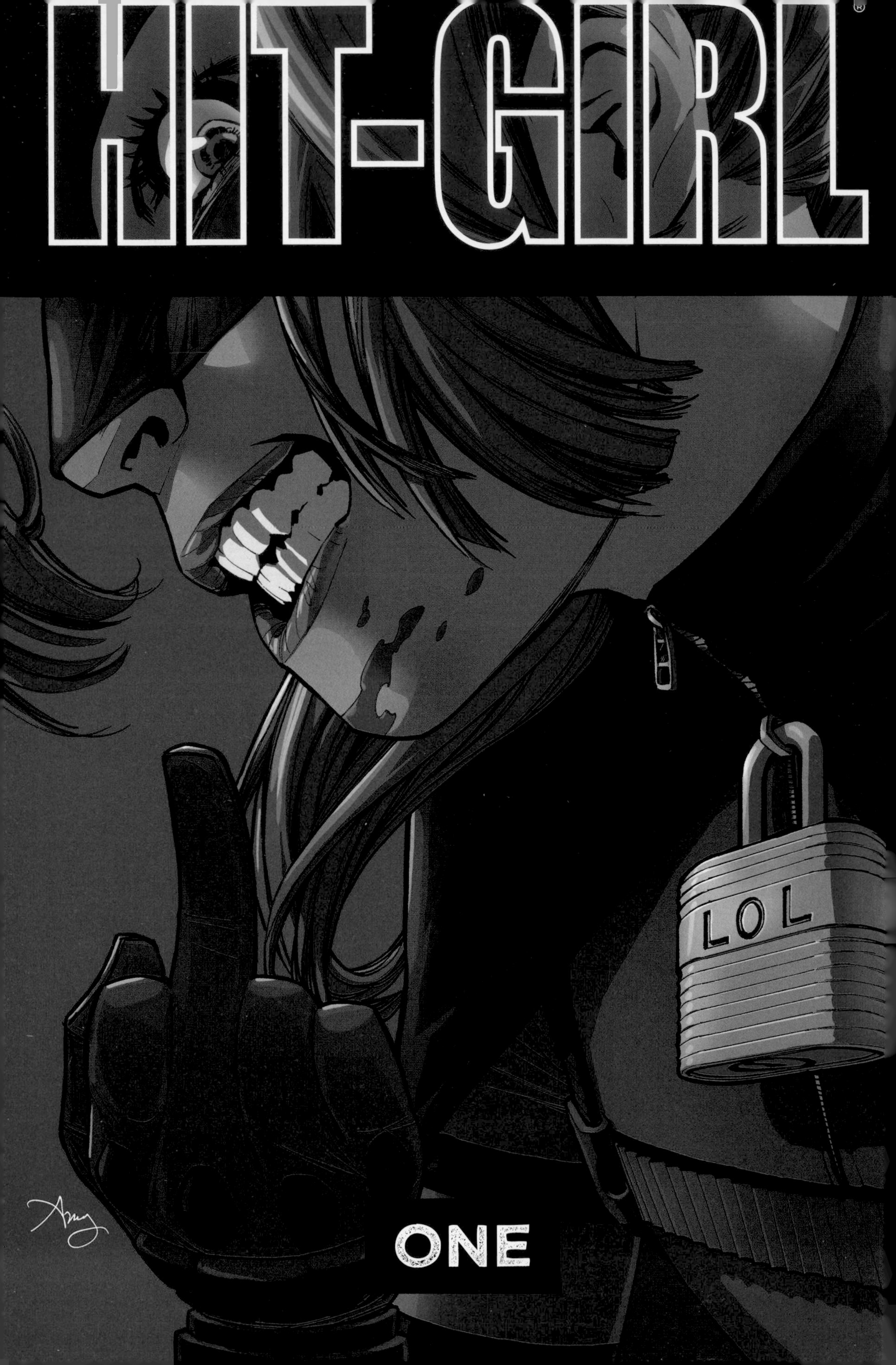
HIT-GIRL®
LOL
ONE

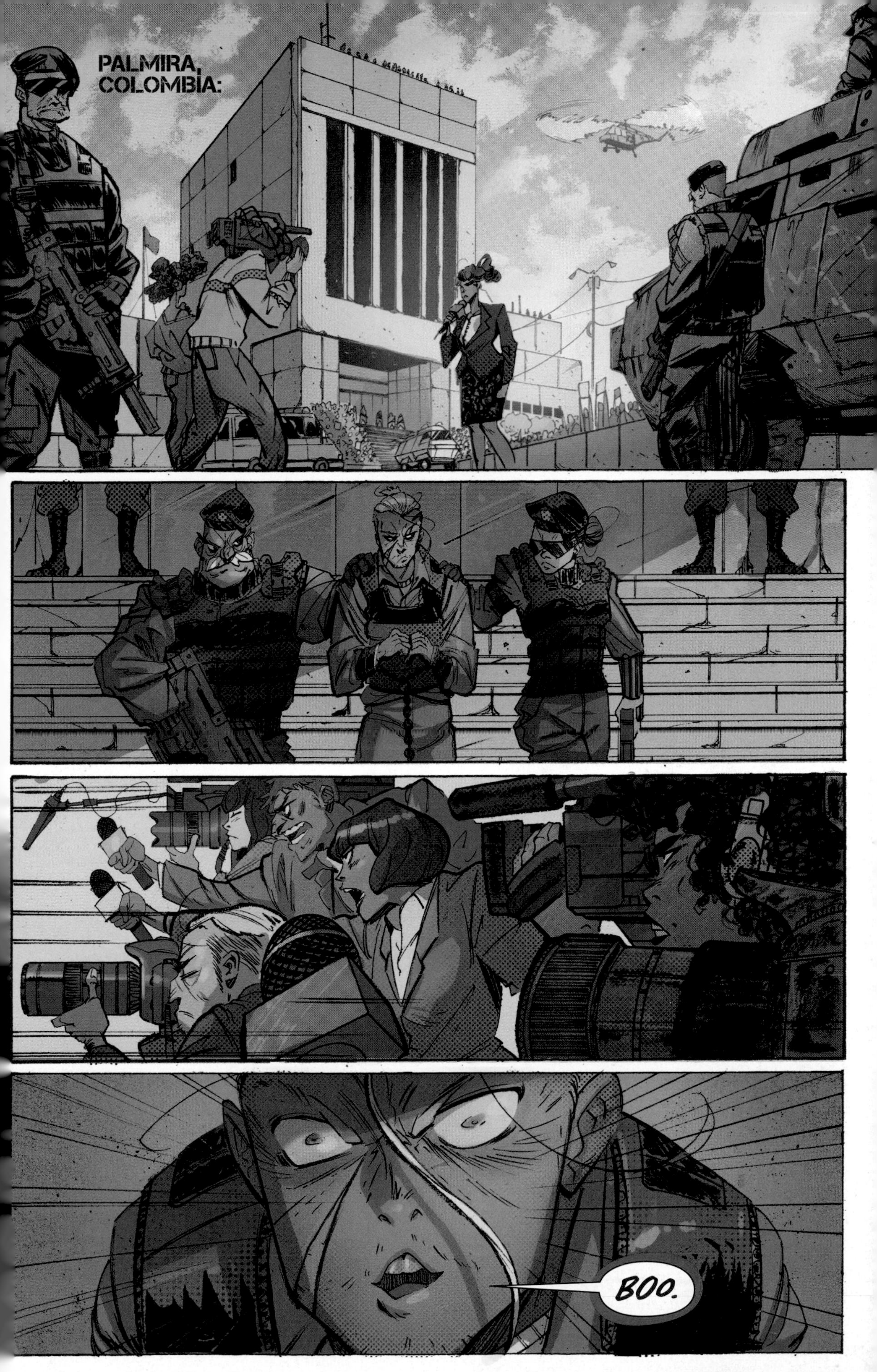
PALMIRA, COLOMBIA:
BOO.

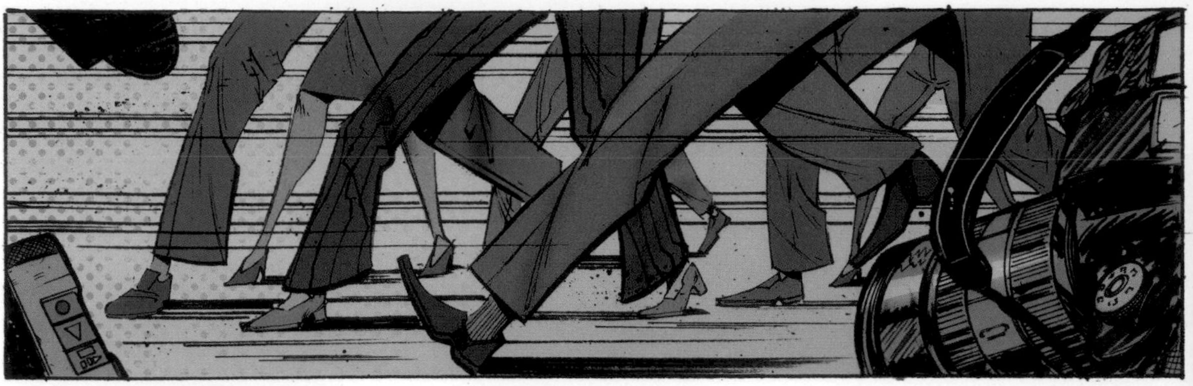

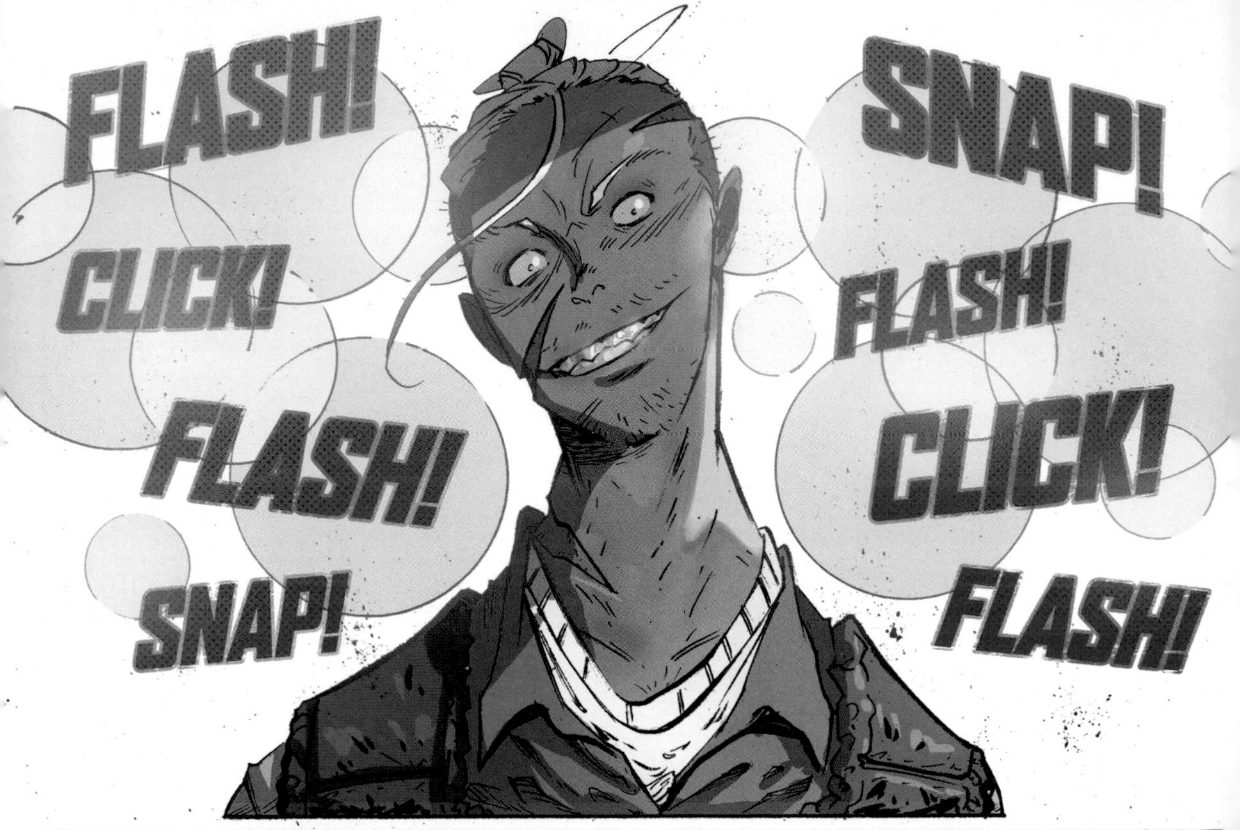
FLASH!
CLICK!
FLASH!
SNAP!
SNAP!
FLASH!
CLICK!
FLASH!

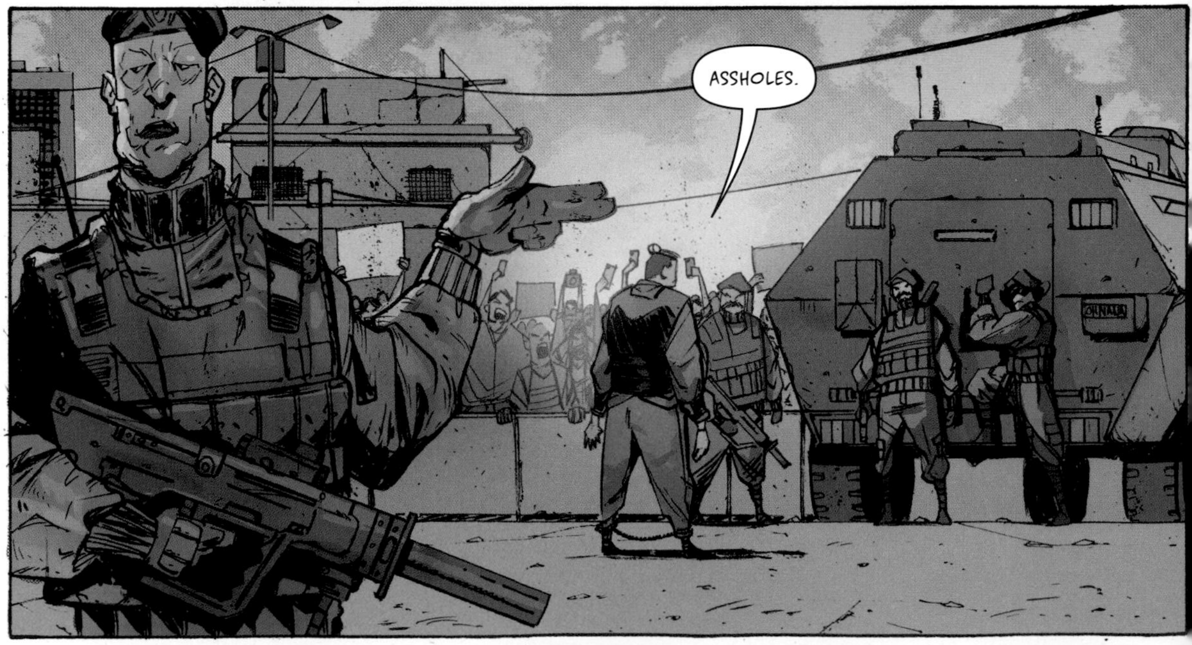
ASSHOLES.

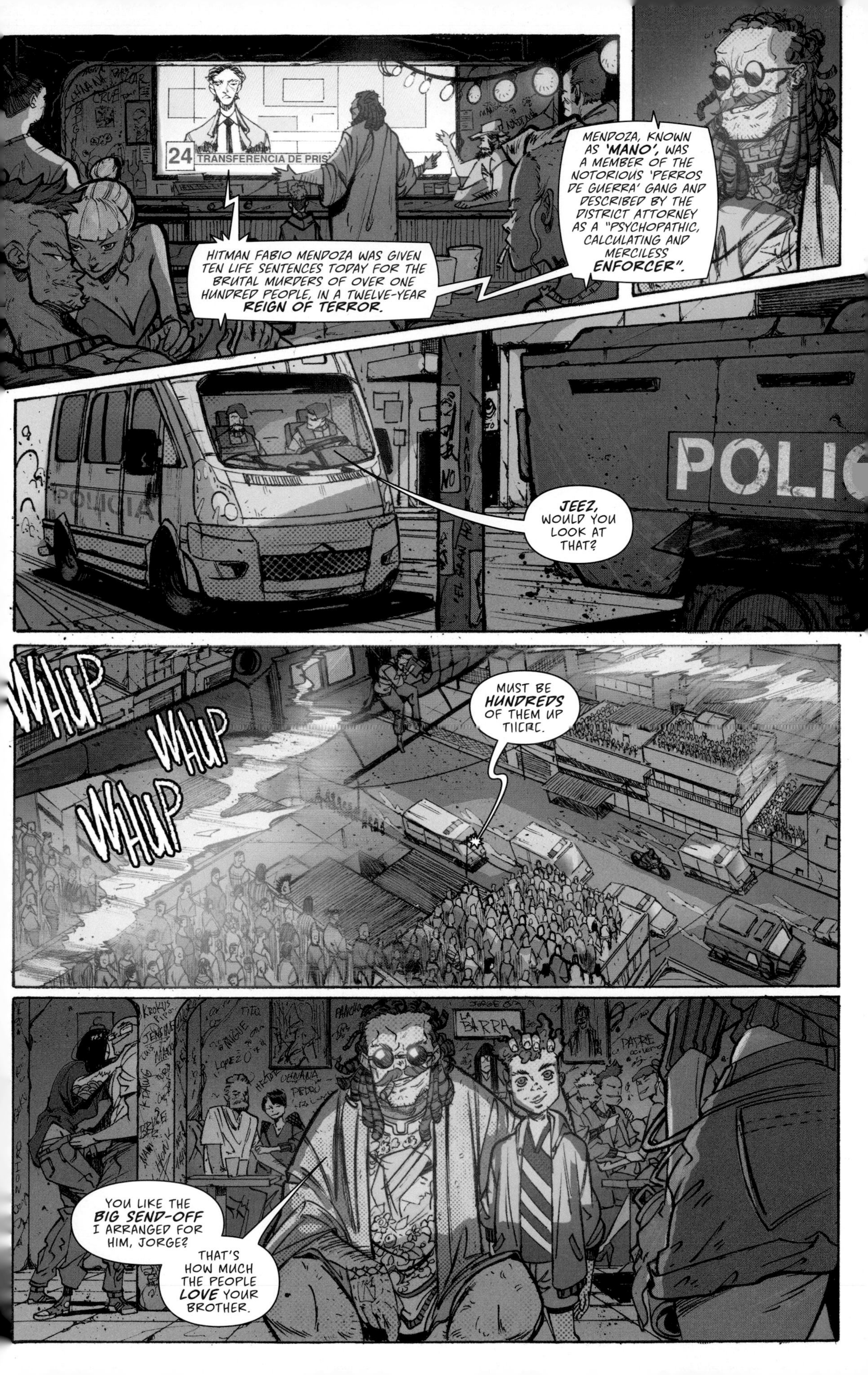
24 TRANSFERENCIA DE PRIS
HITMAN FABIO MENDOZA WAS GIVEN TEN LIFE SENTENCES TODAY FOR THE BRUTAL MURDERS OF OVER ONE HUNDRED PEOPLE, IN A TWELVE-YEAR REIGN OF TERROR.
MENDOZA, KNOWN AS 'MANO', WAS A MEMBER OF THE NOTORIOUS 'PERROS DE GUERRA' GANG AND DESCRIBED BY THE DISTRICT ATTORNEY AS A "PSYCHOPATHIC, CALCULATING AND MERCILESS ENFORCER".
POLICIA
POLIC
JEEZ, WOULD YOU LOOK AT THAT?
WHUP
WHUP
WHUP
MUST BE HUNDREDS OF THEM UP THERE.
LA BARRA
YOU LIKE THE BIG SEND-OFF I ARRANGED FOR HIM, JORGE?
THAT'S HOW MUCH THE PEOPLE LOVE YOUR BROTHER.

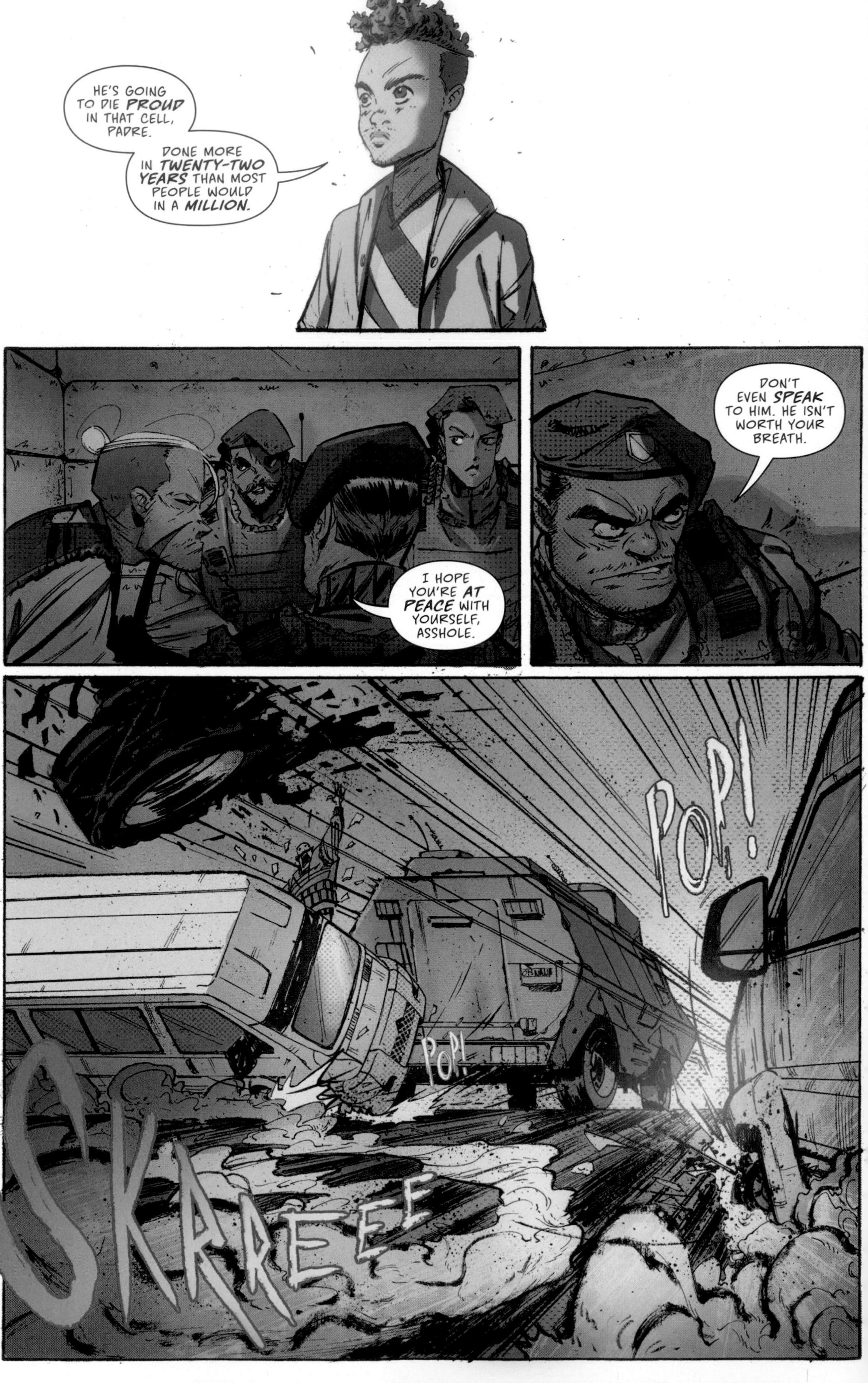
HE'S GOING TO DIE PROUD IN THAT CELL, PADRE.
DONE MORE IN TWENTY-TWO YEARS THAN MOST PEOPLE WOULD IN A MILLION.
I HOPE YOU'RE AT PEACE WITH YOURSELF, ASSHOLE.
DON'T EVEN SPEAK TO HIM. HE ISN'T WORTH YOUR BREATH.
POP!
POP!
SKRREEEE

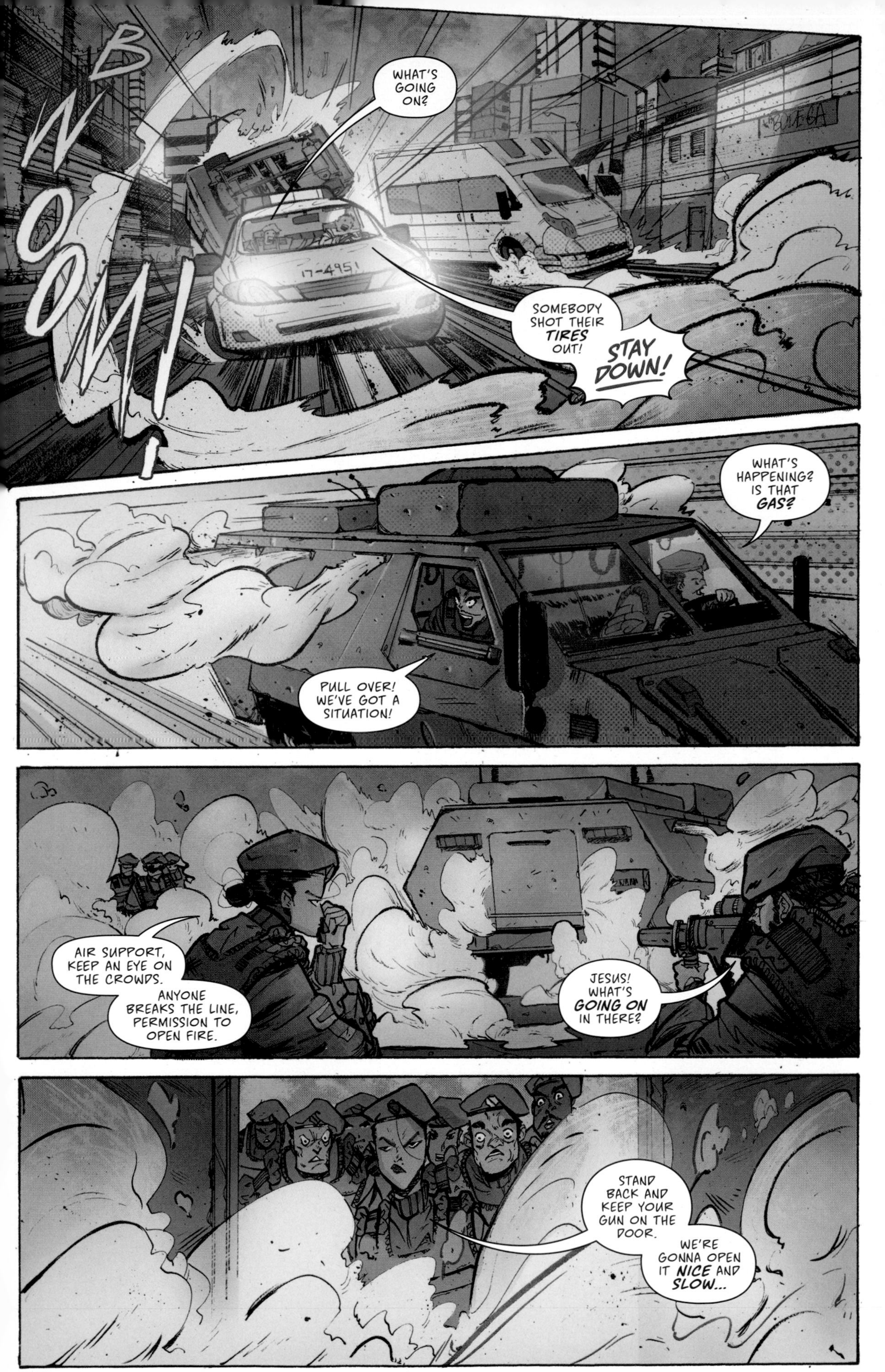BWOOM!
WHAT'S GOING ON?
SOMEBODY SHOT THEIR TIRES OUT!
STAY DOWN!
WHAT'S HAPPENING? IS THAT GAS?
PULL OVER! WE'VE GOT A SITUATION!
AIR SUPPORT, KEEP AN EYE ON THE CROWDS.
ANYONE BREAKS THE LINE, PERMISSION TO OPEN FIRE.
JESUS! WHAT'S GOING ON IN THERE?
STAND BACK AND KEEP YOUR GUN ON THE DOOR.
WE'RE GONNA OPEN IT NICE AND SLOW...

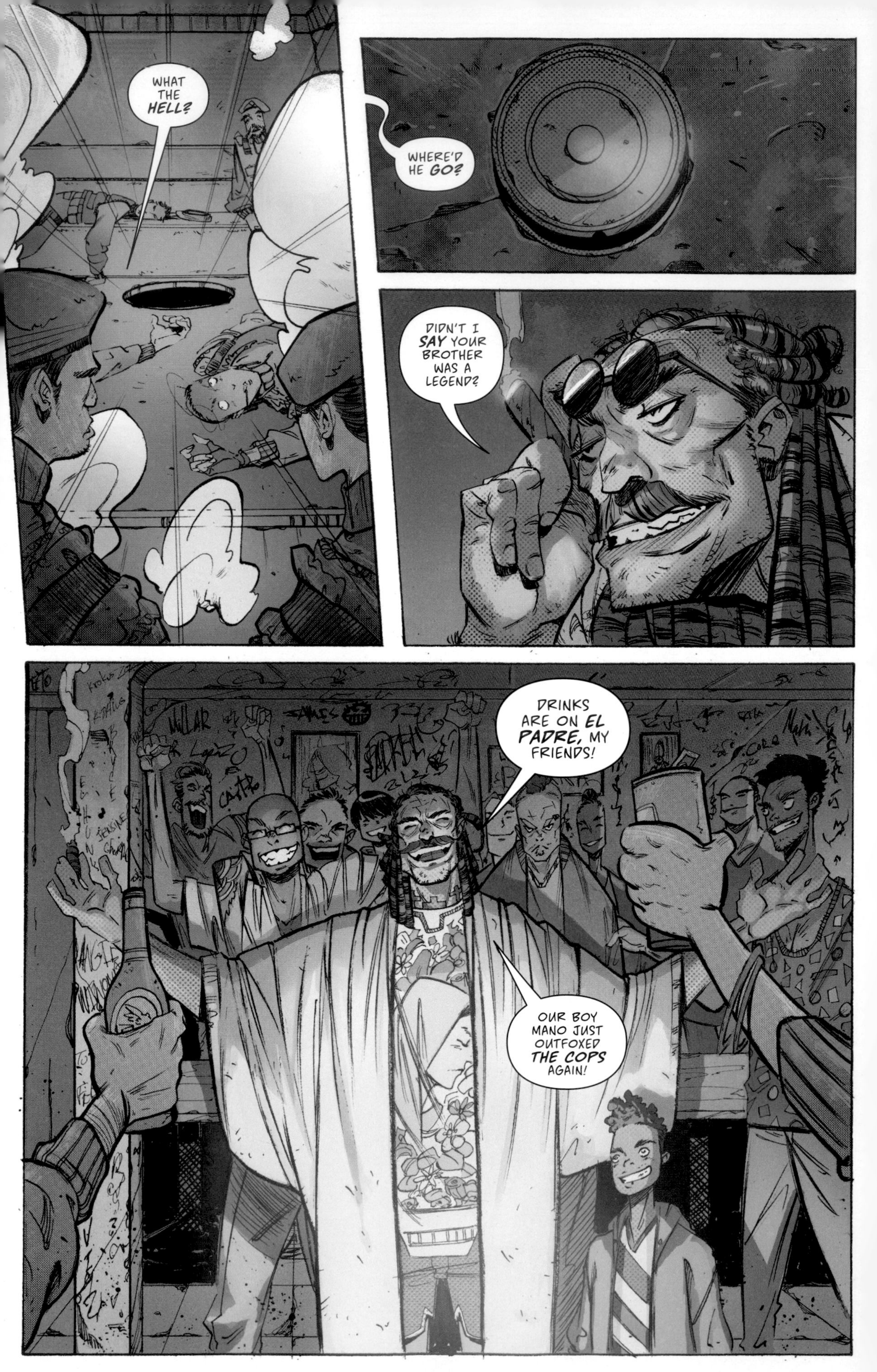
WHAT THE HELL?
WHERE'D HE GO?
DIDN'T I SAY YOUR BROTHER WAS A LEGEND?
DRINKS ARE ON EL PADRE, MY FRIENDS!
OUR BOY MANO JUST OUTFOXED THE COPS AGAIN!

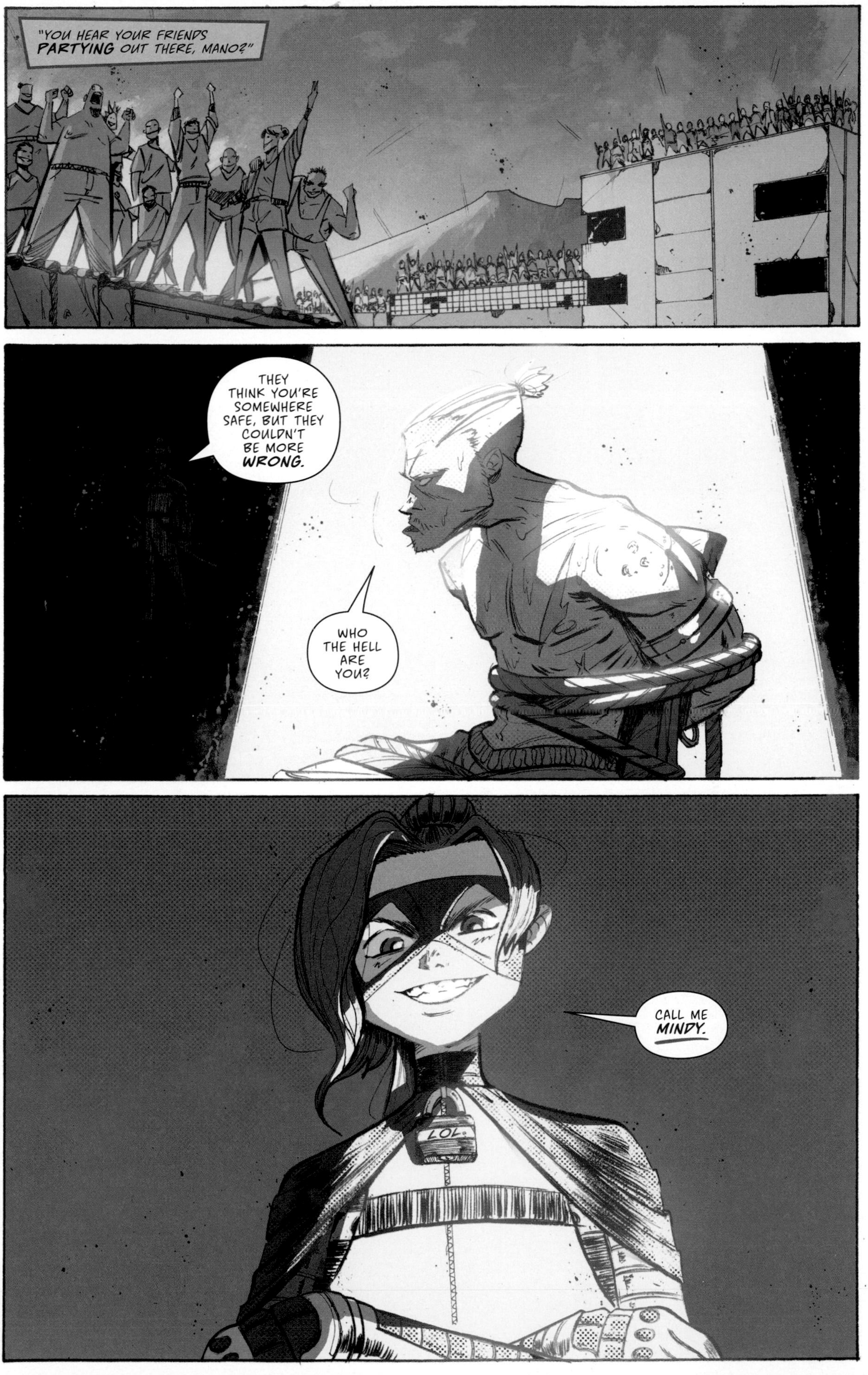
"YOU HEAR YOUR FRIENDS PARTYING OUT THERE, MANO?"
THEY THINK YOU'RE SOMEWHERE SAFE, BUT THEY COULDN'T BE MORE WRONG.
WHO THE HELL ARE YOU?
CALL ME MINDY.
LOL.

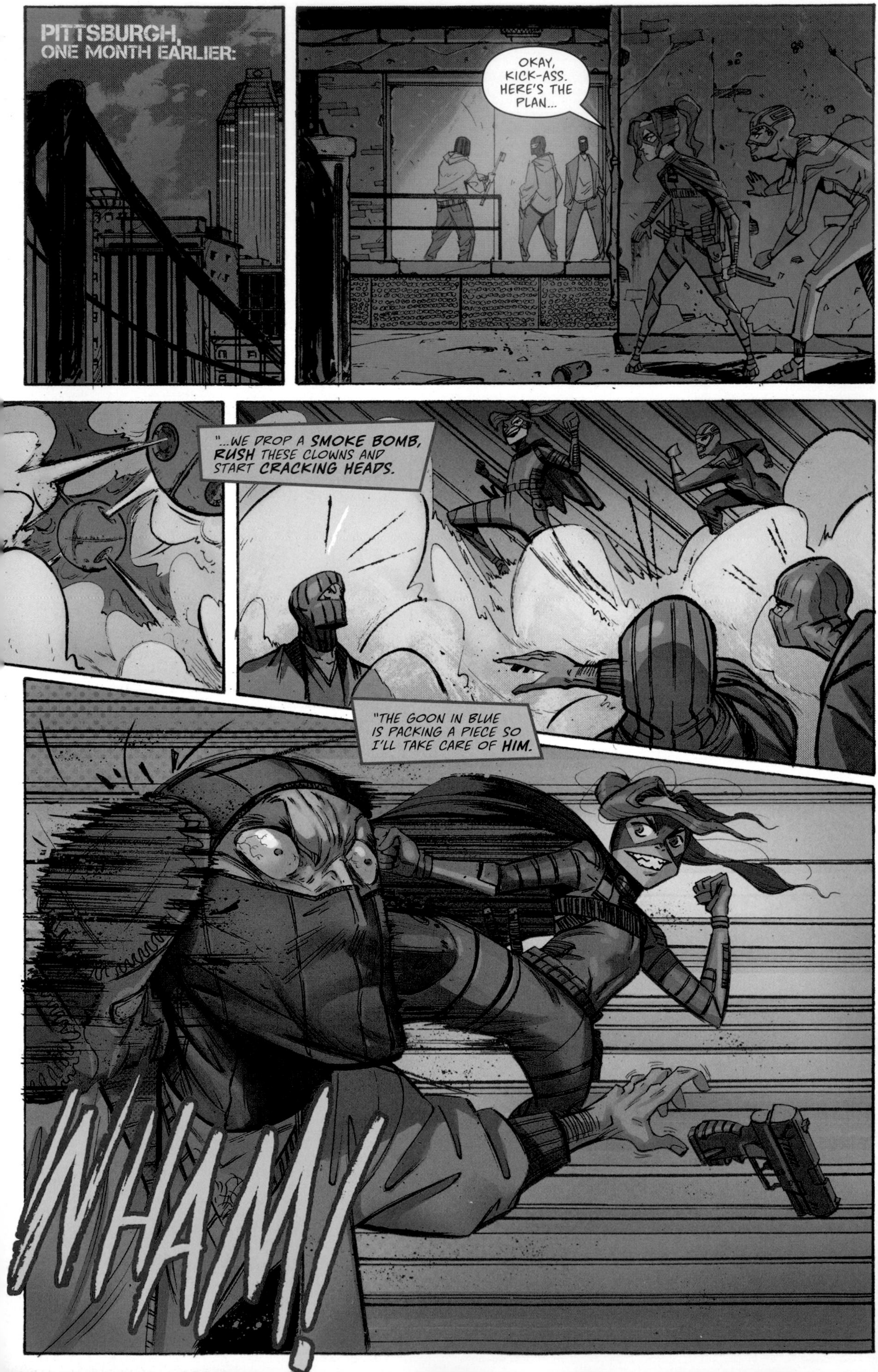
PITTSBURGH, ONE MONTH EARLIER:
OKAY, KICK-ASS. HERE'S THE PLAN...
"...WE DROP A SMOKE BOMB, RUSH THESE CLOWNS AND START CRACKING HEADS.
"THE GOON IN BLUE IS PACKING A PIECE SO I'LL TAKE CARE OF HIM.
WHAM!

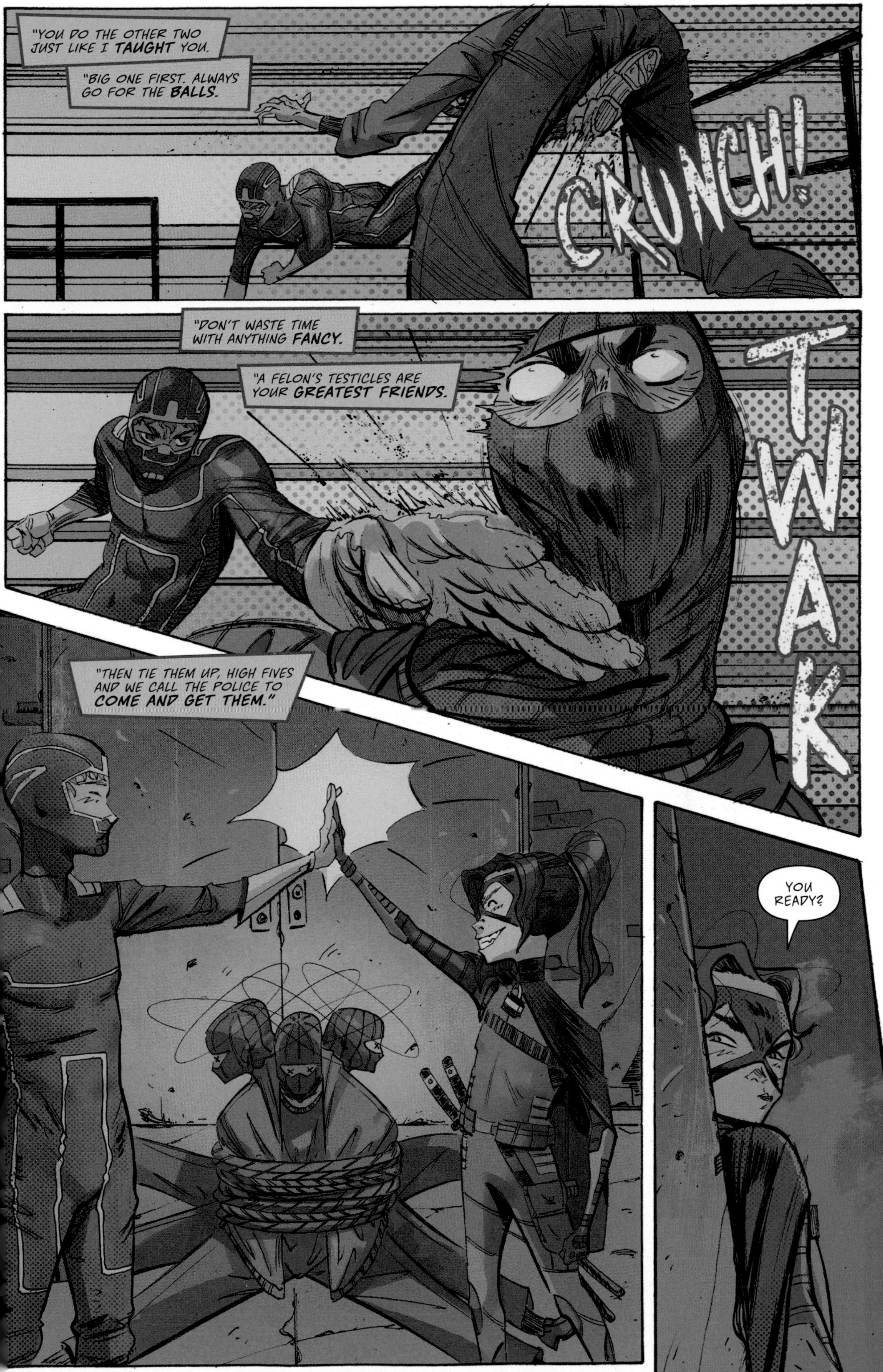
"YOU DO THE OTHER TWO JUST LIKE I TAUGHT YOU.
"BIG ONE FIRST. ALWAYS GO FOR THE BALLS.
CRUNCH!
"DON'T WASTE TIME WITH ANYTHING FANCY.
"A FELON'S TESTICLES ARE YOUR GREATEST FRIENDS.
TWAK
"THEN TIE THEM UP, HIGH FIVES AND WE CALL THE POLICE TO COME AND GET THEM."
YOU READY?

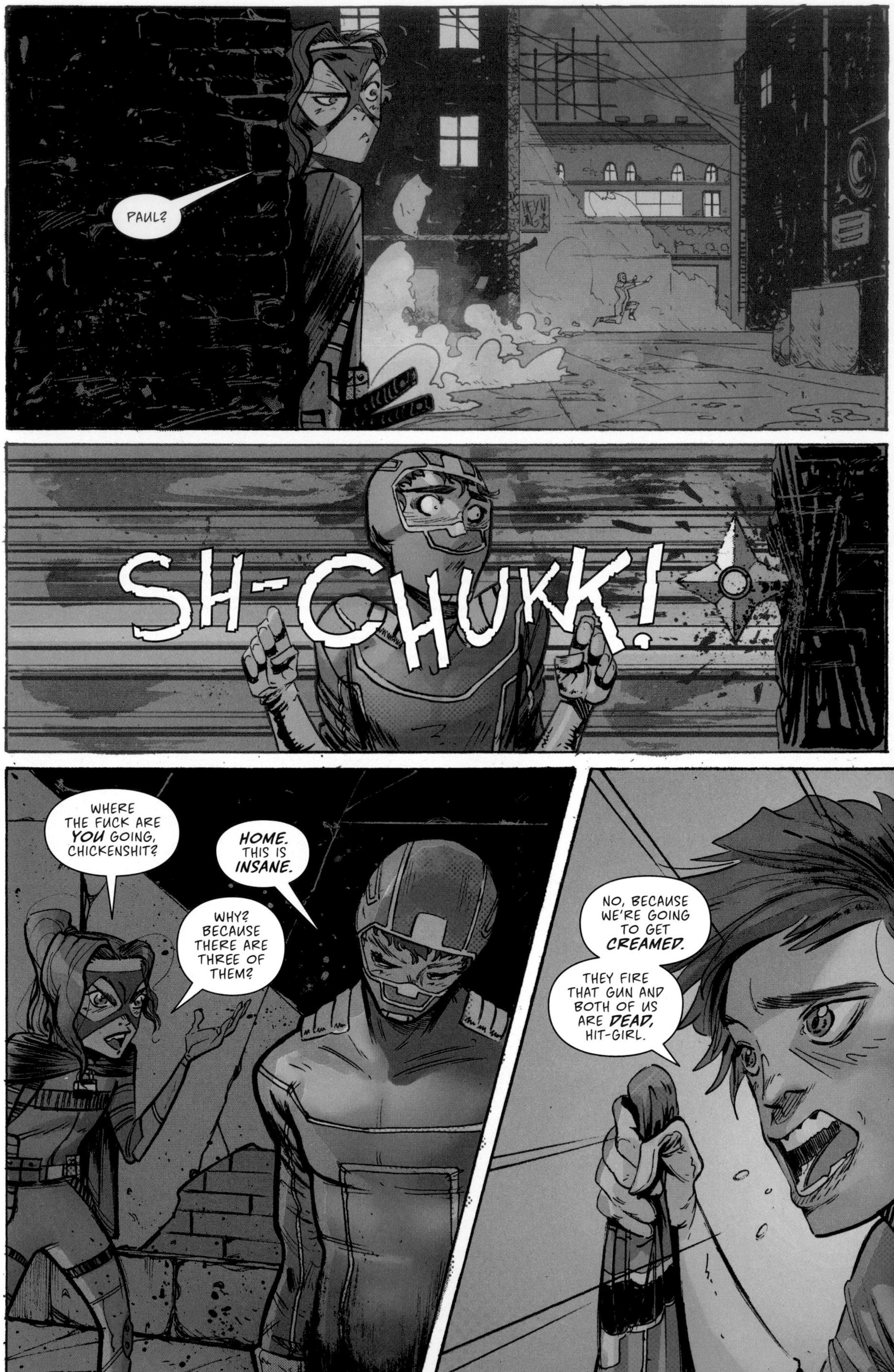
PAUL?
SH-CHUKK!
WHERE THE FUCK ARE YOU GOING, CHICKENSHIT?
HOME. THIS IS INSANE.
WHY? BECAUSE THERE ARE THREE OF THEM?
NO, BECAUSE WE'RE GOING TO GET CREAMED.
THEY FIRE THAT GUN AND BOTH OF US ARE DEAD, HIT-GIRL.

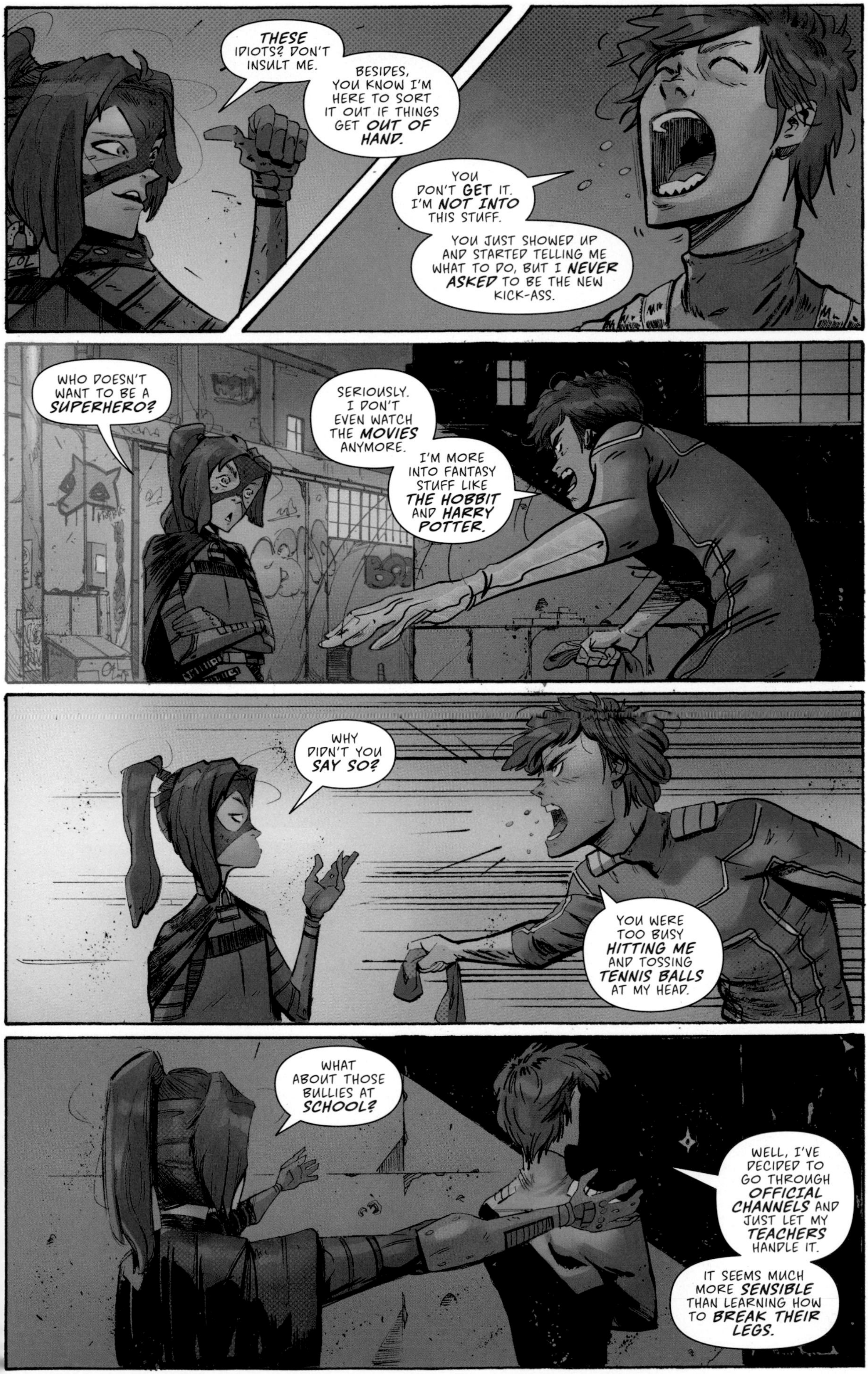

THESE IDIOTS? DON'T INSULT ME.
BESIDES, YOU KNOW I'M HERE TO SORT IT OUT IF THINGS GET OUT OF HAND.
YOU DON'T GET IT. I'M NOT INTO THIS STUFF.
YOU JUST SHOWED UP AND STARTED TELLING ME WHAT TO DO, BUT I NEVER ASKED TO BE THE NEW KICK-ASS.
WHO DOESN'T WANT TO BE A SUPERHERO?
SERIOUSLY. I DON'T EVEN WATCH THE MOVIES ANYMORE.
I'M MORE INTO FANTASY STUFF LIKE THE HOBBIT AND HARRY POTTER.
WHY DIDN'T YOU SAY SO?
YOU WERE TOO BUSY HITTING ME AND TOSSING TENNIS BALLS AT MY HEAD.
WHAT ABOUT THOSE BULLIES AT SCHOOL?
WELL, I'VE DECIDED TO GO THROUGH OFFICIAL CHANNELS AND JUST LET MY TEACHERS HANDLE IT.
IT SEEMS MUCH MORE SENSIBLE THAN LEARNING HOW TO BREAK THEIR LEGS.

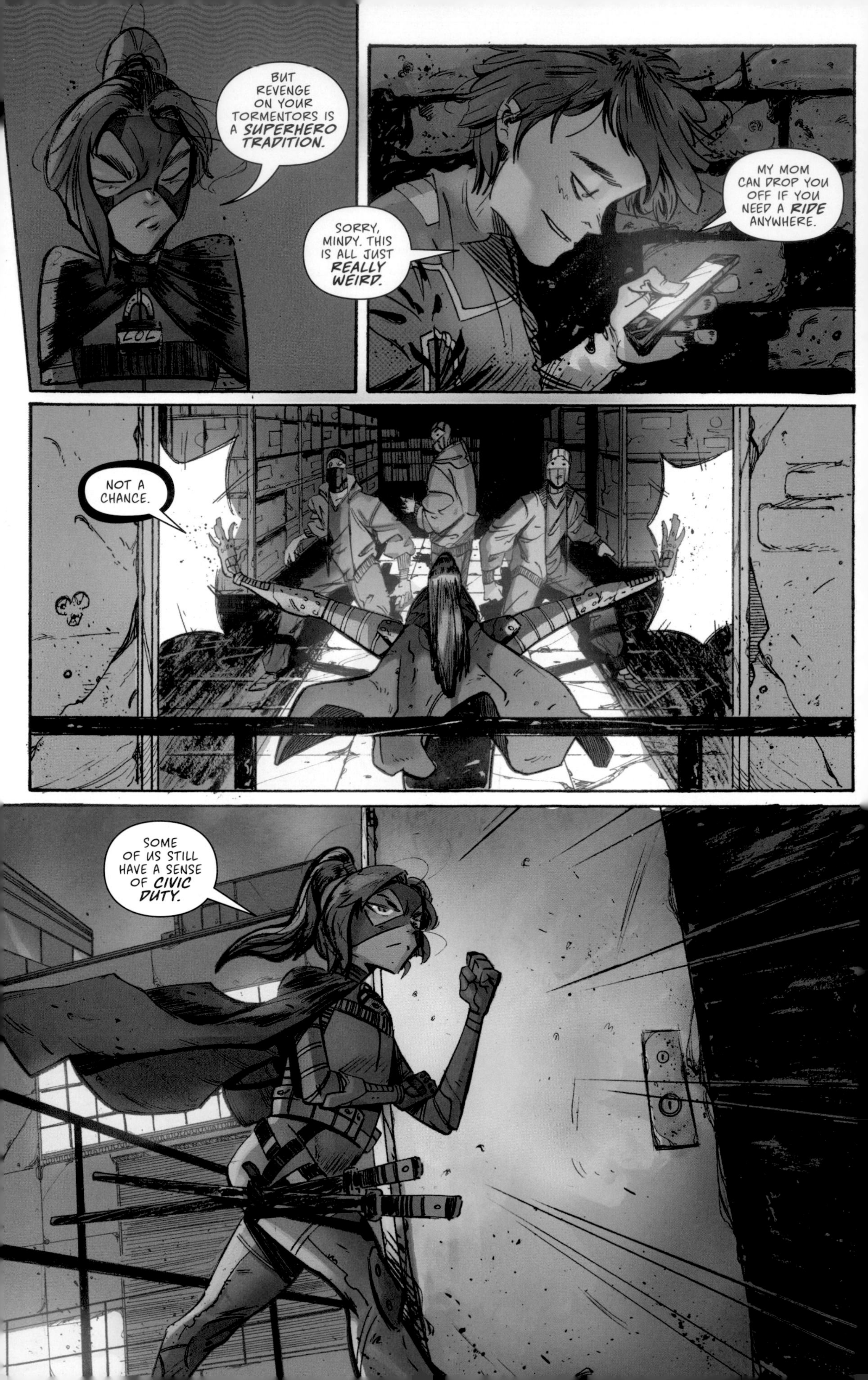

BUT REVENGE ON YOUR TORMENTORS IS A SUPERHERO TRADITION.
SORRY, MINDY. THIS IS ALL JUST REALLY WEIRD.
MY MOM CAN DROP YOU OFF IF YOU NEED A RIDE ANYWHERE.
NOT A CHANCE.
SOME OF US STILL HAVE A SENSE OF CIVIC DUTY.

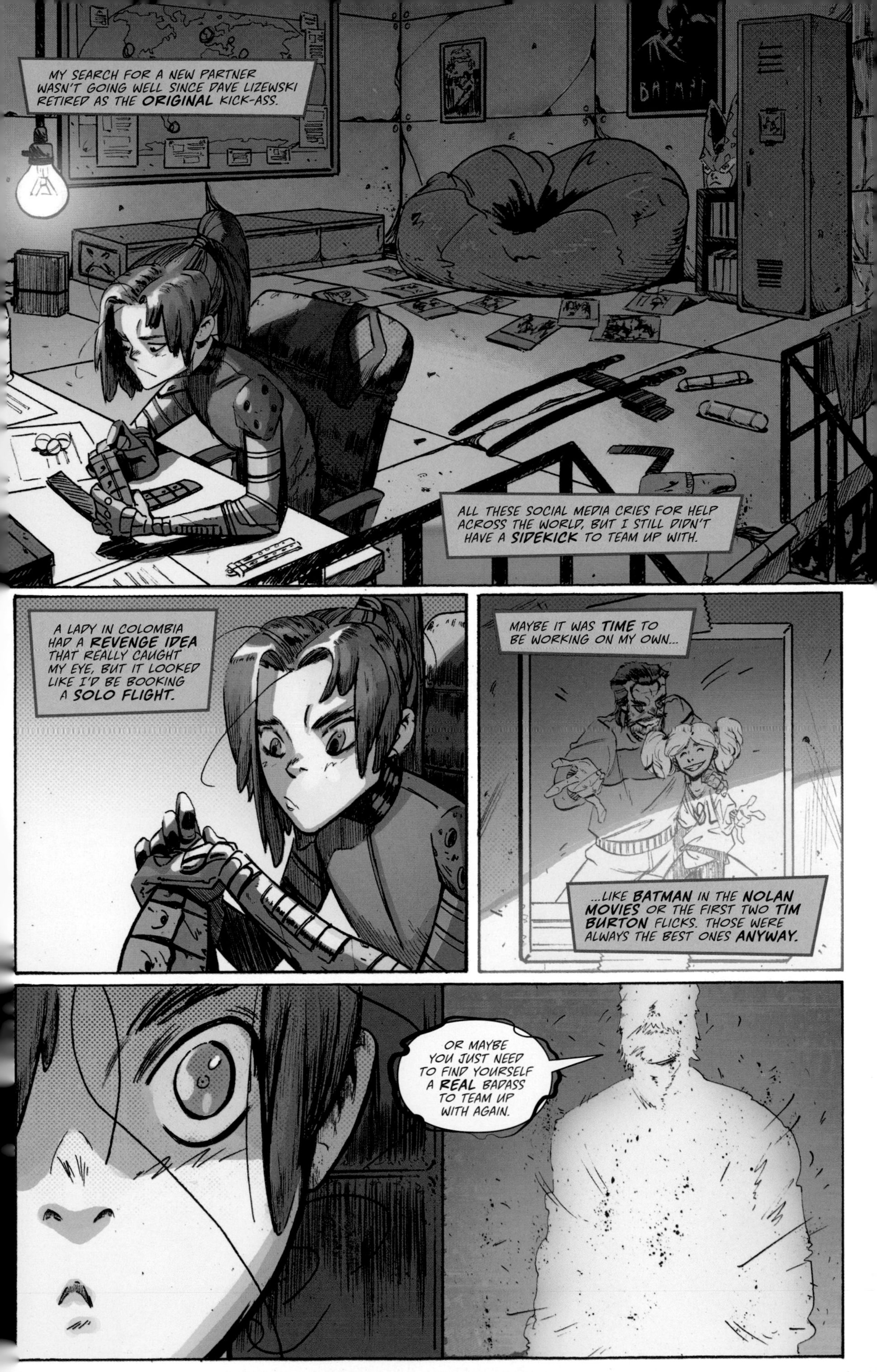
MY SEARCH FOR A NEW PARTNER WASN'T GOING WELL SINCE DAVE LIZEWSKI RETIRED AS THE ORIGINAL KICK-ASS.
BATMAN
ALL THESE SOCIAL MEDIA CRIES FOR HELP ACROSS THE WORLD, BUT I STILL DIDN'T HAVE A SIDEKICK TO TEAM UP WITH.
A LADY IN COLOMBIA HAD A REVENGE IDEA THAT REALLY CAUGHT MY EYE, BUT IT LOOKED LIKE I'D BE BOOKING A SOLO FLIGHT.
MAYBE IT WAS TIME TO BE WORKING ON MY OWN...
...LIKE BATMAN IN THE NOLAN MOVIES OR THE FIRST TWO TIM BURTON FLICKS. THOSE WERE ALWAYS THE BEST ONES ANYWAY.
OR MAYBE YOU JUST NEED TO FIND YOURSELF A REAL BADASS TO TEAM UP WITH AGAIN.

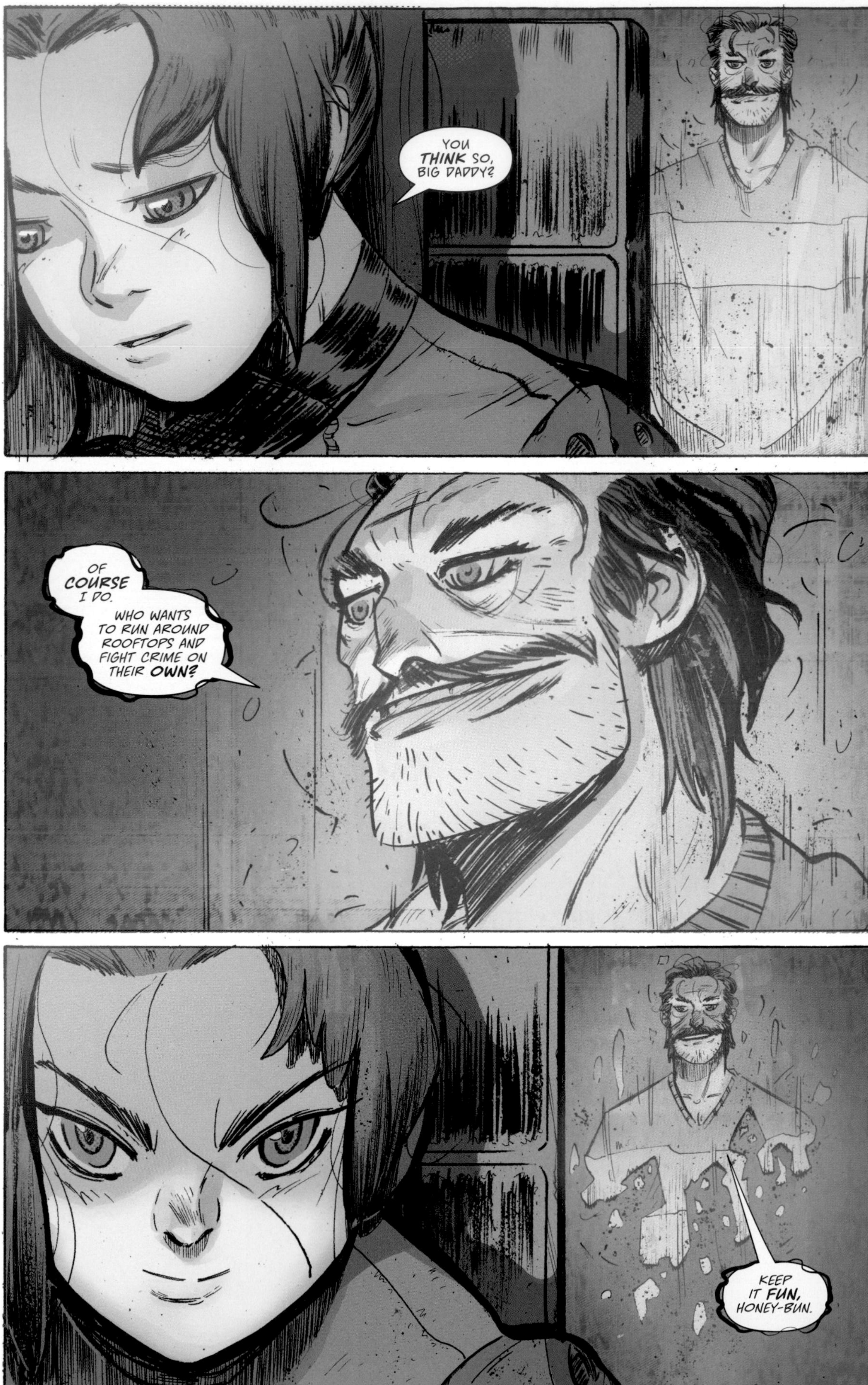
YOU THINK SO, BIG DADDY?
OF COURSE I DO.
WHO WANTS TO RUN AROUND ROOFTOPS AND FIGHT CRIME ON THEIR OWN?
KEEP IT FUN, HONEY-BUN.

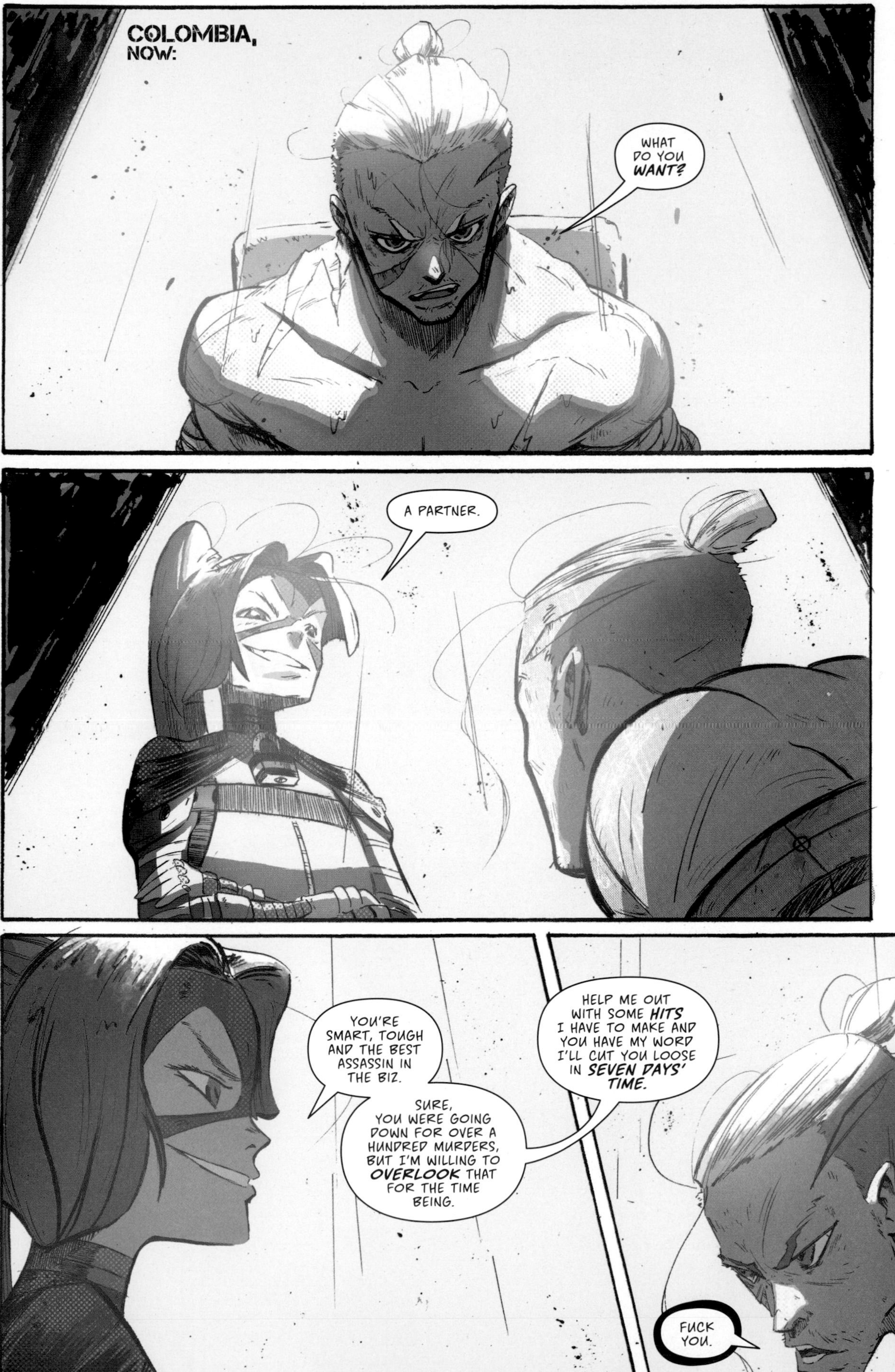
COLOMBIA, NOW:
WHAT DO YOU WANT?
A PARTNER.
YOU'RE SMART, TOUGH AND THE BEST ASSASSIN IN THE BIZ.
SURE, YOU WERE GOING DOWN FOR OVER A HUNDRED MURDERS, BUT I'M WILLING TO OVERLOOK THAT FOR THE TIME BEING.
HELP ME OUT WITH SOME HITS I HAVE TO MAKE AND YOU HAVE MY WORD I'LL CUT YOU LOOSE IN SEVEN DAYS' TIME.
FUCK YOU.

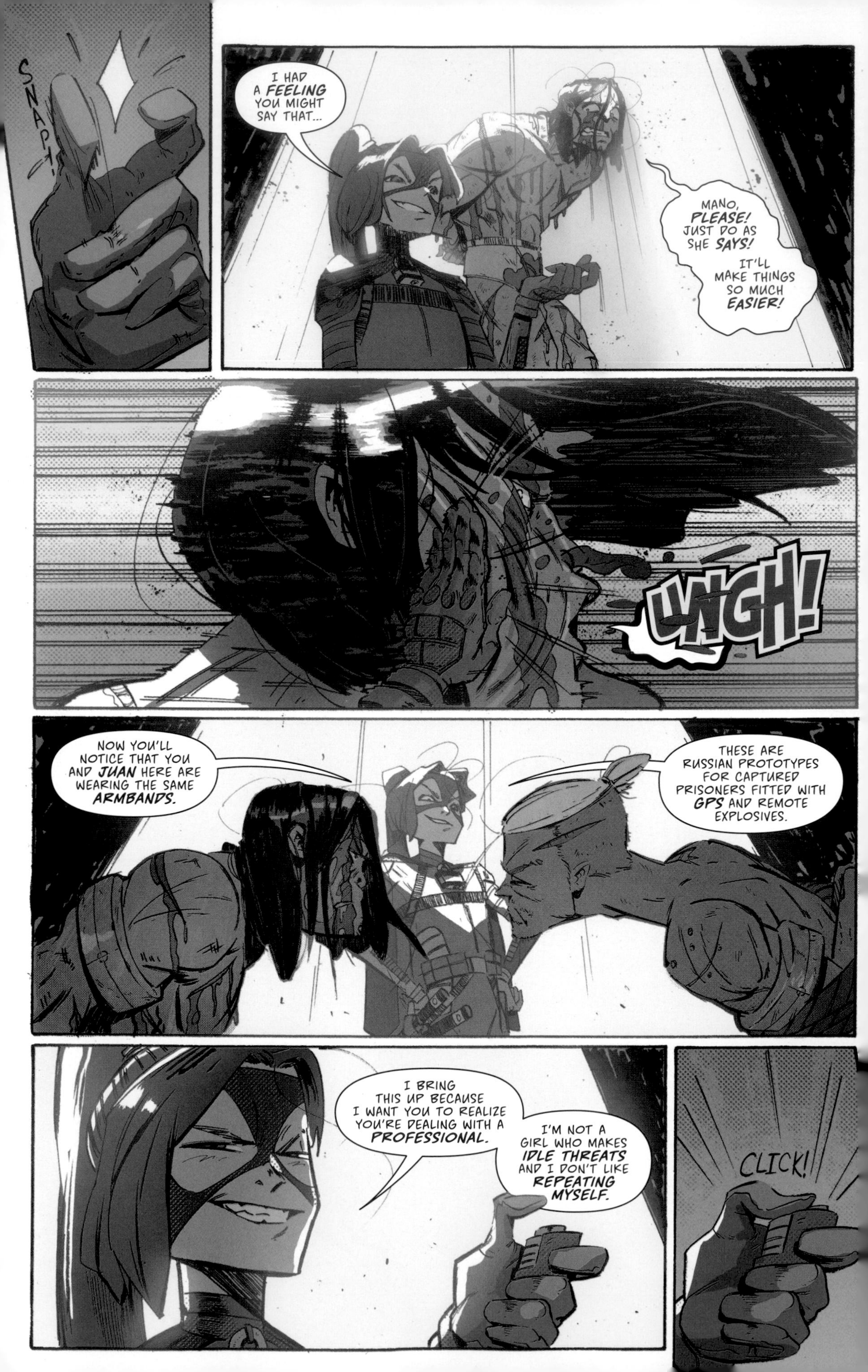
SNAP!
I HAD A FEELING YOU MIGHT SAY THAT...
MANO, PLEASE! JUST DO AS SHE SAYS!
IT'LL MAKE THINGS SO MUCH EASIER!
UGH!
NOW YOU'LL NOTICE THAT YOU AND JUAN HERE ARE WEARING THE SAME ARMBANDS.
THESE ARE RUSSIAN PROTOTYPES FOR CAPTURED PRISONERS FITTED WITH GPS AND REMOTE EXPLOSIVES.
I BRING THIS UP BECAUSE I WANT YOU TO REALIZE YOU'RE DEALING WITH A PROFESSIONAL.
I'M NOT A GIRL WHO MAKES IDLE THREATS AND I DON'T LIKE REPEATING MYSELF.
CLICK!

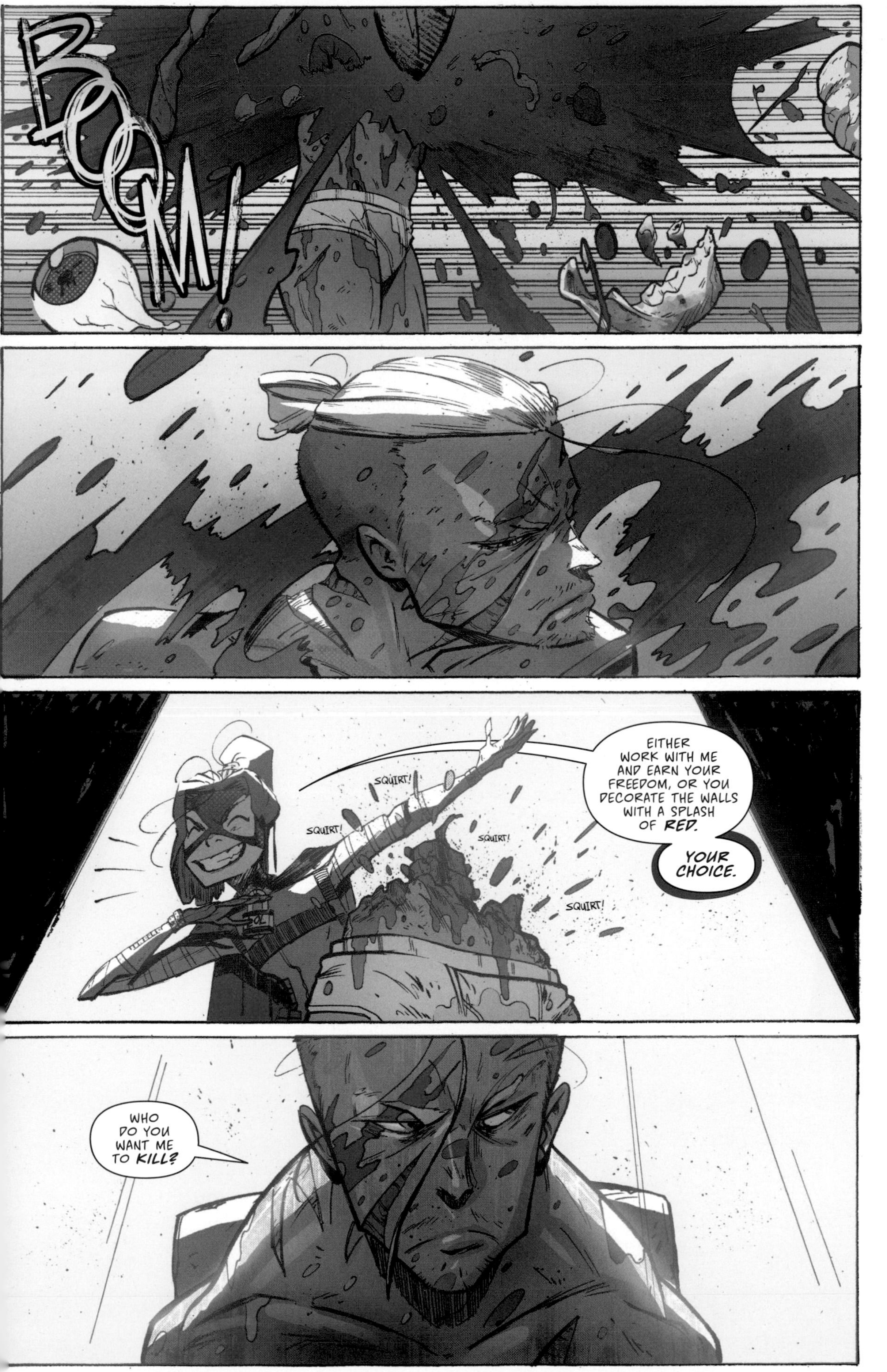
BOOM!
SQUIRT!
SQUIRT!
SQUIRT!
SQUIRT!
EITHER WORK WITH ME AND EARN YOUR FREEDOM, OR YOU DECORATE THE WALLS WITH A SPLASH OF RED.
YOUR CHOICE.
WHO DO YOU WANT ME TO KILL?

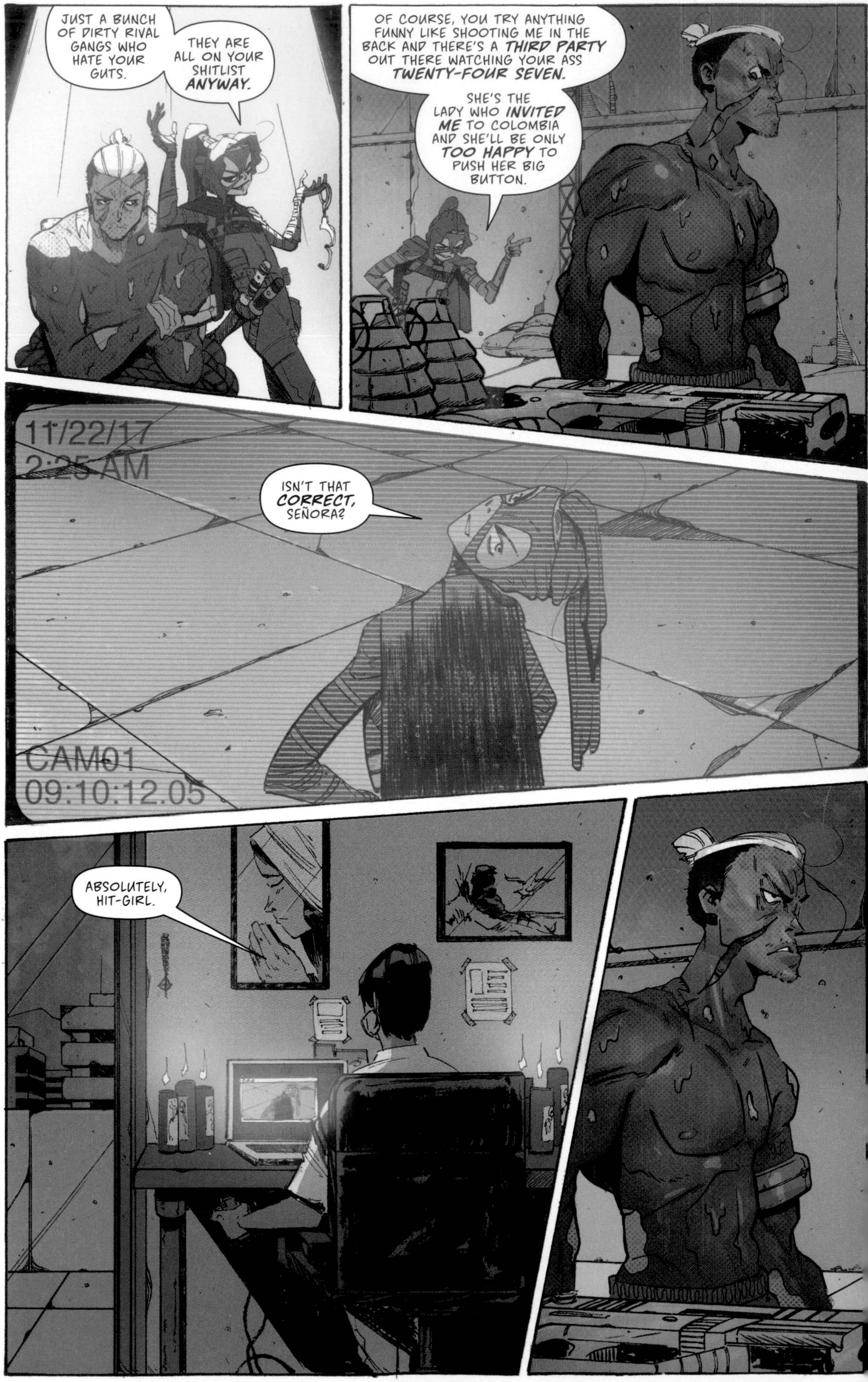
JUST A BUNCH OF DIRTY RIVAL GANGS WHO HATE YOUR GUTS.
THEY ARE ALL ON YOUR SHITLIST ANYWAY.
OF COURSE, YOU TRY ANYTHING FUNNY LIKE SHOOTING ME IN THE BACK AND THERE'S A THIRD PARTY OUT THERE WATCHING YOUR ASS TWENTY-FOUR SEVEN.
SHE'S THE LADY WHO INVITED ME TO COLOMBIA AND SHE'LL BE ONLY TOO HAPPY TO PUSH HER BIG BUTTON.
11/22/17
2:25 AM
ISN'T THAT CORRECT, SEÑORA?
CAM01
09:10:12.05
ABSOLUTELY, HIT-GIRL.

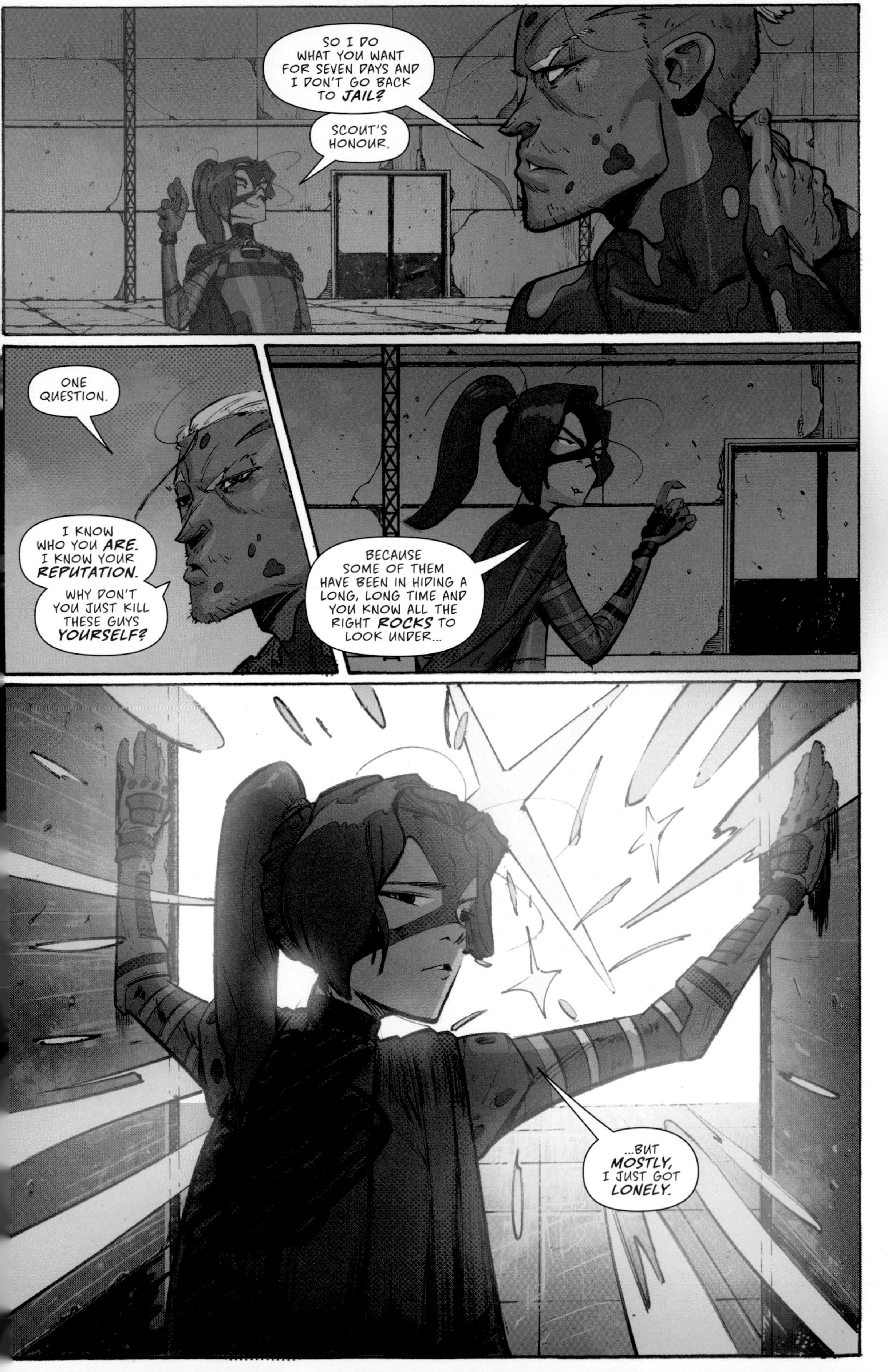
SO I DO WHAT YOU WANT FOR SEVEN DAYS AND I DON'T GO BACK TO JAIL?
SCOUT'S HONOUR.
ONE QUESTION.
I KNOW WHO YOU ARE. I KNOW YOUR REPUTATION.
WHY DON'T YOU JUST KILL THESE GUYS YOURSELF?
BECAUSE SOME OF THEM HAVE BEEN IN HIDING A LONG, LONG TIME AND YOU KNOW ALL THE RIGHT ROCKS TO LOOK UNDER...
...BUT MOSTLY, I JUST GOT LONELY.

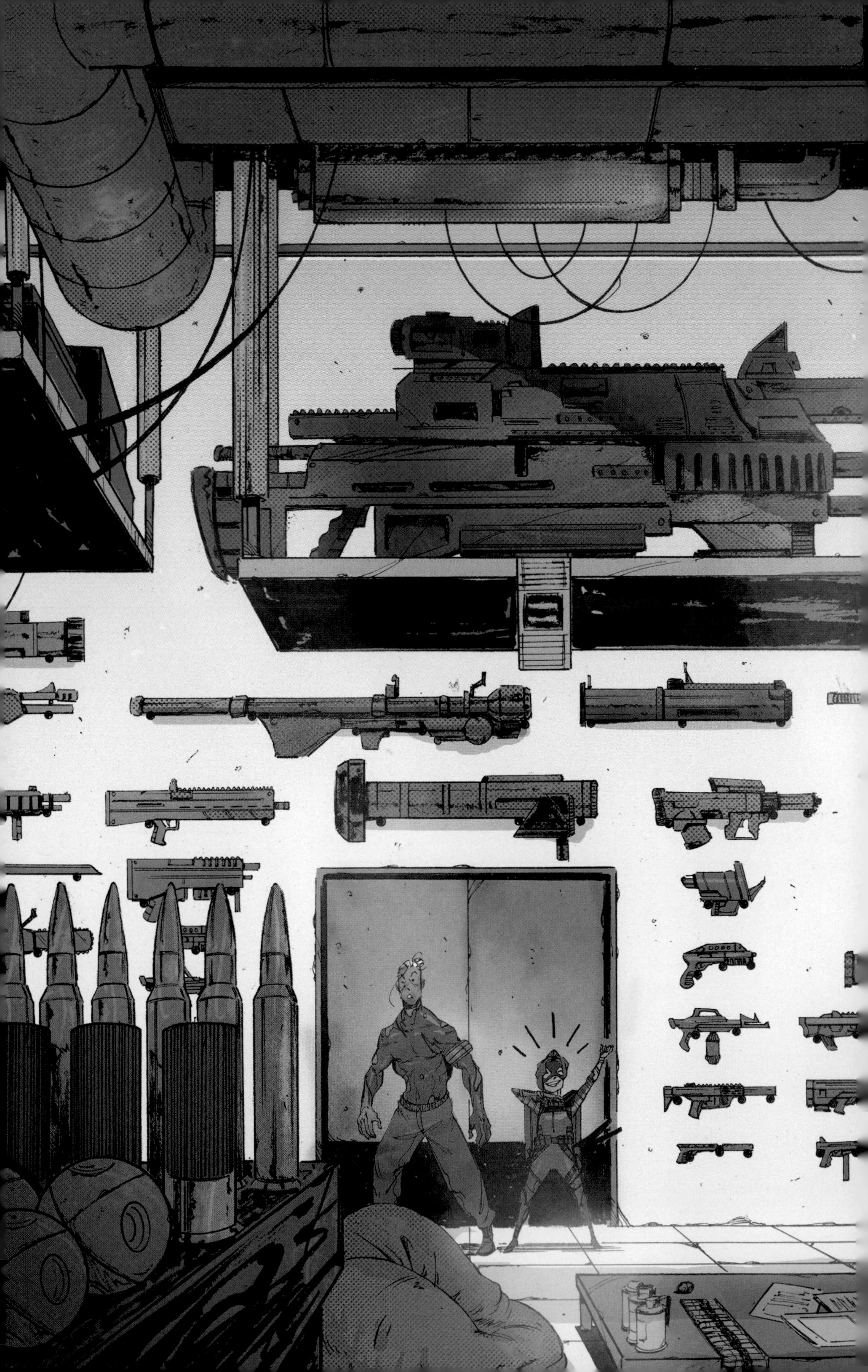

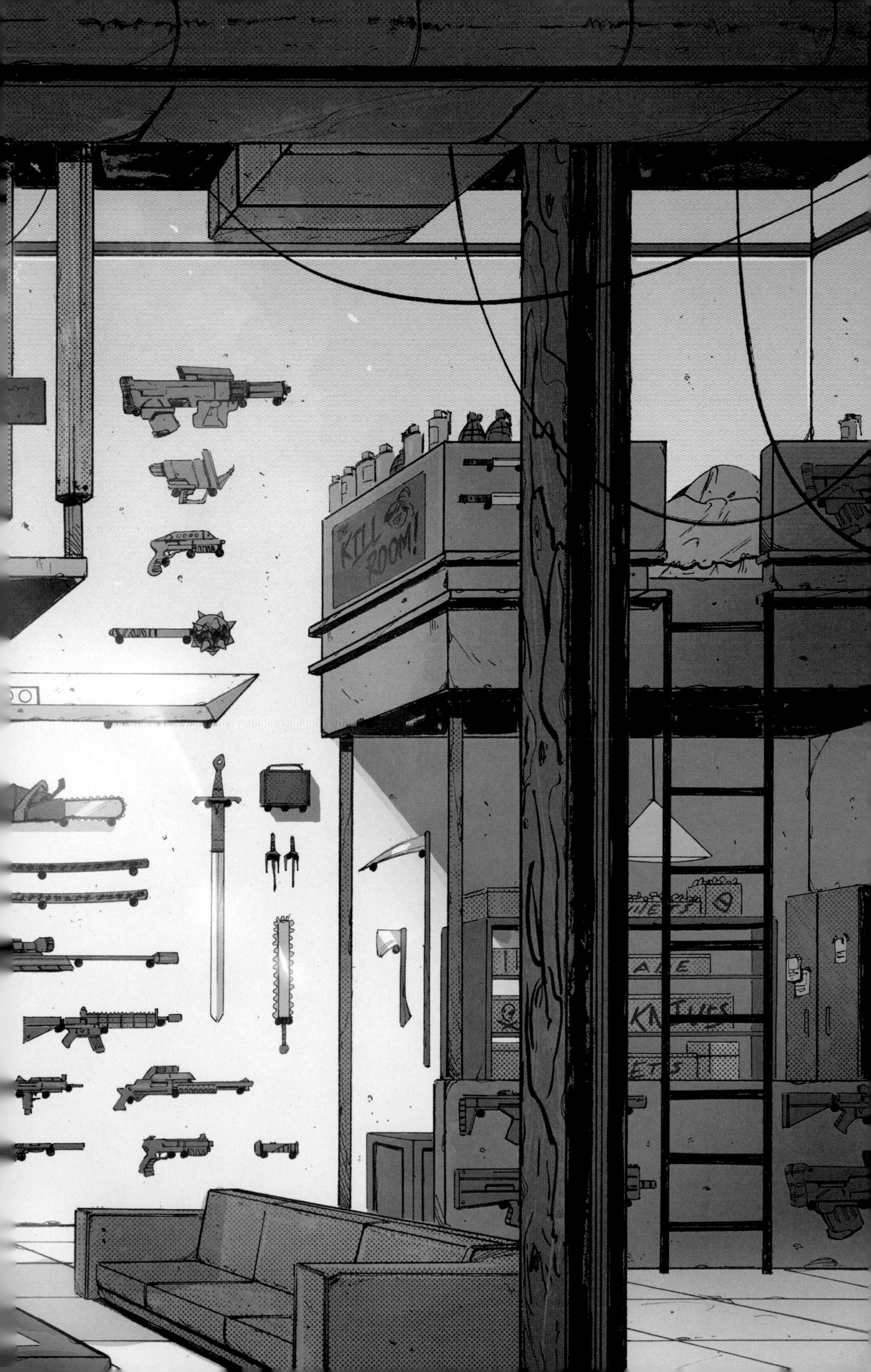
THE KILL ROOM!

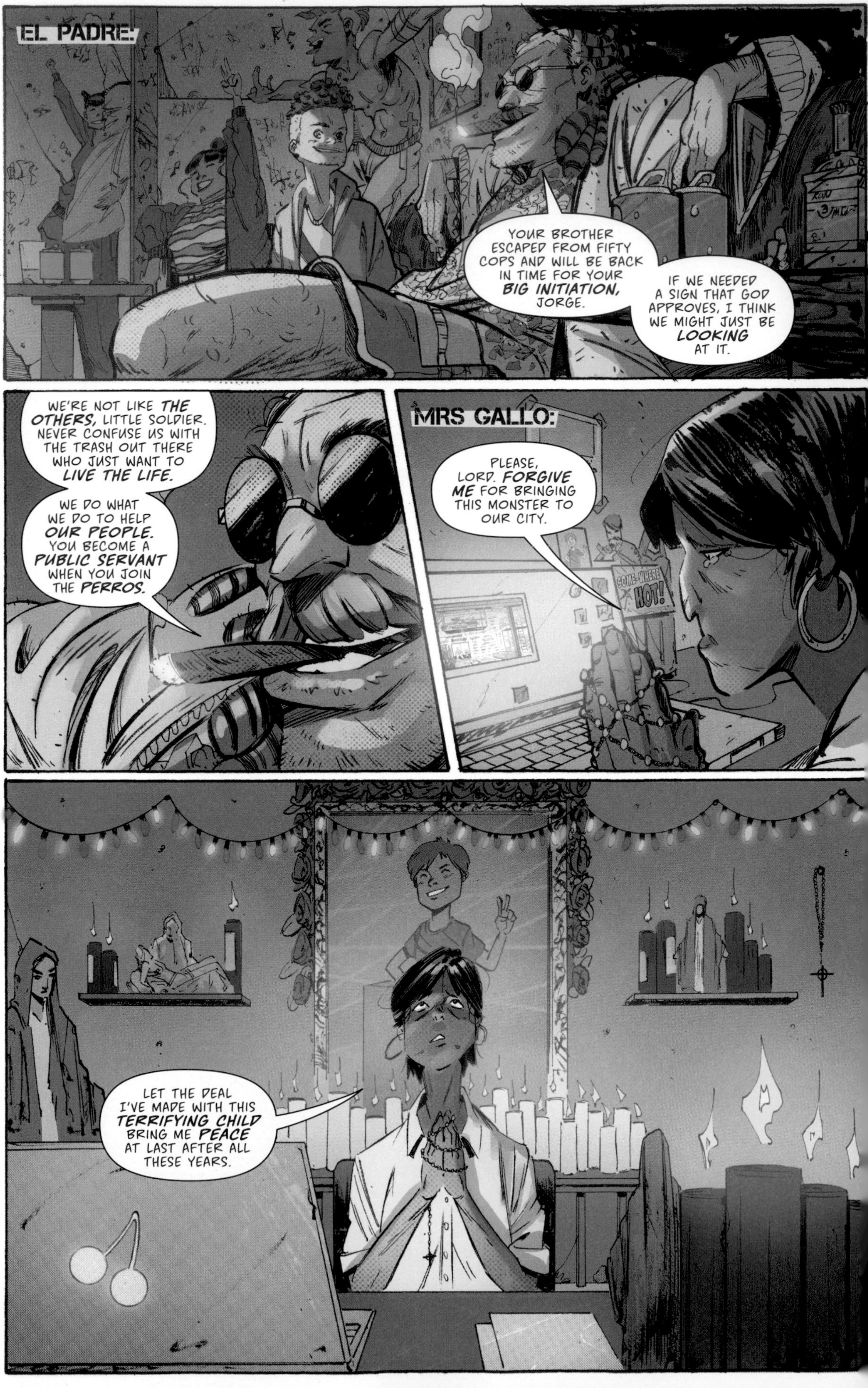
EL PADRE:
YOUR BROTHER ESCAPED FROM FIFTY COPS AND WILL BE BACK IN TIME FOR YOUR BIG INITIATION, JORGE.
IF WE NEEDED A SIGN THAT GOD APPROVES, I THINK WE MIGHT JUST BE LOOKING AT IT.
WE'RE NOT LIKE THE OTHERS, LITTLE SOLDIER. NEVER CONFUSE US WITH THE TRASH OUT THERE WHO JUST WANT TO LIVE THE LIFE.
WE DO WHAT WE DO TO HELP OUR PEOPLE. YOU BECOME A PUBLIC SERVANT WHEN YOU JOIN THE PERROS.
MRS GALLO:
PLEASE, LORD. FORGIVE ME FOR BRINGING THIS MONSTER TO OUR CITY.
COME-WHERE HOT!
LET THE DEAL I'VE MADE WITH THIS TERRIFYING CHILD BRING ME PEACE AT LAST AFTER ALL THESE YEARS.

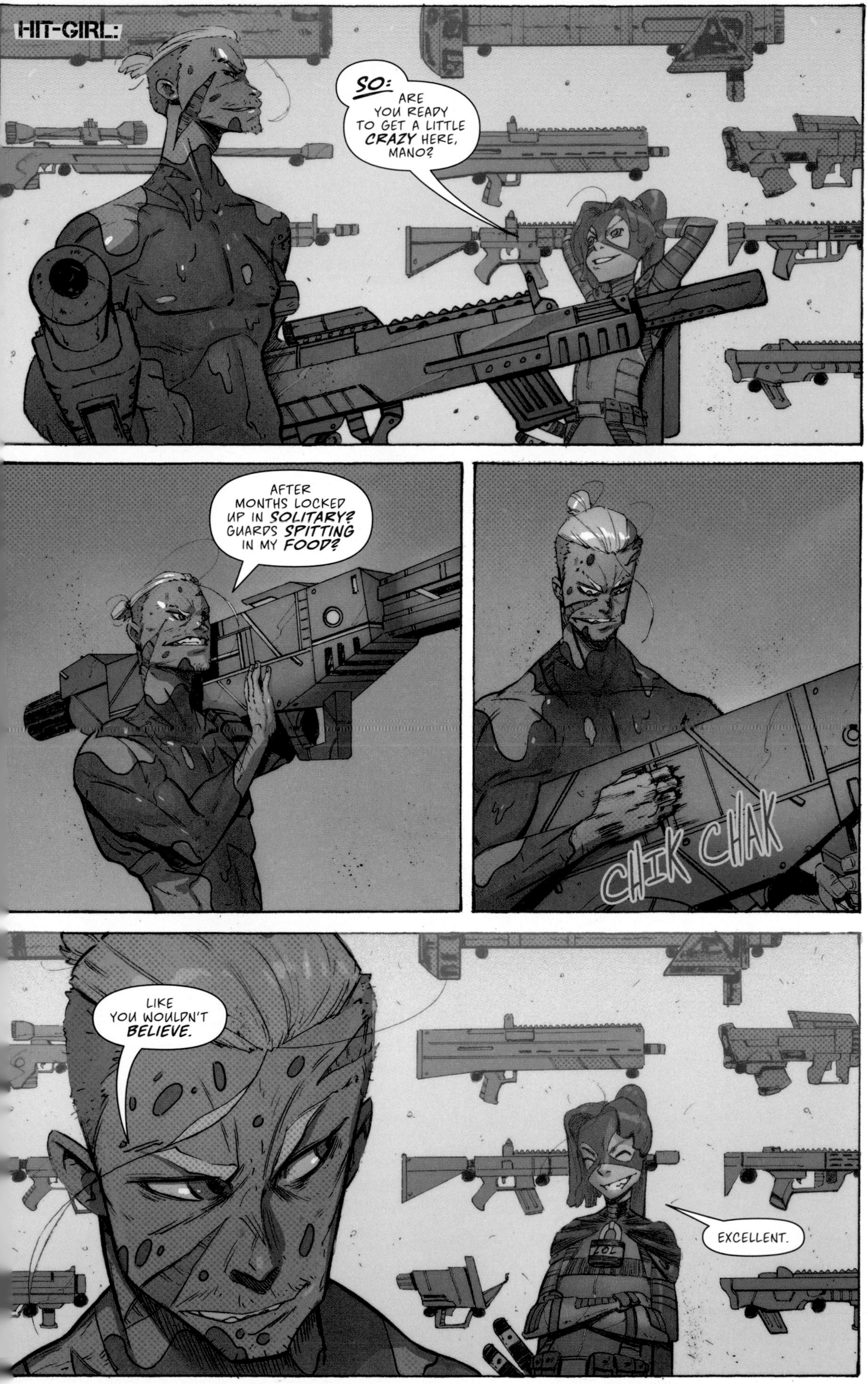
HIT-GIRL:
SO: ARE YOU READY TO GET A LITTLE CRAZY HERE, MANO?
AFTER MONTHS LOCKED UP IN SOLITARY? GUARDS SPITTING IN MY FOOD?
CHIK CHAK
LIKE YOU WOULDN'T BELIEVE.
EXCELLENT.

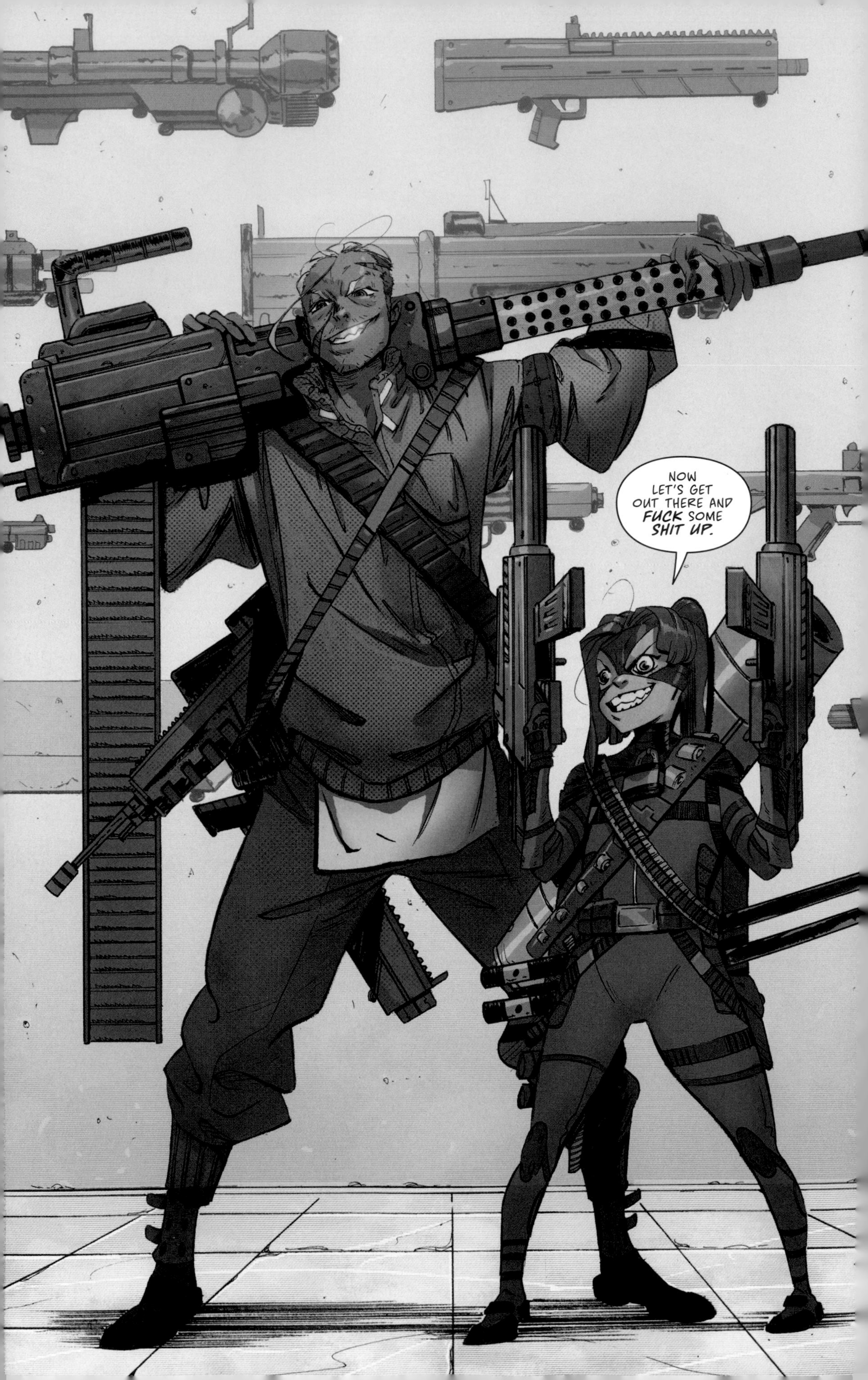
NOW LET'S GET OUT THERE AND FUCK SOME SHIT UP.

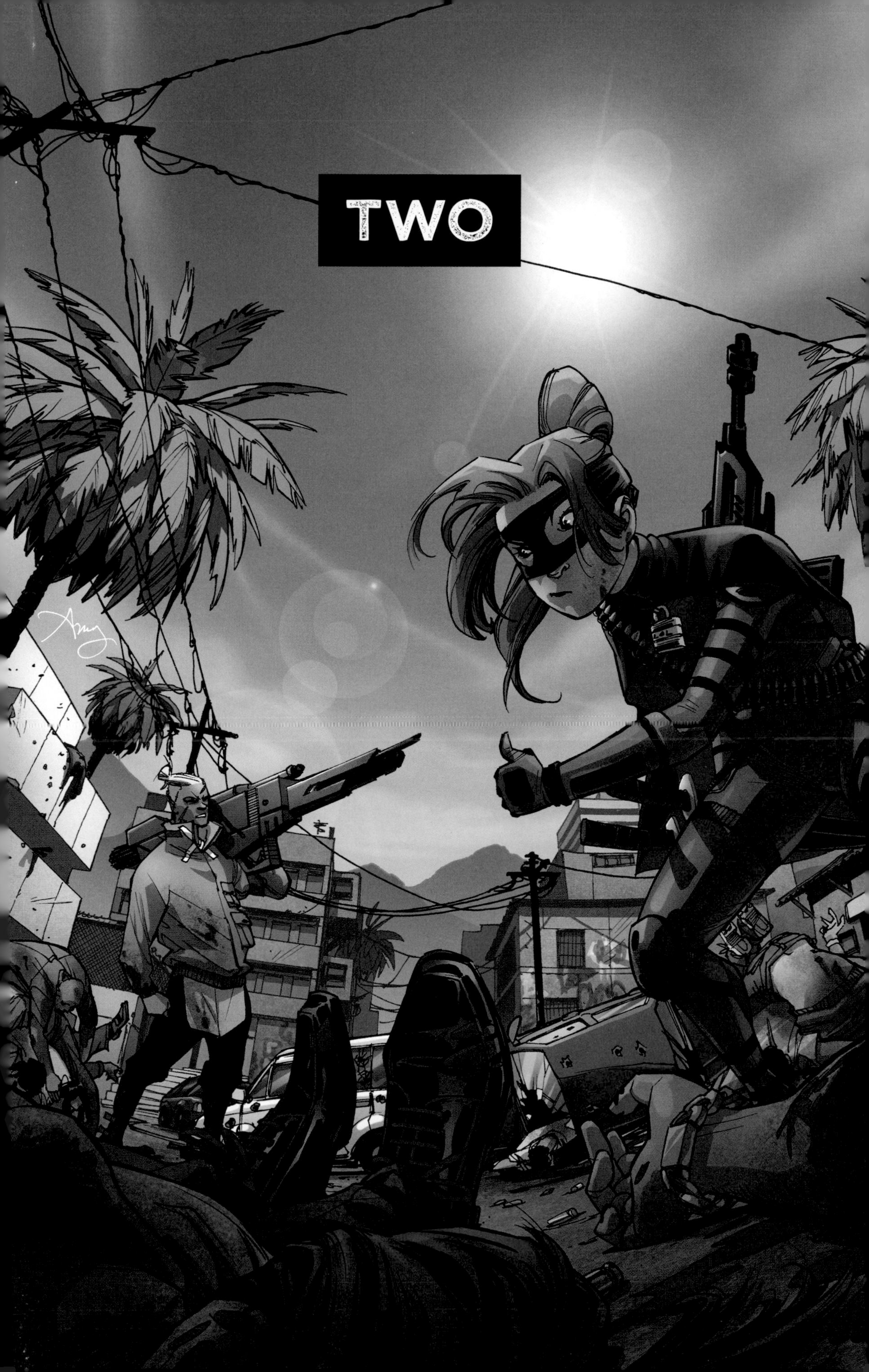
TWO

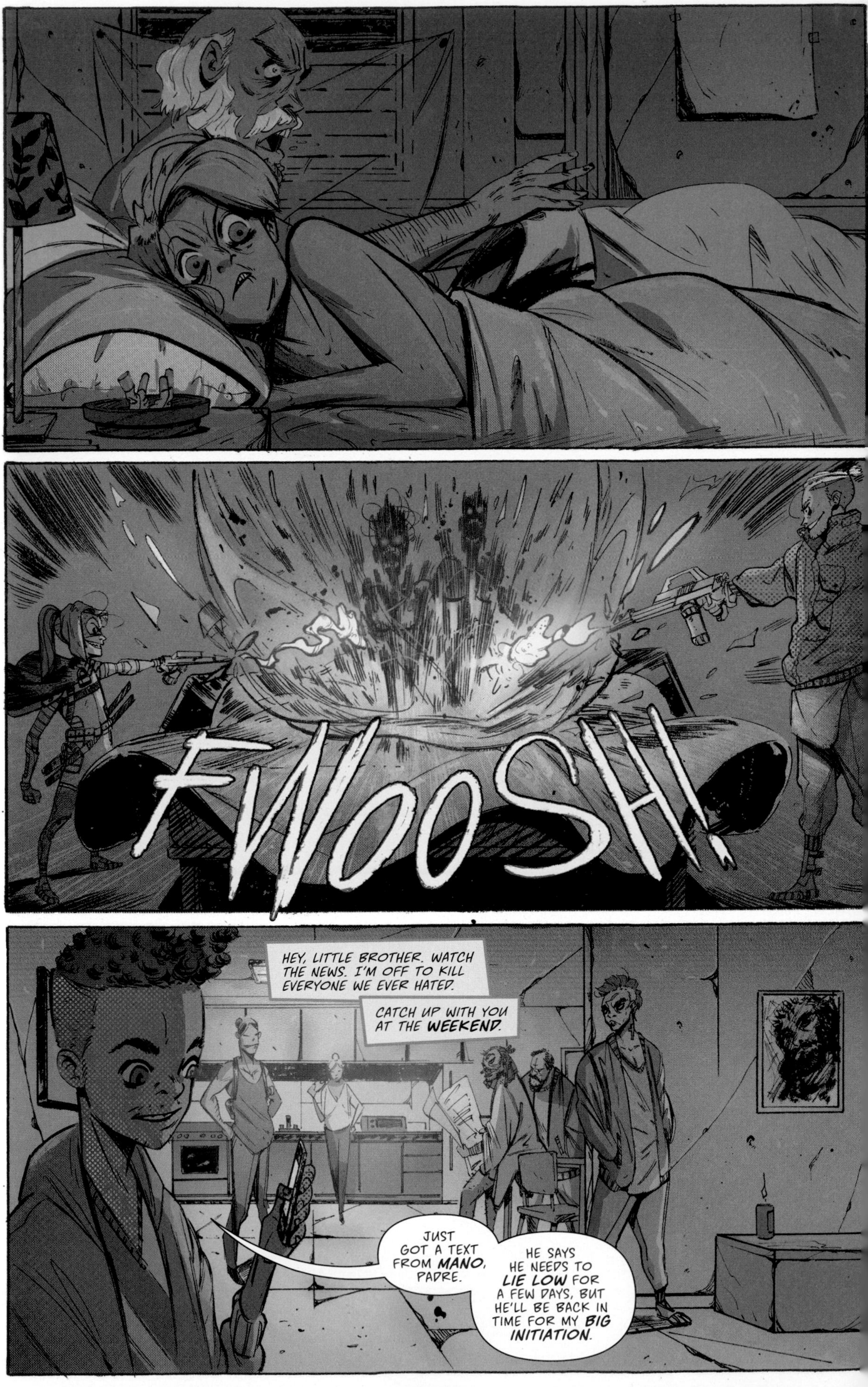
FWOOSH!
HEY, LITTLE BROTHER. WATCH THE NEWS. I'M OFF TO KILL EVERYONE WE EVER HATED.
CATCH UP WITH YOU AT THE WEEKEND.
JUST GOT A TEXT FROM MANO, PADRE.
HE SAYS HE NEEDS TO LIE LOW FOR A FEW DAYS, BUT HE'LL BE BACK IN TIME FOR MY BIG INITIATION.

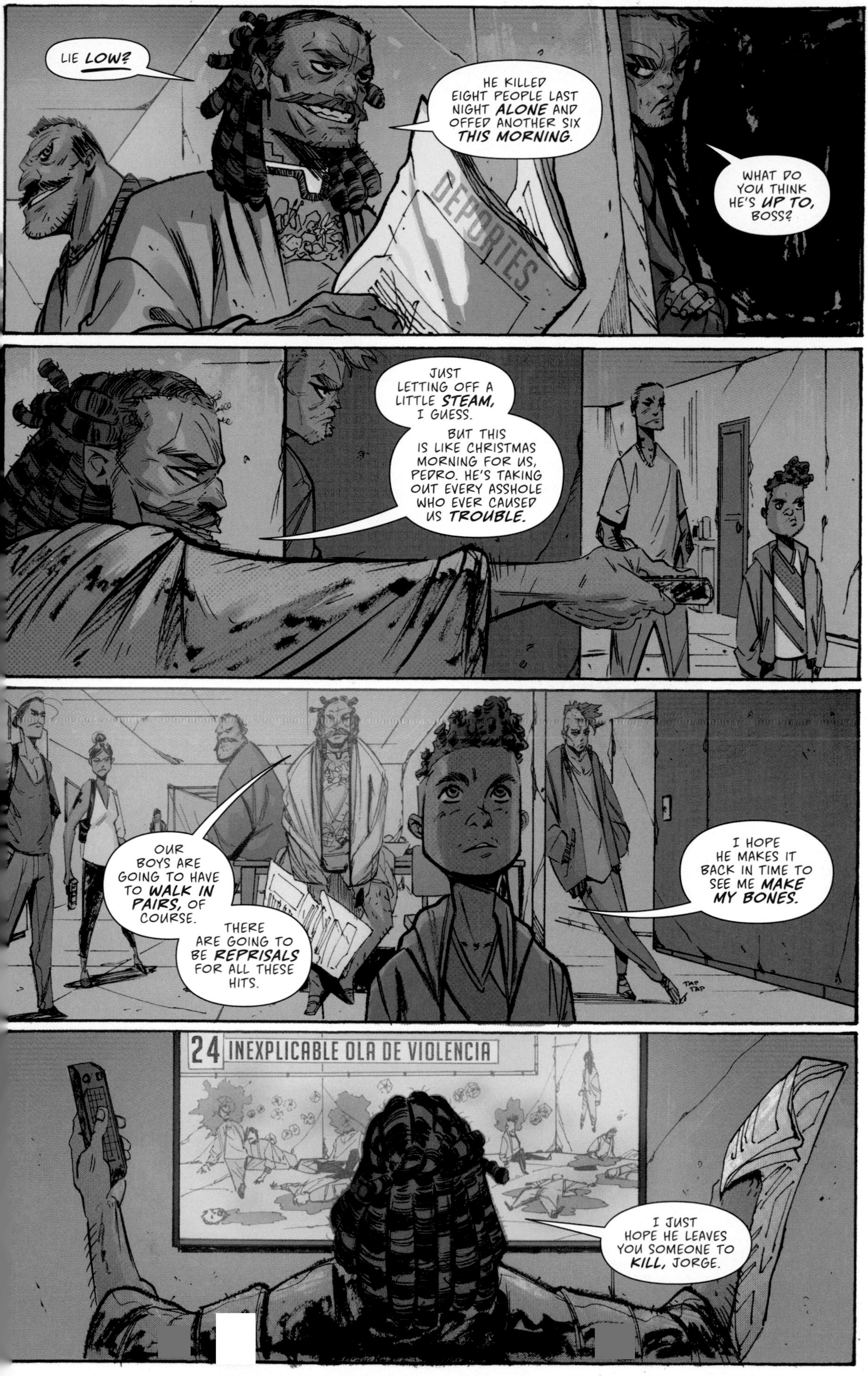
LIE LOW?
HE KILLED EIGHT PEOPLE LAST NIGHT ALONE AND OFFED ANOTHER SIX THIS MORNING.
DEPORTES
WHAT DO YOU THINK HE'S UP TO, BOSS?
JUST LETTING OFF A LITTLE STEAM, I GUESS.
BUT THIS IS LIKE CHRISTMAS MORNING FOR US, PEDRO. HE'S TAKING OUT EVERY ASSHOLE WHO EVER CAUSED US TROUBLE.
OUR BOYS ARE GOING TO HAVE TO WALK IN PAIRS, OF COURSE.
THERE ARE GOING TO BE REPRISALS FOR ALL THESE HITS.
I HOPE HE MAKES IT BACK IN TIME TO SEE ME MAKE MY BONES.
TAP TAP
24 INEXPLICABLE OLA DE VIOLENCIA
I JUST HOPE HE LEAVES YOU SOMEONE TO KILL, JORGE.

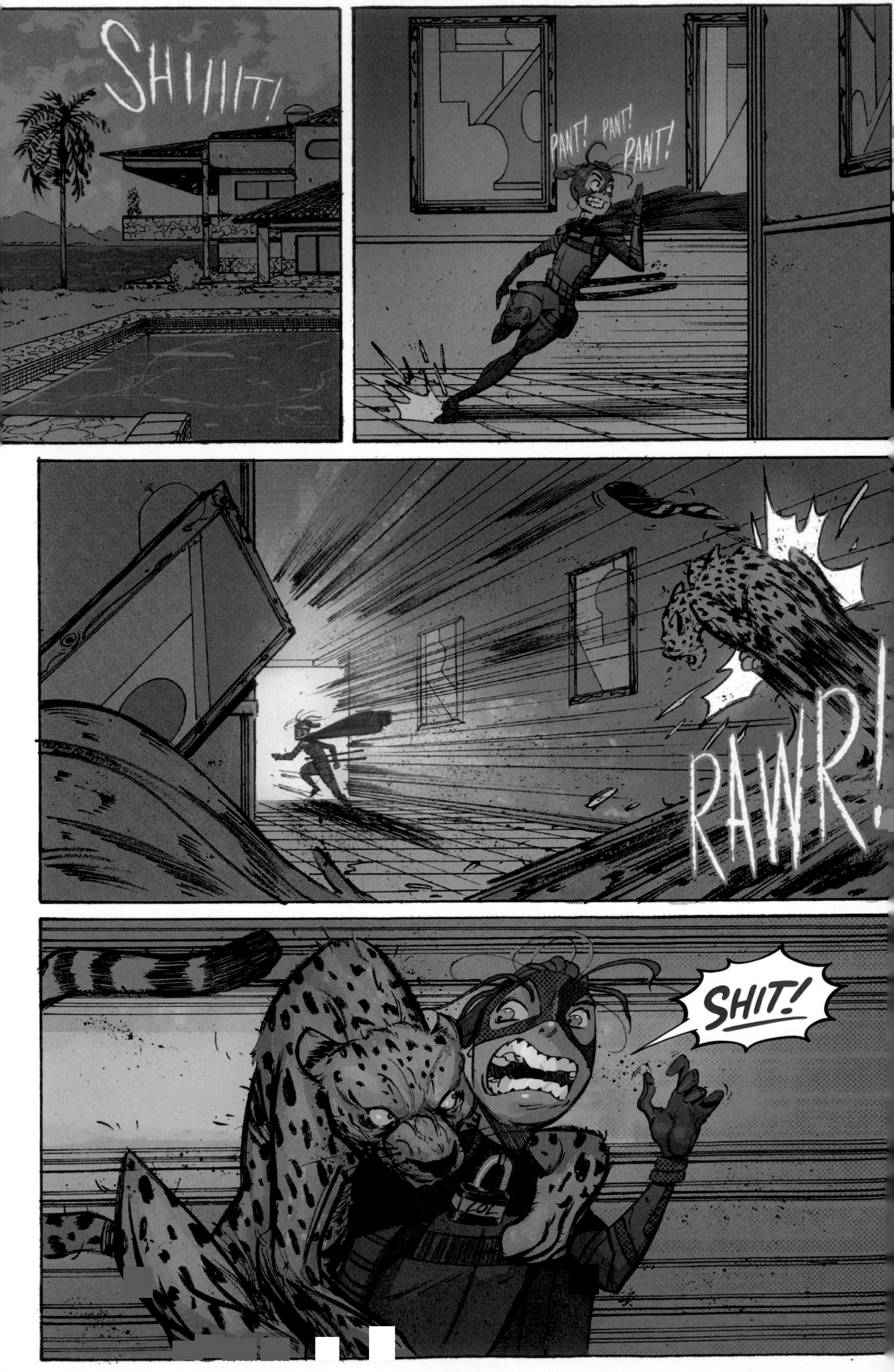
SHIIIIT!
PANT! PANT! PANT!
RAWR!
SHIT!

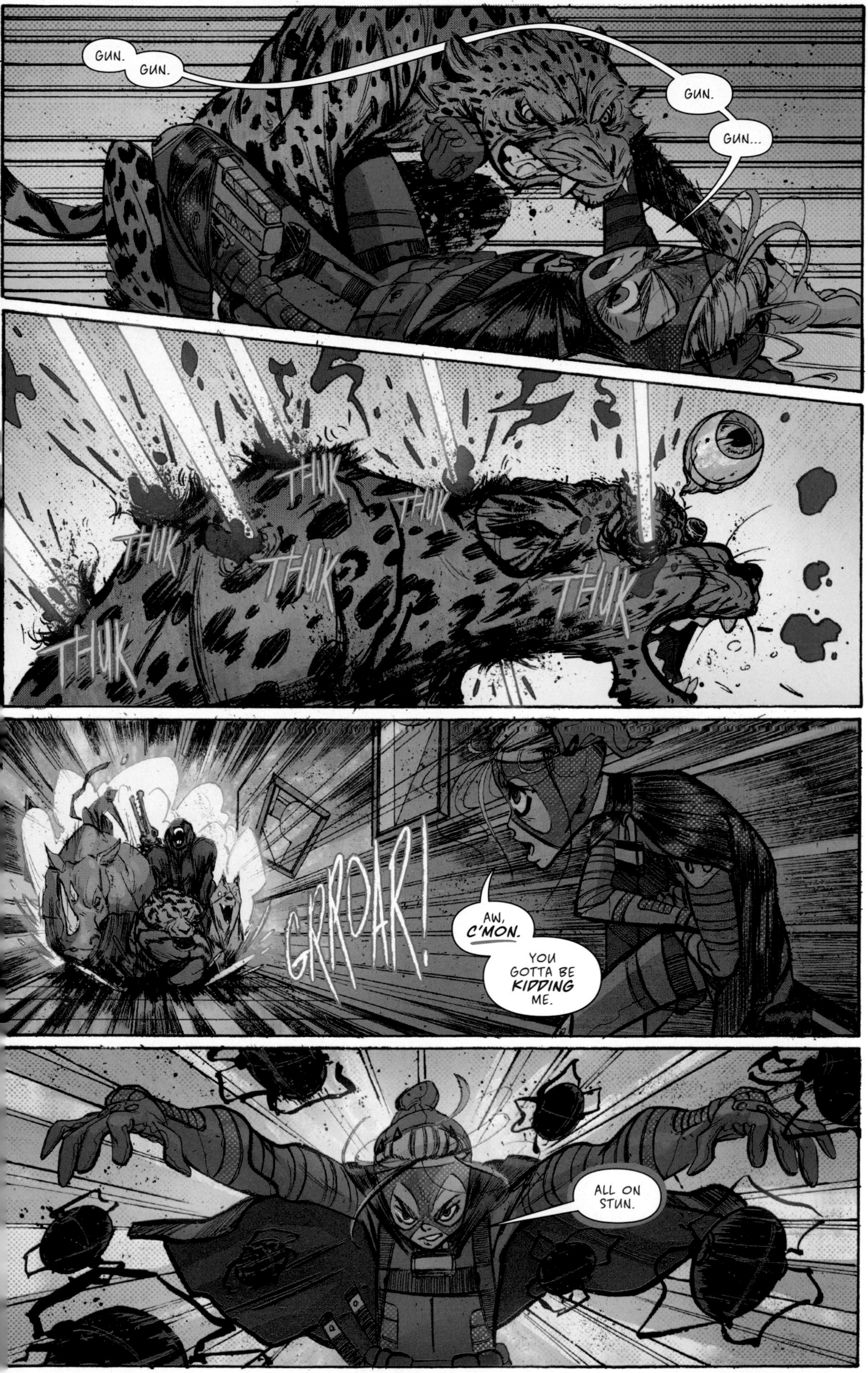
GUN.
GUN.
GUN.
GUN...
THUK
THUK
THUK
THUK
THUK
THUK
GRROAR!
AW, C'MON.
YOU GOTTA BE KIDDING ME.
ALL ON STUN.

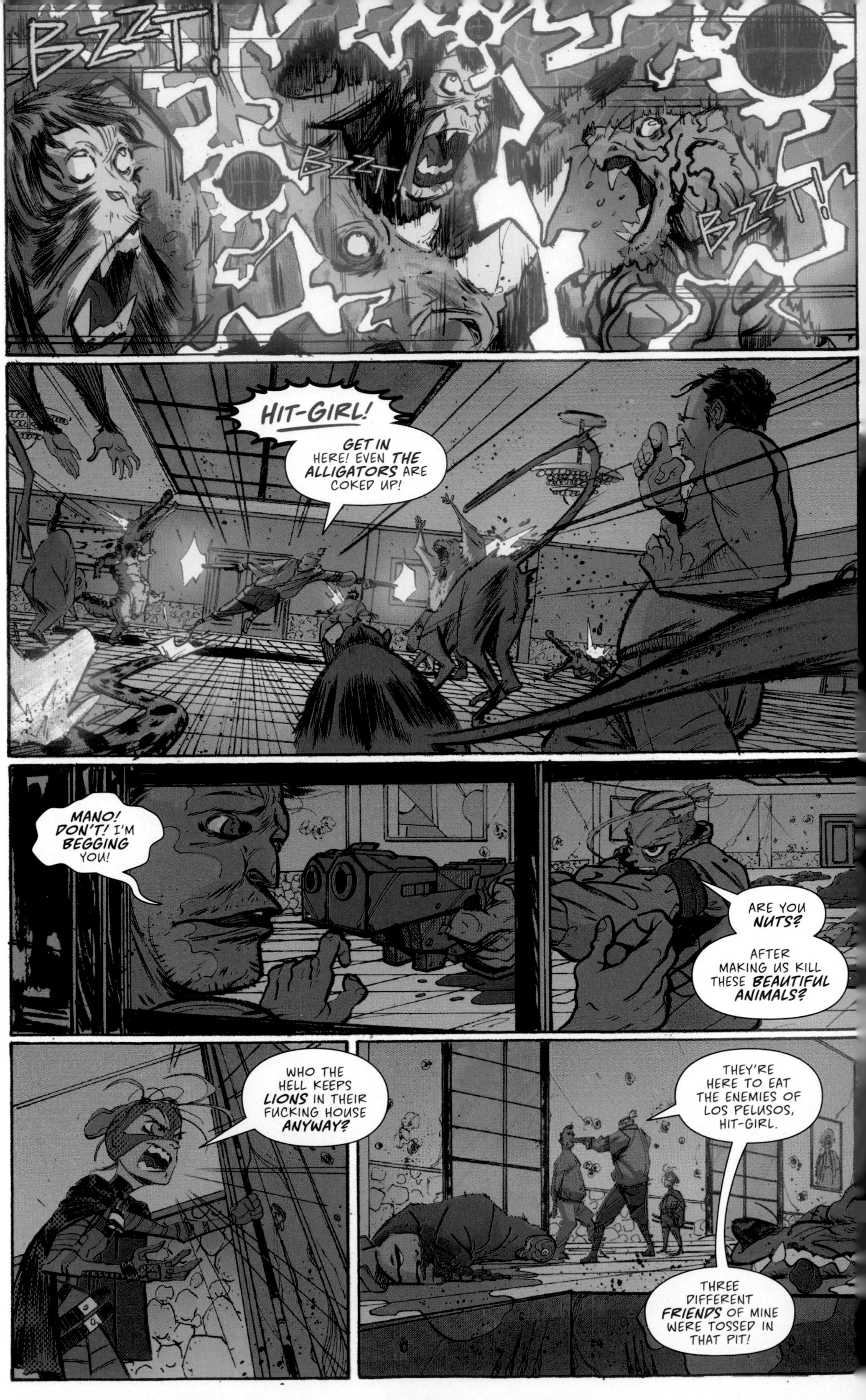
BZZT!
BZZT!
BZZT!
HIT-GIRL!
GET IN HERE! EVEN THE ALLIGATORS ARE COKED UP!
MANO! DON'T! I'M BEGGING YOU!
ARE YOU NUTS?
AFTER MAKING US KILL THESE BEAUTIFUL ANIMALS?
WHO THE HELL KEEPS LIONS IN THEIR FUCKING HOUSE ANYWAY?
THEY'RE HERE TO EAT THE ENEMIES OF LOS PELUSOS, HIT-GIRL.
THREE DIFFERENT FRIENDS OF MINE WERE TOSSED IN THAT PIT!

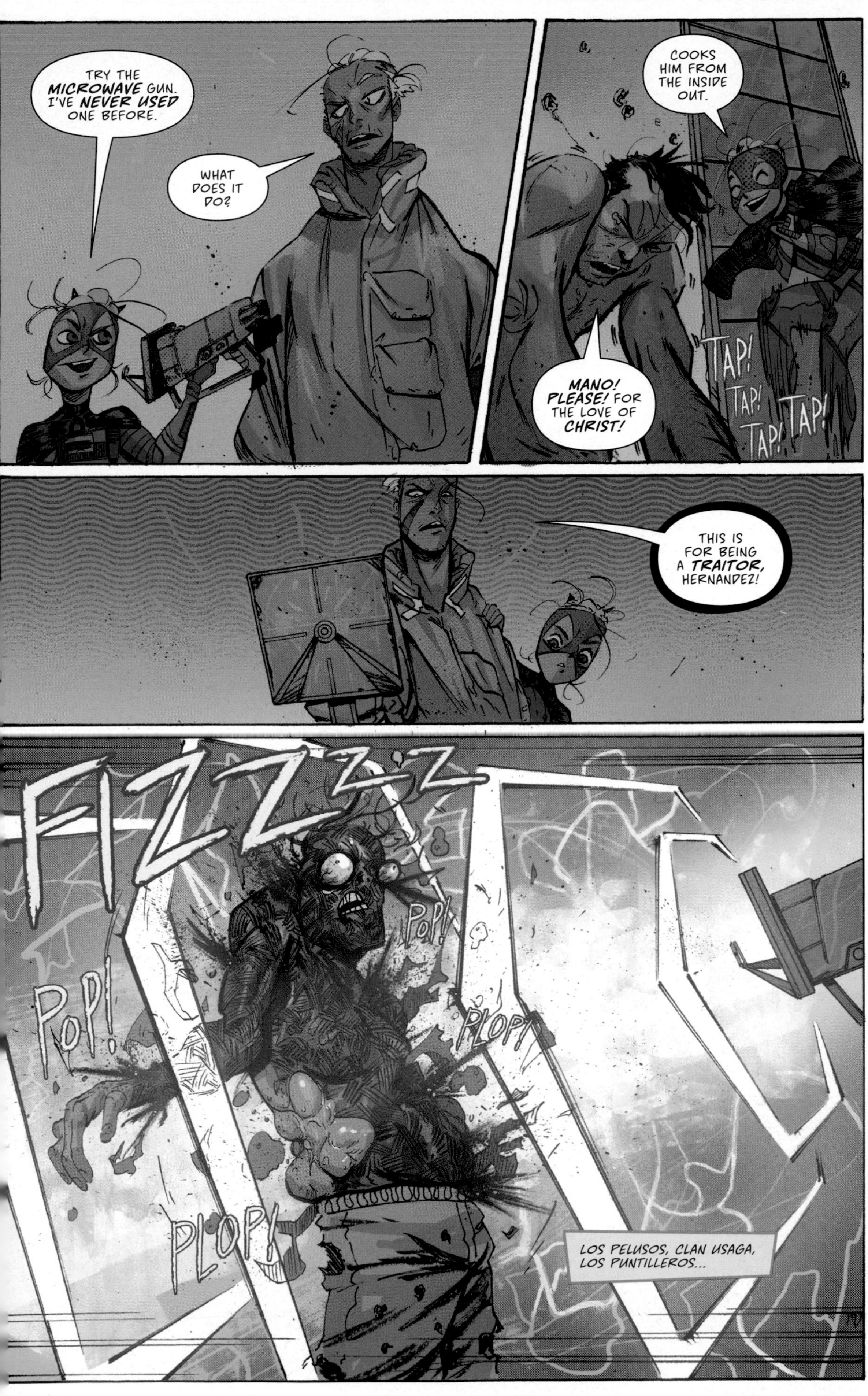
TRY THE MICROWAVE GUN. I'VE NEVER USED ONE BEFORE.
WHAT DOES IT DO?
COOKS HIM FROM THE INSIDE OUT.
MANO! PLEASE! FOR THE LOVE OF CHRIST!
TAP! TAP! TAP! TAP!
THIS IS FOR BEING A TRAITOR, HERNANDEZ!
FIZZZZZ
POP!
POP!
PLOP!
PLOP!
LOS PELUSOS, CLAN USAGA, LOS PUNTILLEROS...

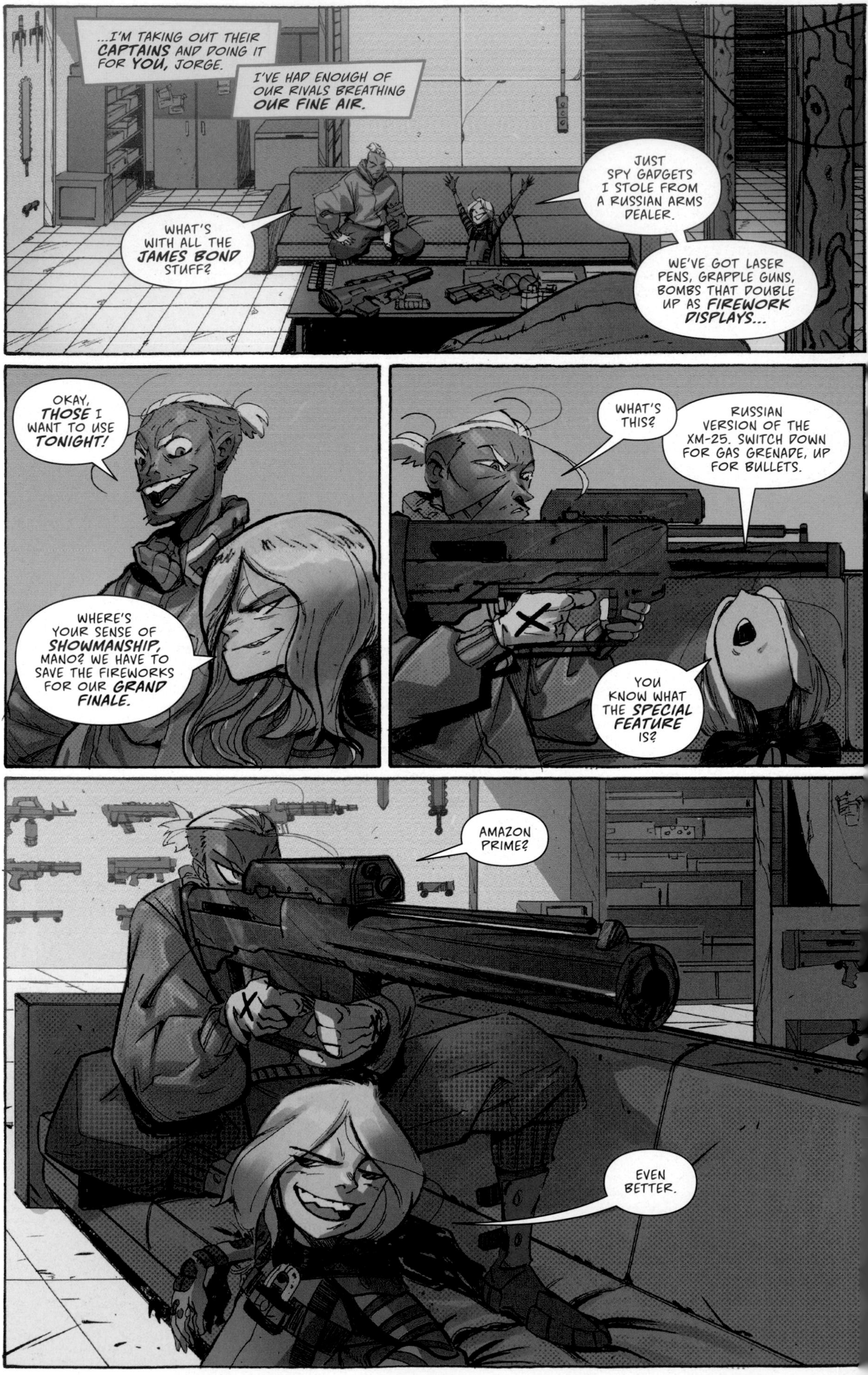
...I'M TAKING OUT THEIR CAPTAINS AND DOING IT FOR YOU, JORGE.
I'VE HAD ENOUGH OF OUR RIVALS BREATHING OUR FINE AIR.
WHAT'S WITH ALL THE JAMES BOND STUFF?
JUST SPY GADGETS I STOLE FROM A RUSSIAN ARMS DEALER.
WE'VE GOT LASER PENS, GRAPPLE GUNS, BOMBS THAT DOUBLE UP AS FIREWORK DISPLAYS...
OKAY, THOSE I WANT TO USE TONIGHT!
WHERE'S YOUR SENSE OF SHOWMANSHIP, MANO? WE HAVE TO SAVE THE FIREWORKS FOR OUR GRAND FINALE.
WHAT'S THIS?
RUSSIAN VERSION OF THE XM-25. SWITCH DOWN FOR GAS GRENADE, UP FOR BULLETS.
YOU KNOW WHAT THE SPECIAL FEATURE IS?
AMAZON PRIME?
EVEN BETTER.

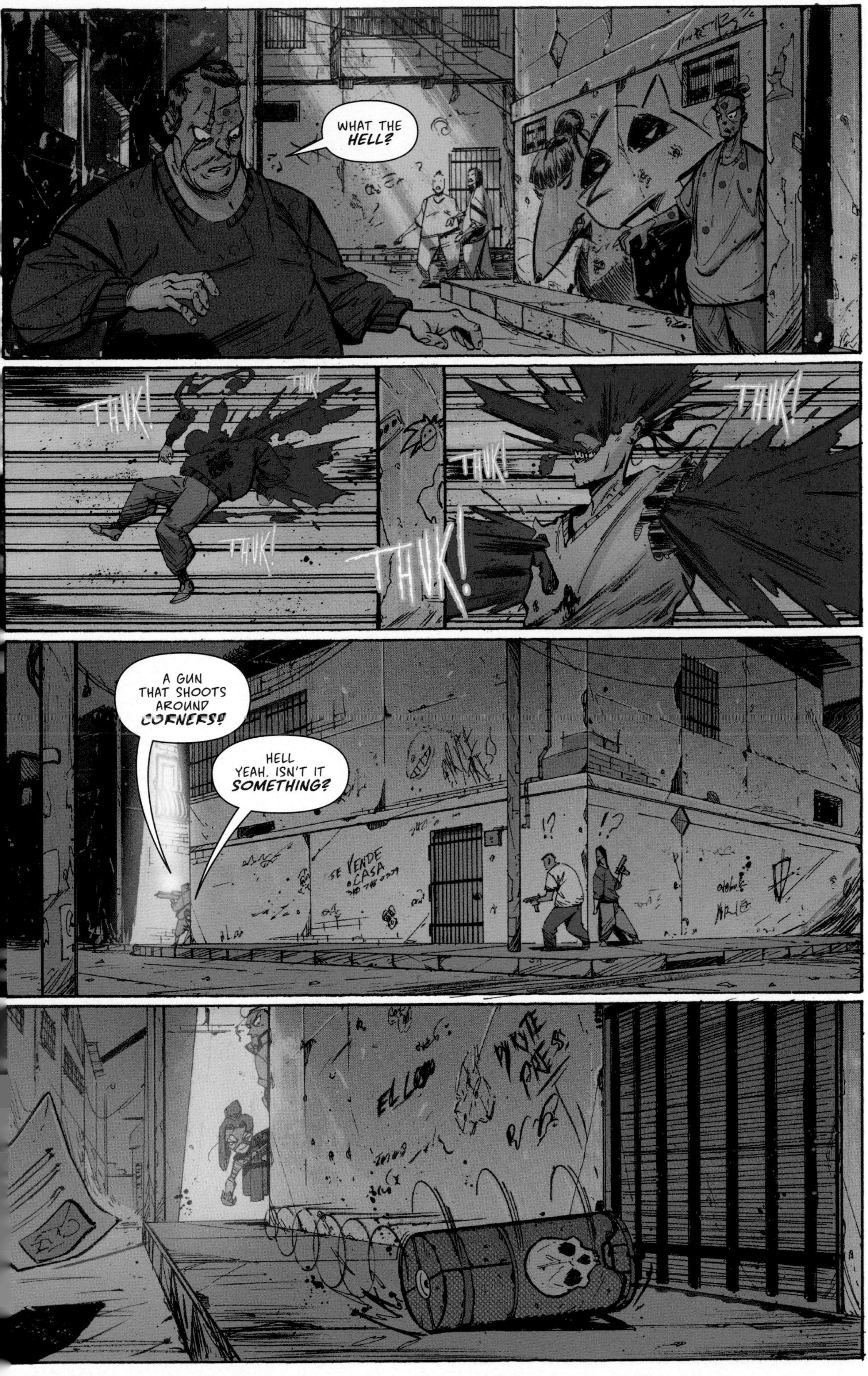
WHAT THE HELL?
THUK!
THUK!
THUK!
THUK!
THUK!
THUK!
A GUN THAT SHOOTS AROUND CORNERS?
HELL YEAH. ISN'T IT SOMETHING?
SE VENDE CASA

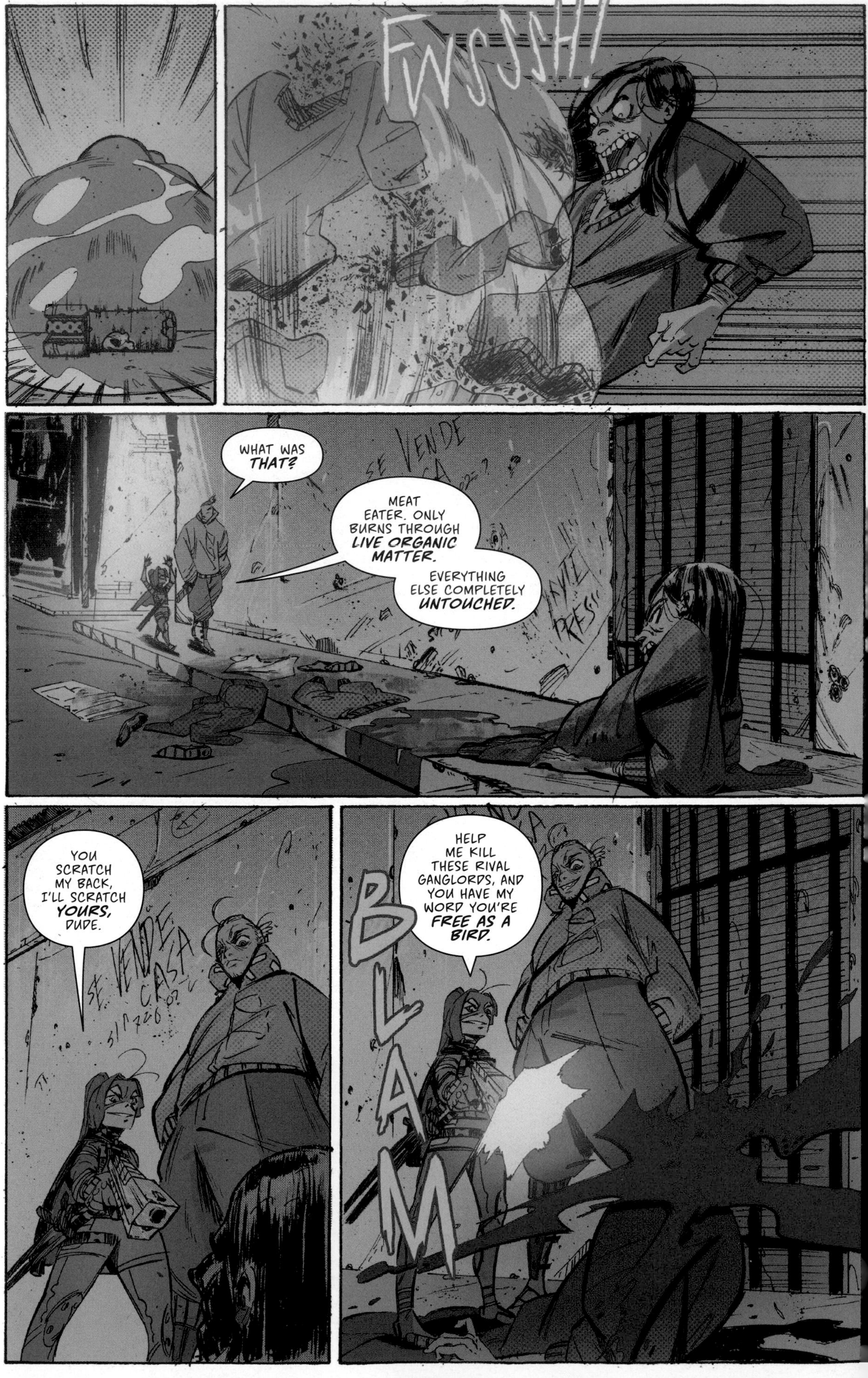
FWSSSH!
WHAT WAS THAT?
MEAT EATER. ONLY BURNS THROUGH LIVE ORGANIC MATTER.
EVERYTHING ELSE COMPLETELY UNTOUCHED.
SE VENDE CASA
YOU SCRATCH MY BACK, I'LL SCRATCH YOURS, DUDE.
HELP ME KILL THESE RIVAL GANGLORDS, AND YOU HAVE MY WORD YOU'RE FREE AS A BIRD.
BLAM

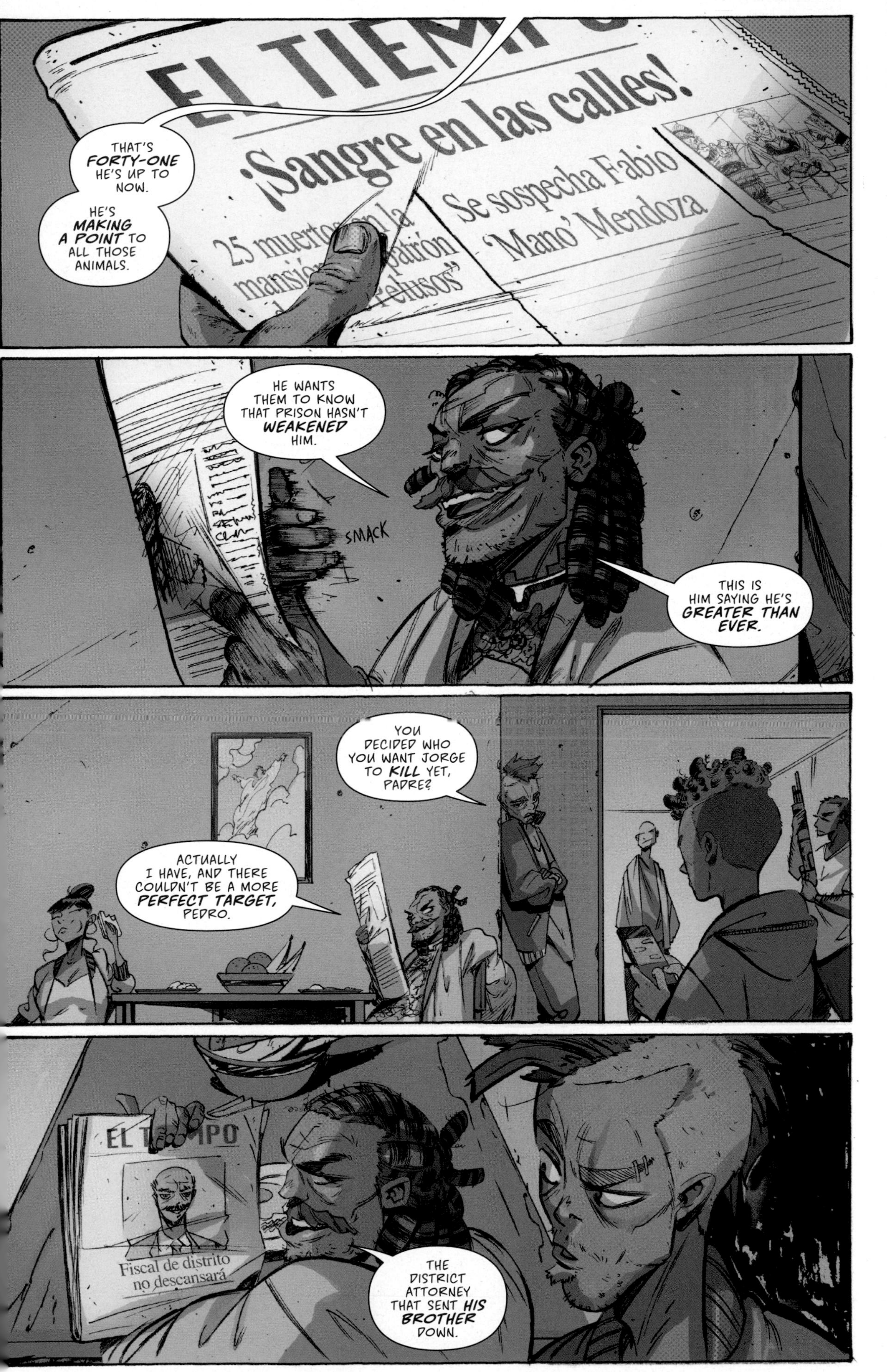
EL TIEMPO
¡Sangre en las calles!
Se sospecha Fabio 'Mano' Mendoza
THAT'S FORTY-ONE HE'S UP TO NOW.
HE'S MAKING A POINT TO ALL THOSE ANIMALS.
HE WANTS THEM TO KNOW THAT PRISON HASN'T WEAKENED HIM.
SMACK
THIS IS HIM SAYING HE'S GREATER THAN EVER.
YOU DECIDED WHO YOU WANT JORGE TO KILL YET, PADRE?
ACTUALLY I HAVE, AND THERE COULDN'T BE A MORE PERFECT TARGET, PEDRO.
Fiscal de distrito no descansará
THE DISTRICT ATTORNEY THAT SENT HIS BROTHER DOWN.

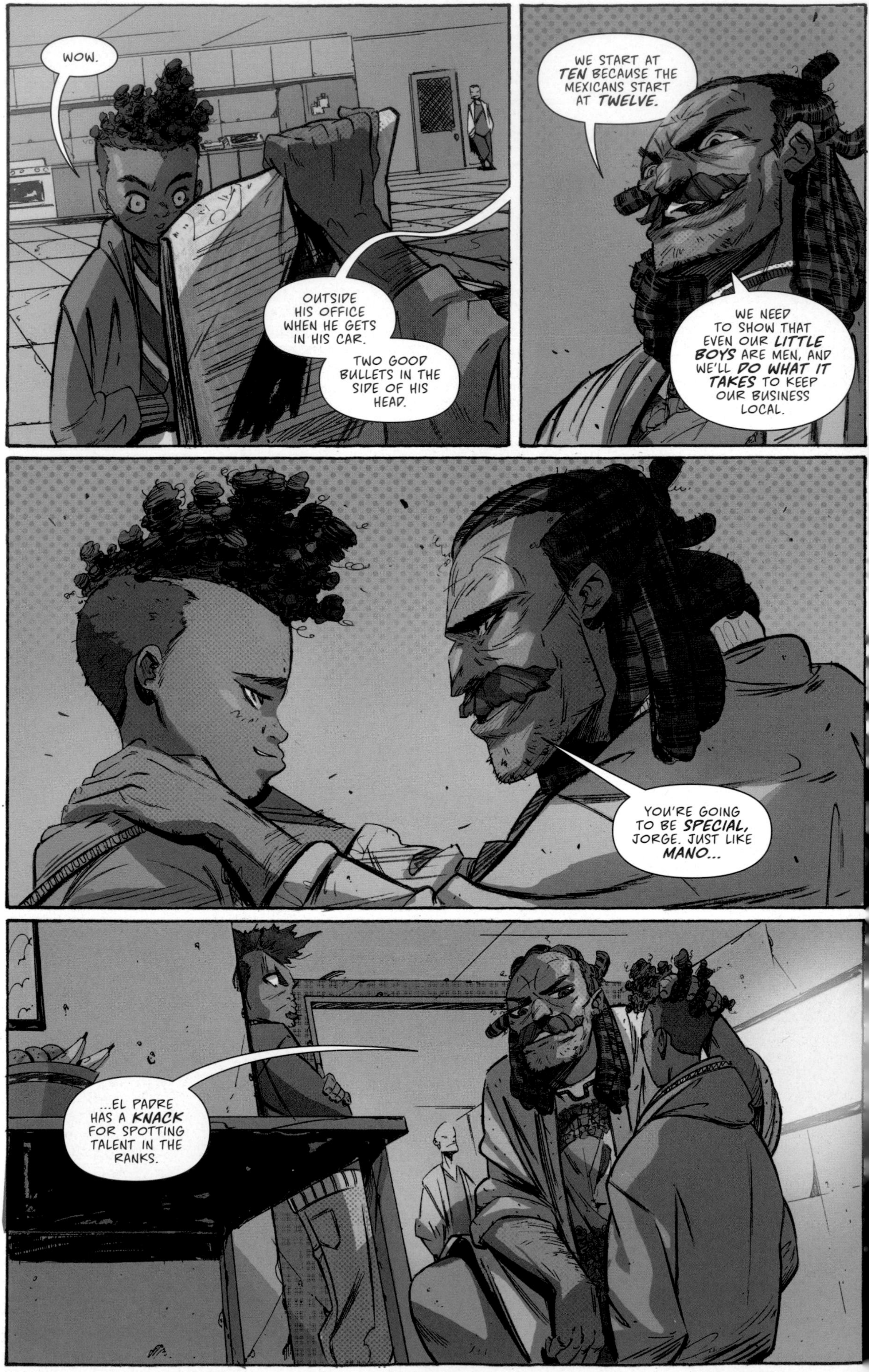
WOW.
OUTSIDE HIS OFFICE WHEN HE GETS IN HIS CAR.
TWO GOOD BULLETS IN THE SIDE OF HIS HEAD.
WE START AT TEN BECAUSE THE MEXICANS START AT TWELVE.
WE NEED TO SHOW THAT EVEN OUR LITTLE BOYS ARE MEN, AND WE'LL DO WHAT IT TAKES TO KEEP OUR BUSINESS LOCAL.
YOU'RE GOING TO BE SPECIAL, JORGE. JUST LIKE MANO...
...EL PADRE HAS A KNACK FOR SPOTTING TALENT IN THE RANKS.

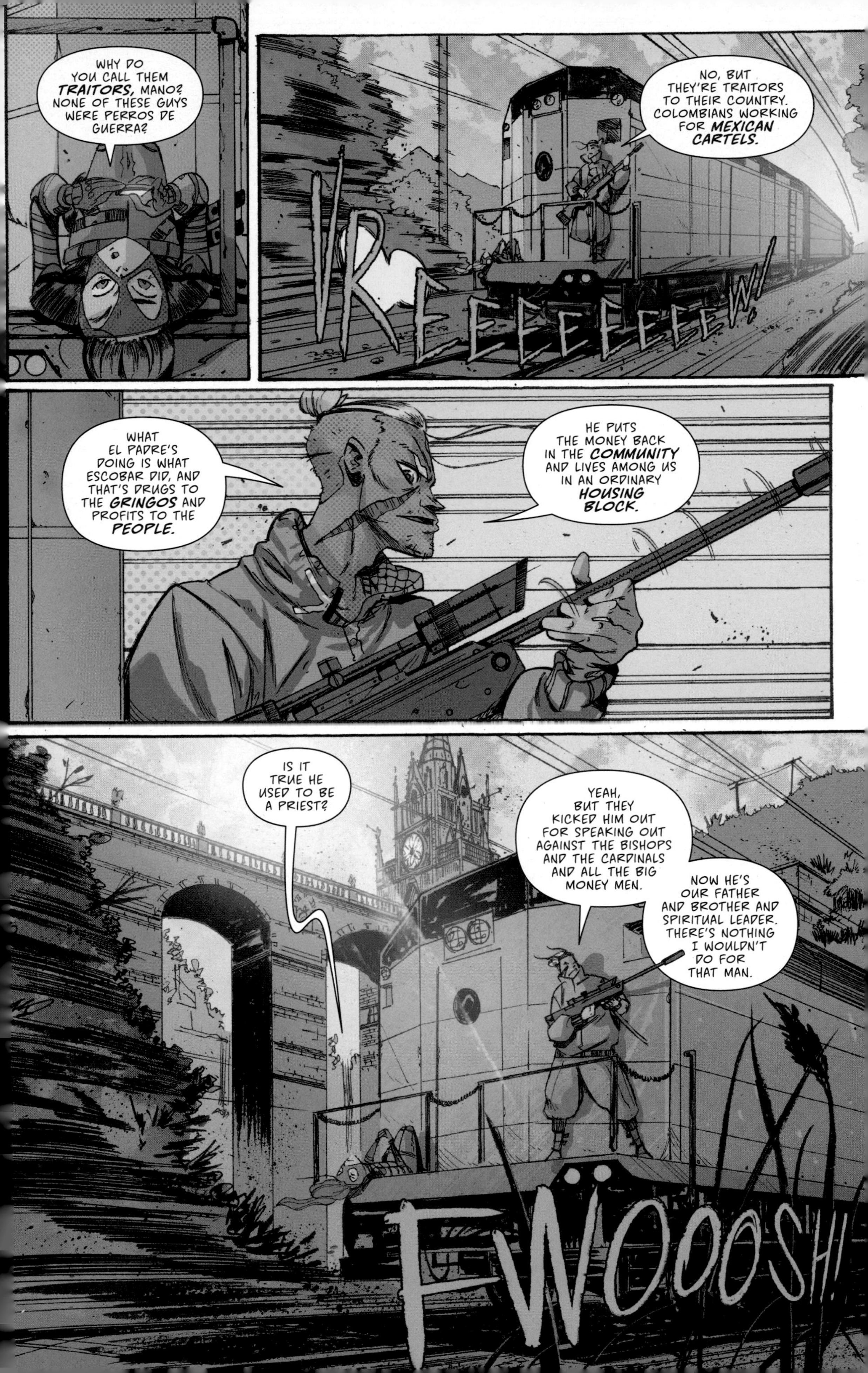
WHY DO YOU CALL THEM TRAITORS, MANO? NONE OF THESE GUYS WERE PERROS DE GUERRA?
NO, BUT THEY'RE TRAITORS TO THEIR COUNTRY. COLOMBIANS WORKING FOR MEXICAN CARTELS.
VREEEEEEEEEW!
WHAT EL PADRE'S DOING IS WHAT ESCOBAR DID, AND THAT'S DRUGS TO THE GRINGOS AND PROFITS TO THE PEOPLE.
HE PUTS THE MONEY BACK IN THE COMMUNITY AND LIVES AMONG US IN AN ORDINARY HOUSING BLOCK.
IS IT TRUE HE USED TO BE A PRIEST?
YEAH, BUT THEY KICKED HIM OUT FOR SPEAKING OUT AGAINST THE BISHOPS AND THE CARDINALS AND ALL THE BIG MONEY MEN.
NOW HE'S OUR FATHER AND BROTHER AND SPIRITUAL LEADER. THERE'S NOTHING I WOULDN'T DO FOR THAT MAN.
FWOOOSH!

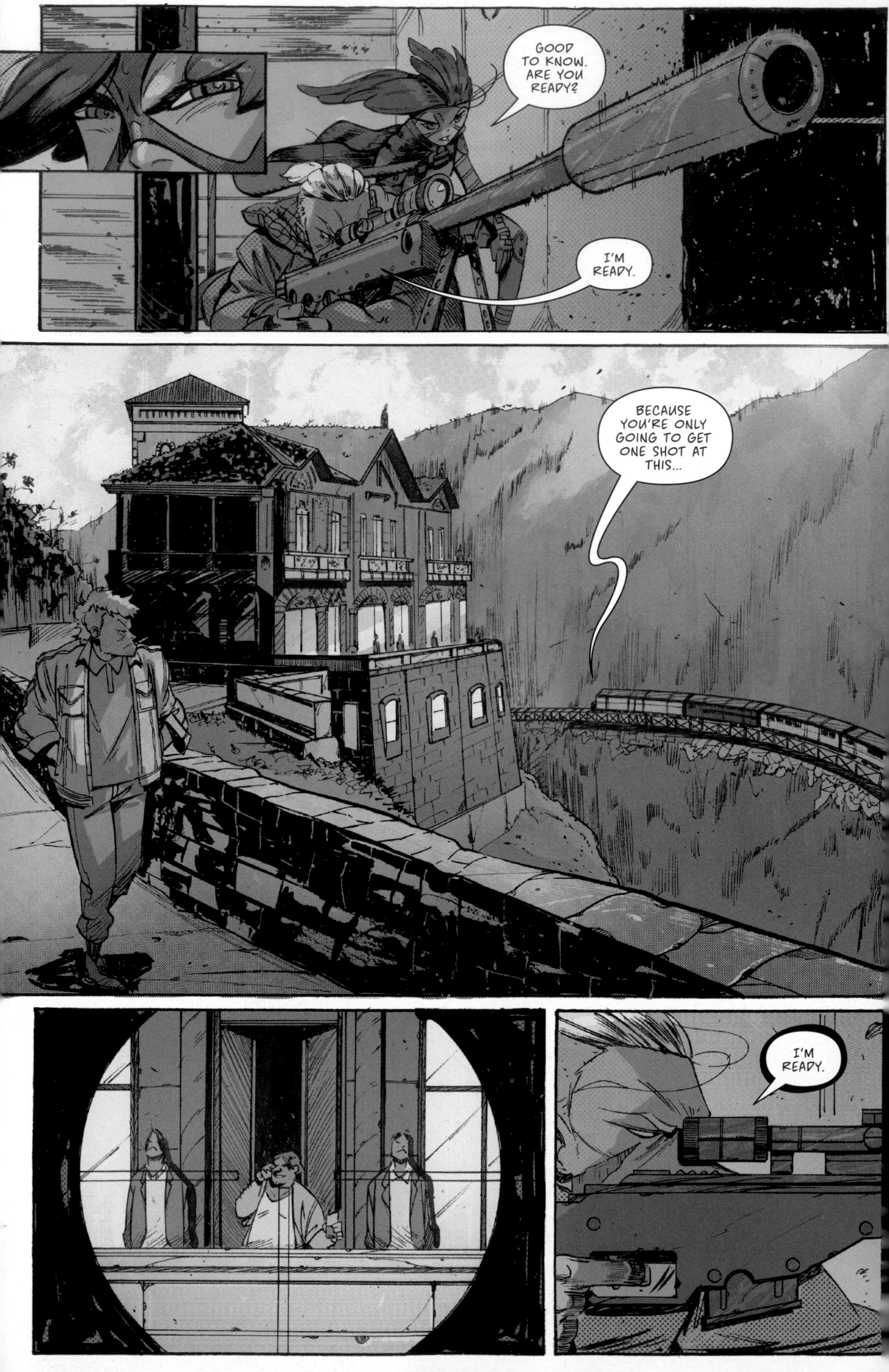
GOOD TO KNOW. ARE YOU READY?
I'M READY.
BECAUSE YOU'RE ONLY GOING TO GET ONE SHOT AT THIS...
I'M READY.

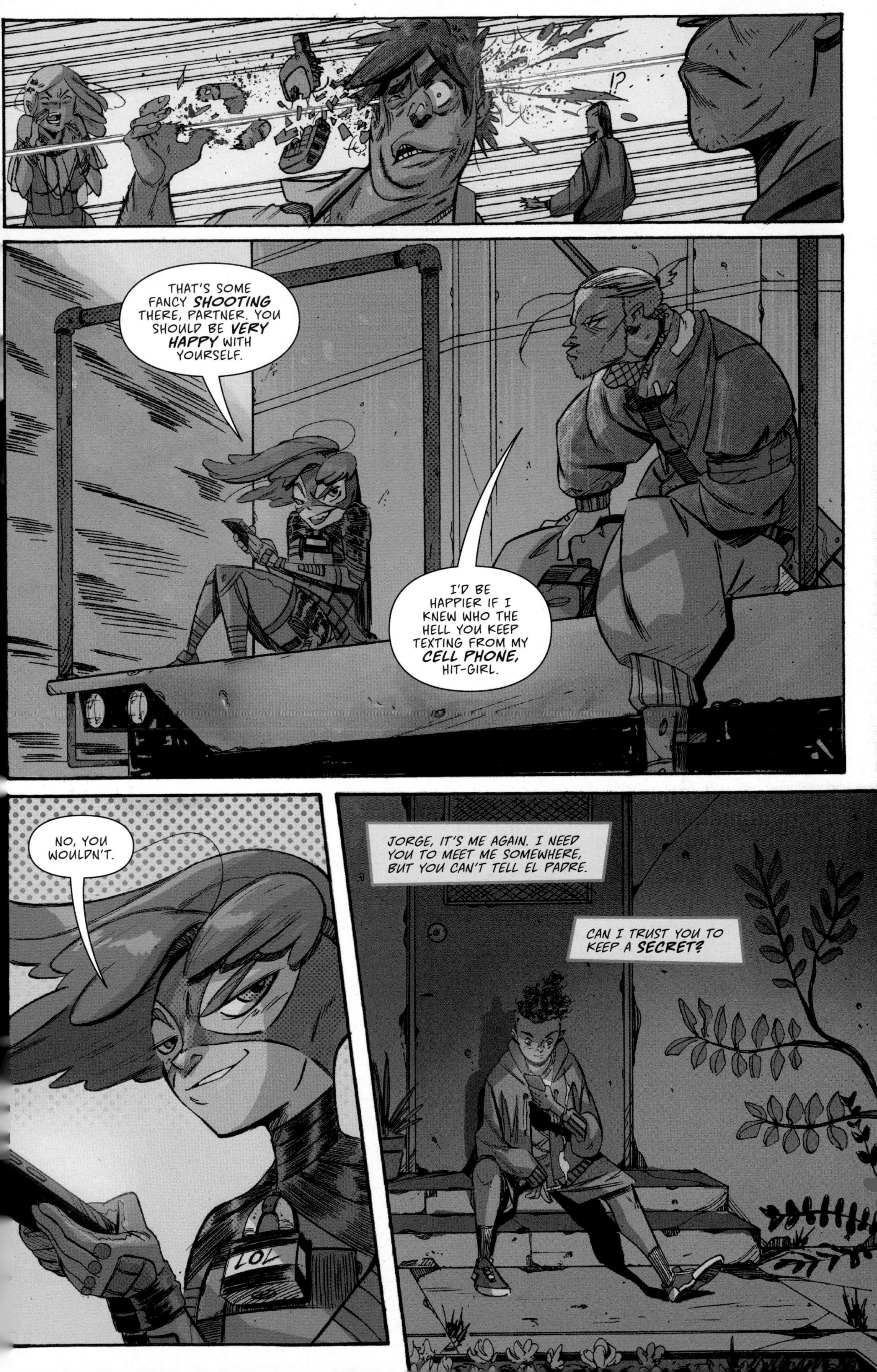
!?
THAT'S SOME FANCY **SHOOTING** THERE, PARTNER. YOU SHOULD BE **VERY HAPPY** WITH YOURSELF.
I'D BE HAPPIER IF I KNEW WHO THE HELL YOU KEEP TEXTING FROM MY **CELL PHONE,** HIT-GIRL.
NO, YOU WOULDN'T.
LOL
JORGE, IT'S ME AGAIN. I NEED YOU TO MEET ME SOMEWHERE, BUT YOU CAN'T TELL EL PADRE.
CAN I TRUST YOU TO KEEP A **SECRET?**

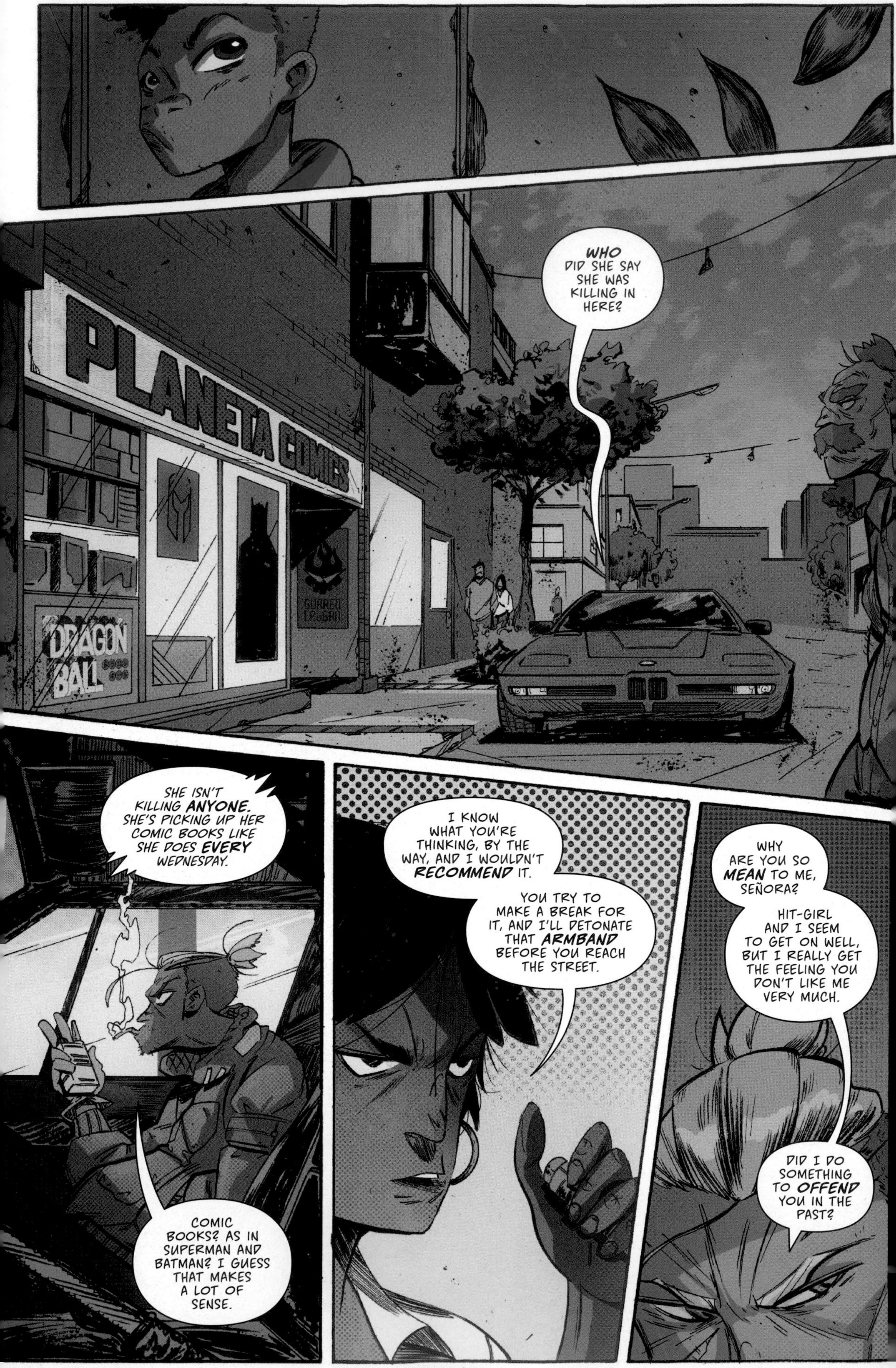

PLANETA COMICS
DRAGON BALL
GURREN LAGANN
WHO DID SHE SAY SHE WAS KILLING IN HERE?
SHE ISN'T KILLING ANYONE. SHE'S PICKING UP HER COMIC BOOKS LIKE SHE DOES EVERY WEDNESDAY.
COMIC BOOKS? AS IN SUPERMAN AND BATMAN? I GUESS THAT MAKES A LOT OF SENSE.
I KNOW WHAT YOU'RE THINKING, BY THE WAY, AND I WOULDN'T RECOMMEND IT.
YOU TRY TO MAKE A BREAK FOR IT, AND I'LL DETONATE THAT ARMBAND BEFORE YOU REACH THE STREET.
WHY ARE YOU SO MEAN TO ME, SEÑORA?
HIT-GIRL AND I SEEM TO GET ON WELL, BUT I REALLY GET THE FEELING YOU DON'T LIKE ME VERY MUCH.
DID I DO SOMETHING TO OFFEND YOU IN THE PAST?

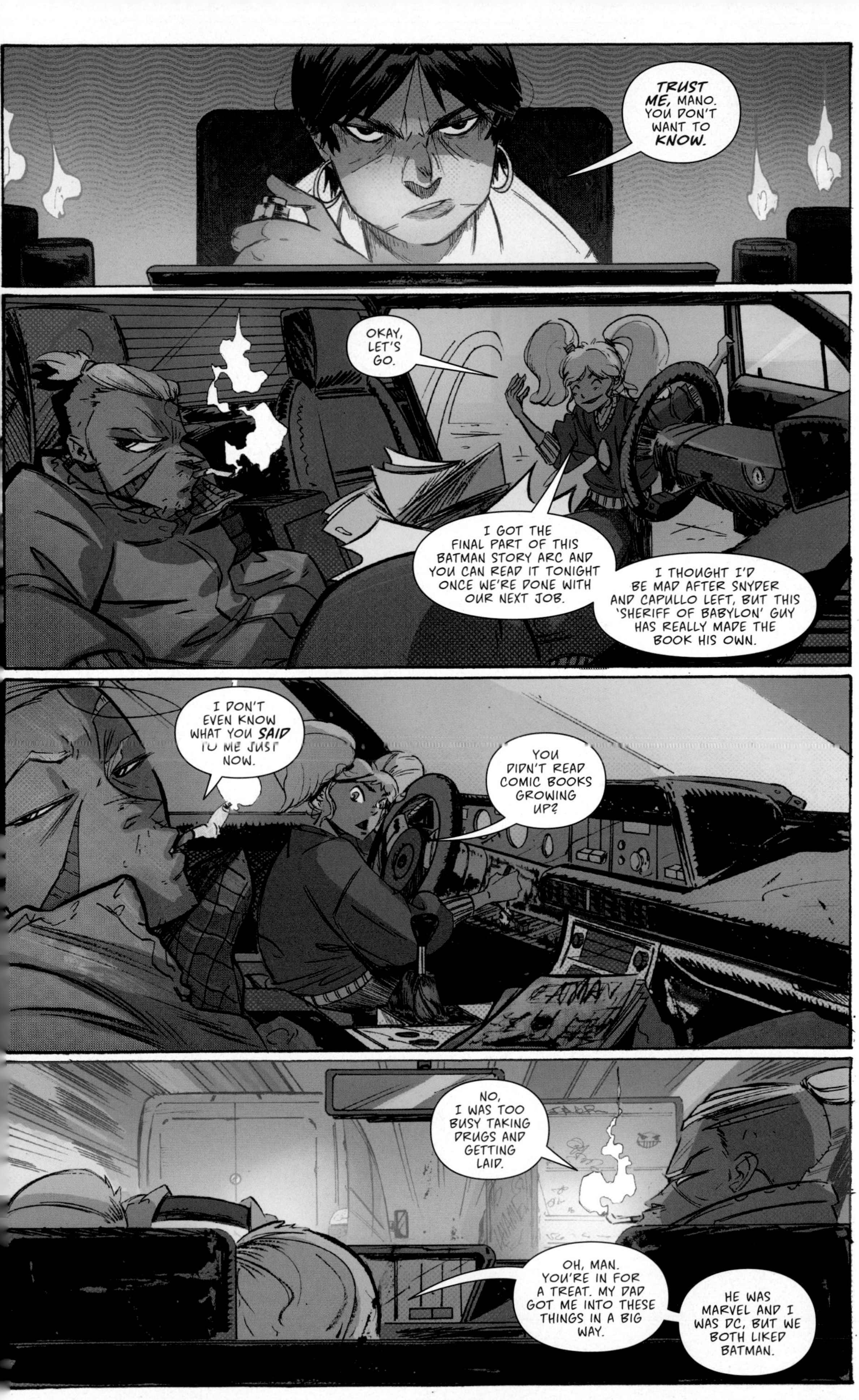
TRUST ME, MANO. YOU DON'T WANT TO KNOW.
OKAY, LET'S GO.
I GOT THE FINAL PART OF THIS BATMAN STORY ARC AND YOU CAN READ IT TONIGHT ONCE WE'RE DONE WITH OUR NEXT JOB.
I THOUGHT I'D BE MAD AFTER SNYDER AND CAPULLO LEFT, BUT THIS 'SHERIFF OF BABYLON' GUY HAS REALLY MADE THE BOOK HIS OWN.
I DON'T EVEN KNOW WHAT YOU SAID TO ME JUST NOW.
YOU DIDN'T READ COMIC BOOKS GROWING UP?
NO, I WAS TOO BUSY TAKING DRUGS AND GETTING LAID.
OH, MAN. YOU'RE IN FOR A TREAT. MY DAD GOT ME INTO THESE THINGS IN A BIG WAY.
HE WAS MARVEL AND I WAS DC, BUT WE BOTH LIKED BATMAN.

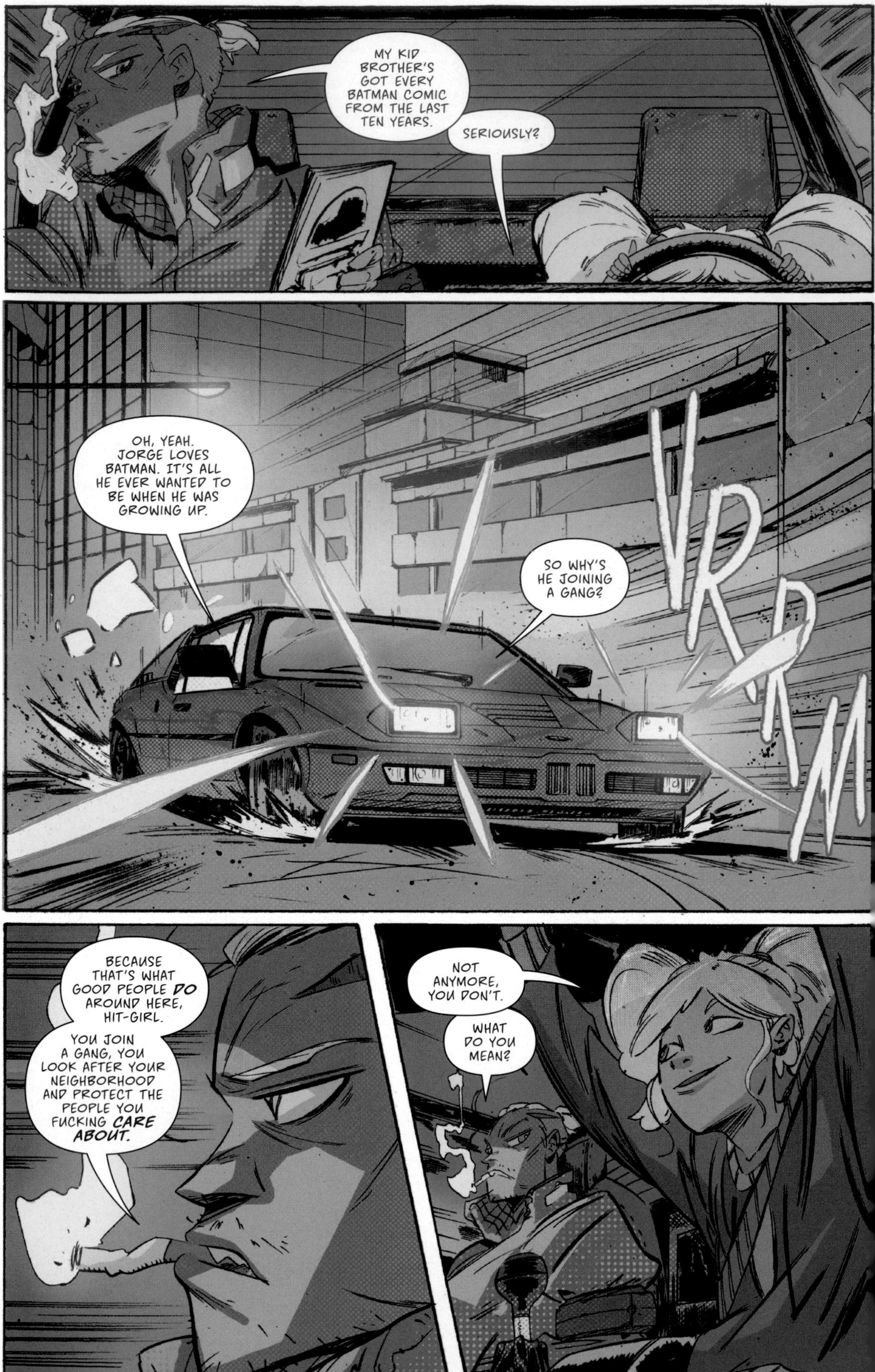

MY KID BROTHER'S GOT EVERY BATMAN COMIC FROM THE LAST TEN YEARS.
SERIOUSLY?
OH, YEAH. JORGE LOVES BATMAN. IT'S ALL HE EVER WANTED TO BE WHEN HE WAS GROWING UP.
SO WHY'S HE JOINING A GANG?
VRRRM
BECAUSE THAT'S WHAT GOOD PEOPLE **DO** AROUND HERE, HIT-GIRL.
YOU JOIN A GANG, YOU LOOK AFTER YOUR NEIGHBORHOOD AND PROTECT THE PEOPLE YOU FUCKING **CARE ABOUT.**
NOT ANYMORE, YOU DON'T.
WHAT DO YOU MEAN?

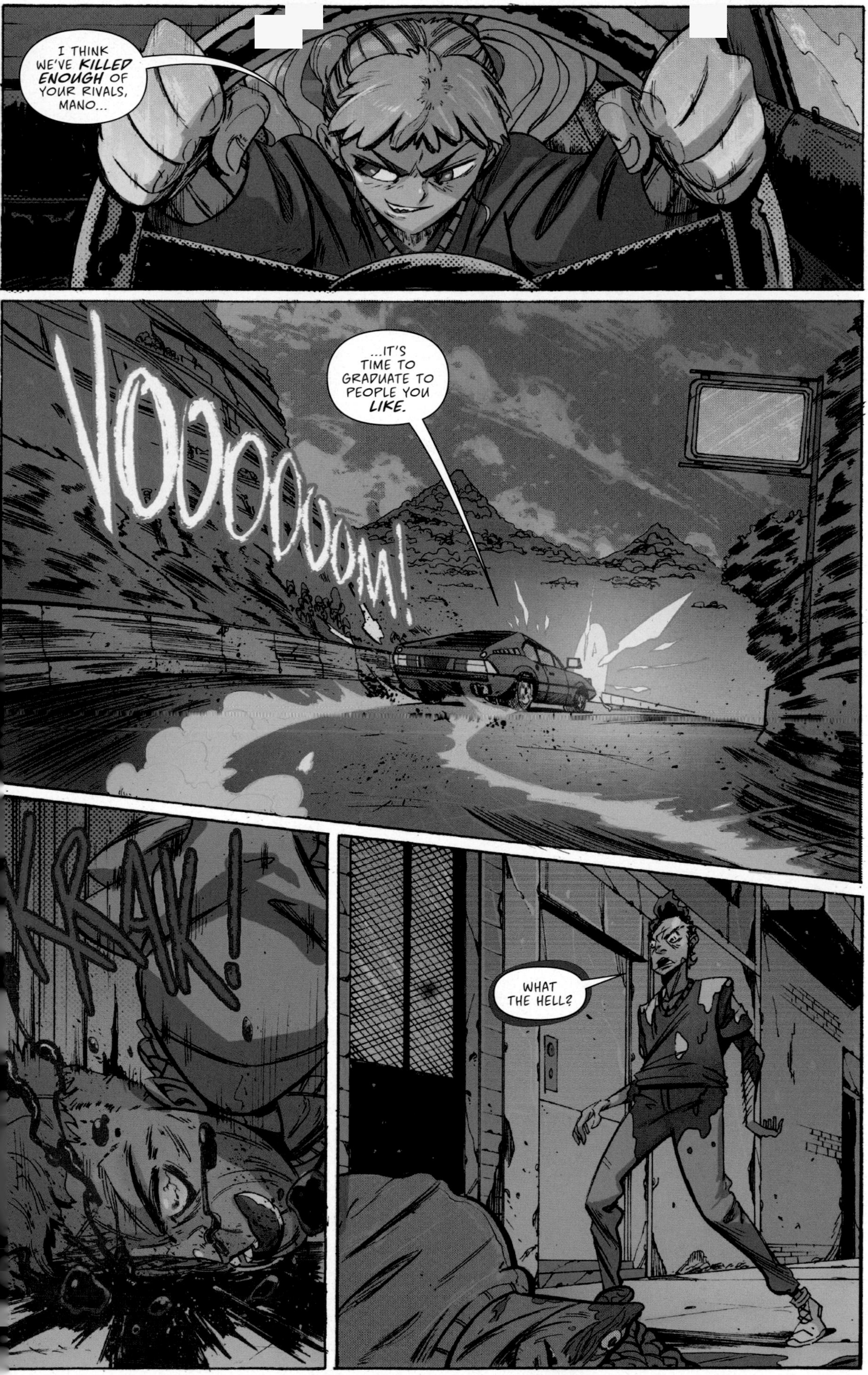
I THINK WE'VE KILLED ENOUGH OF YOUR RIVALS, MANO...
VOOOOOOM!
...IT'S TIME TO GRADUATE TO PEOPLE YOU LIKE.
KRAK!
WHAT THE HELL?

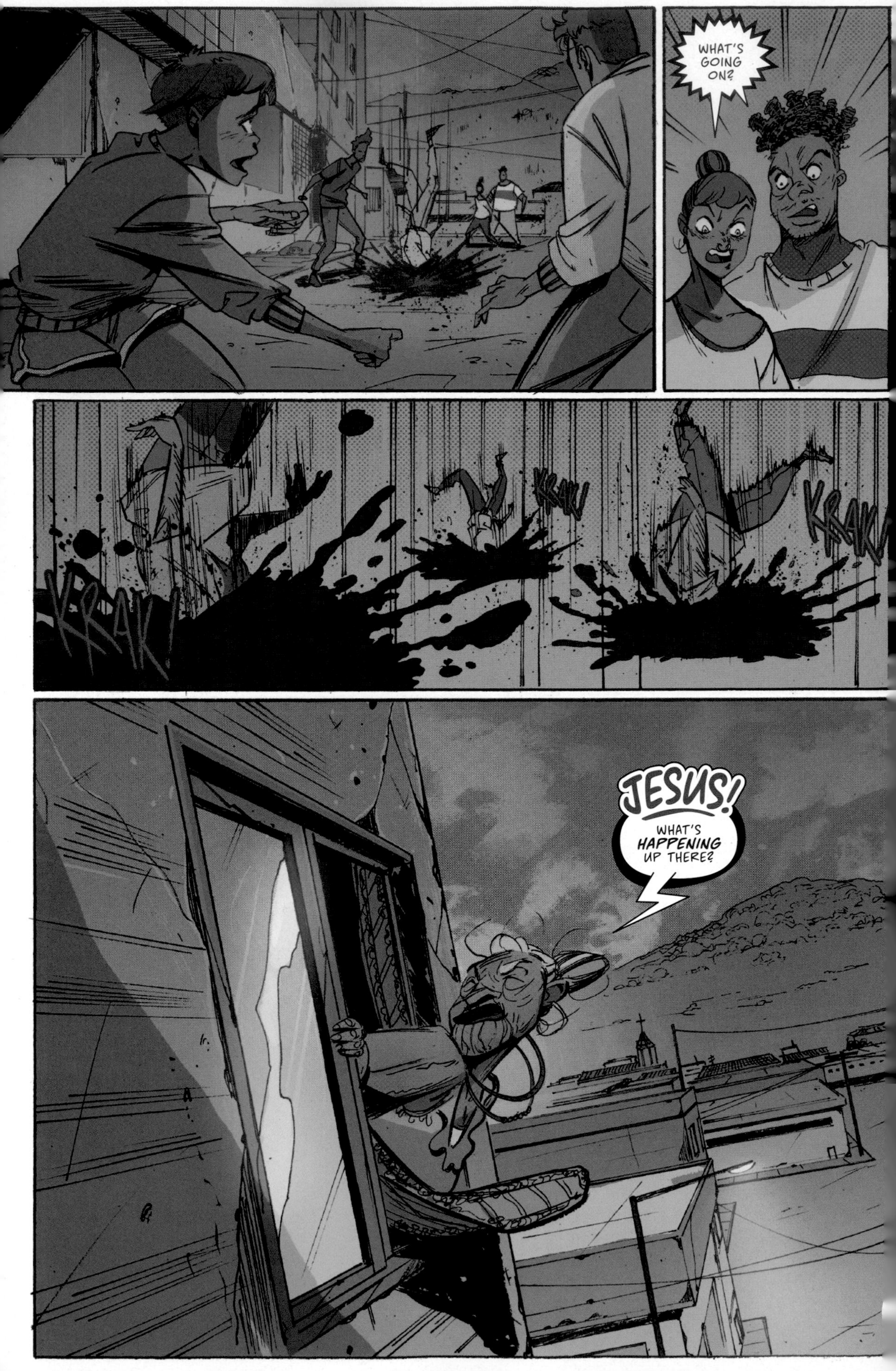
WHAT'S GOING ON?
KRAK!
KRAK!
KRAK!
JESUS!
WHAT'S HAPPENING UP THERE?

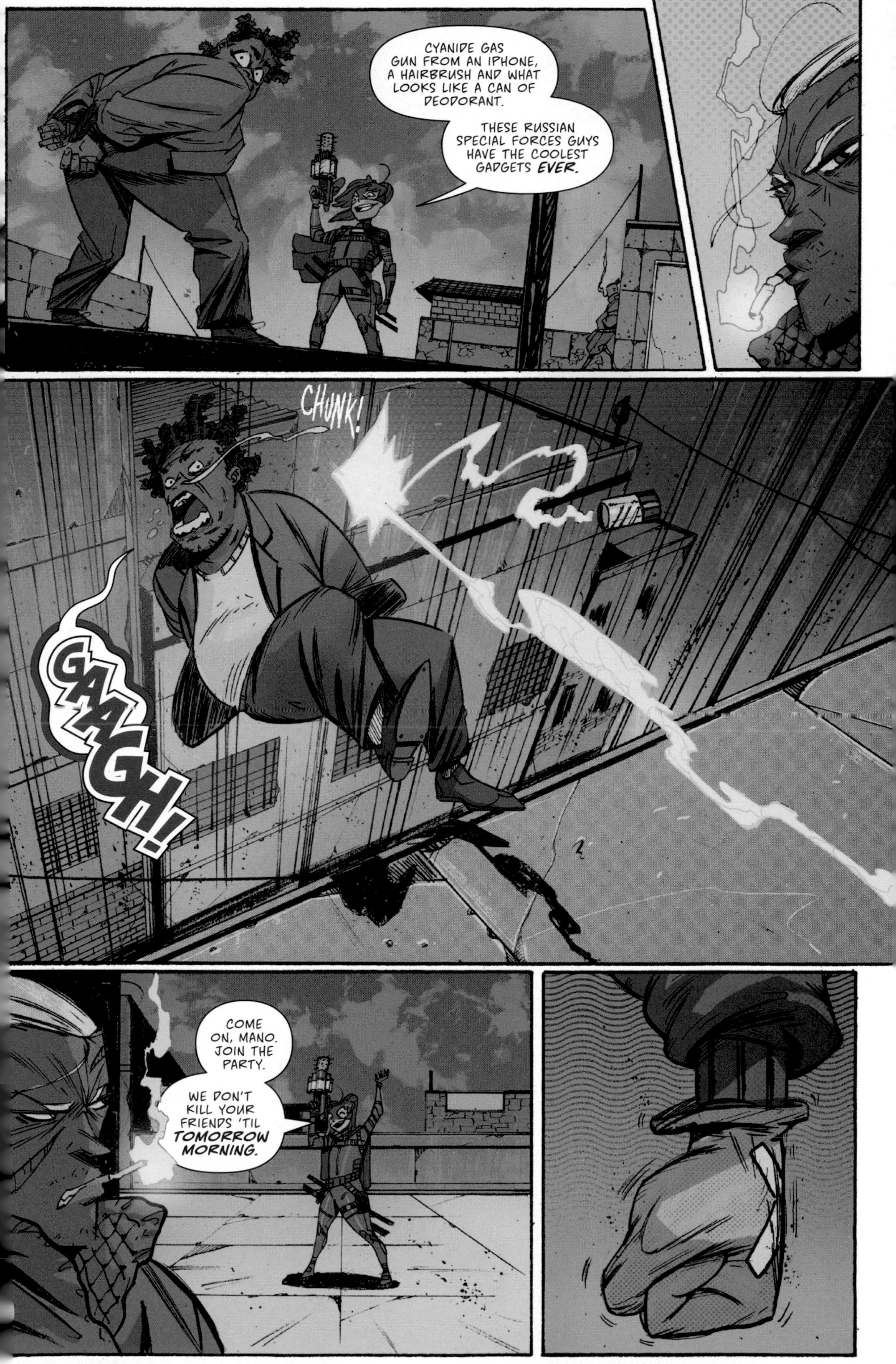

CYANIDE GAS GUN FROM AN IPHONE, A HAIRBRUSH AND WHAT LOOKS LIKE A CAN OF DEODORANT.
THESE RUSSIAN SPECIAL FORCES GUYS HAVE THE COOLEST GADGETS EVER.
CHUNK!
GAAGH!
COME ON, MANO. JOIN THE PARTY.
WE DON'T KILL YOUR FRIENDS 'TIL TOMORROW MORNING.

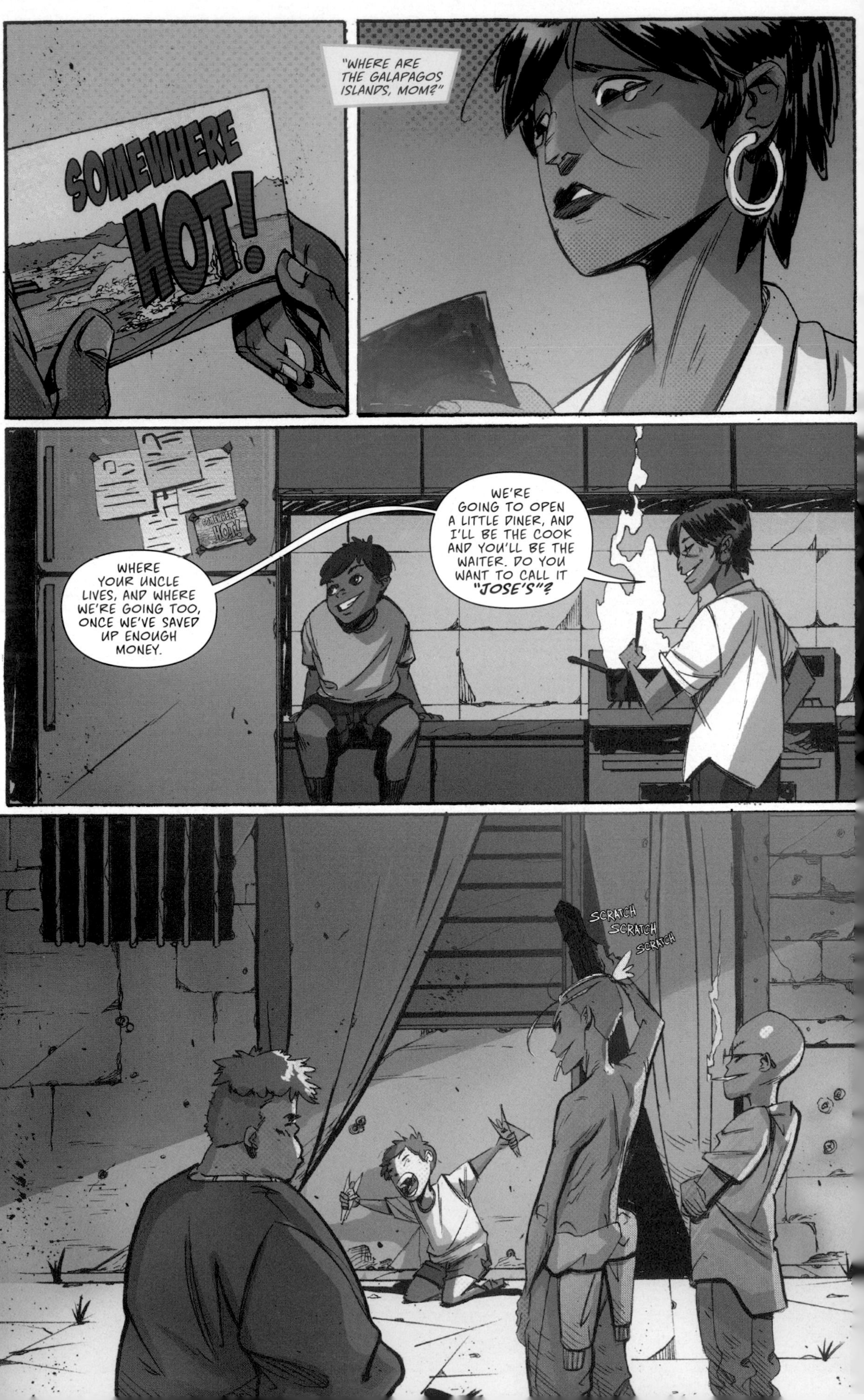
SOMEWHERE HOT!
"WHERE ARE THE GALAPAGOS ISLANDS, MOM?"
SOMEWHERE HOT!
WHERE YOUR UNCLE LIVES, AND WHERE WE'RE GOING TOO, ONCE WE'VE SAVED UP ENOUGH MONEY.
WE'RE GOING TO OPEN A LITTLE DINER, AND I'LL BE THE COOK AND YOU'LL BE THE WAITER. DO YOU WANT TO CALL IT "JOSE'S"?
SCRATCH SCRATCH SCRATCH

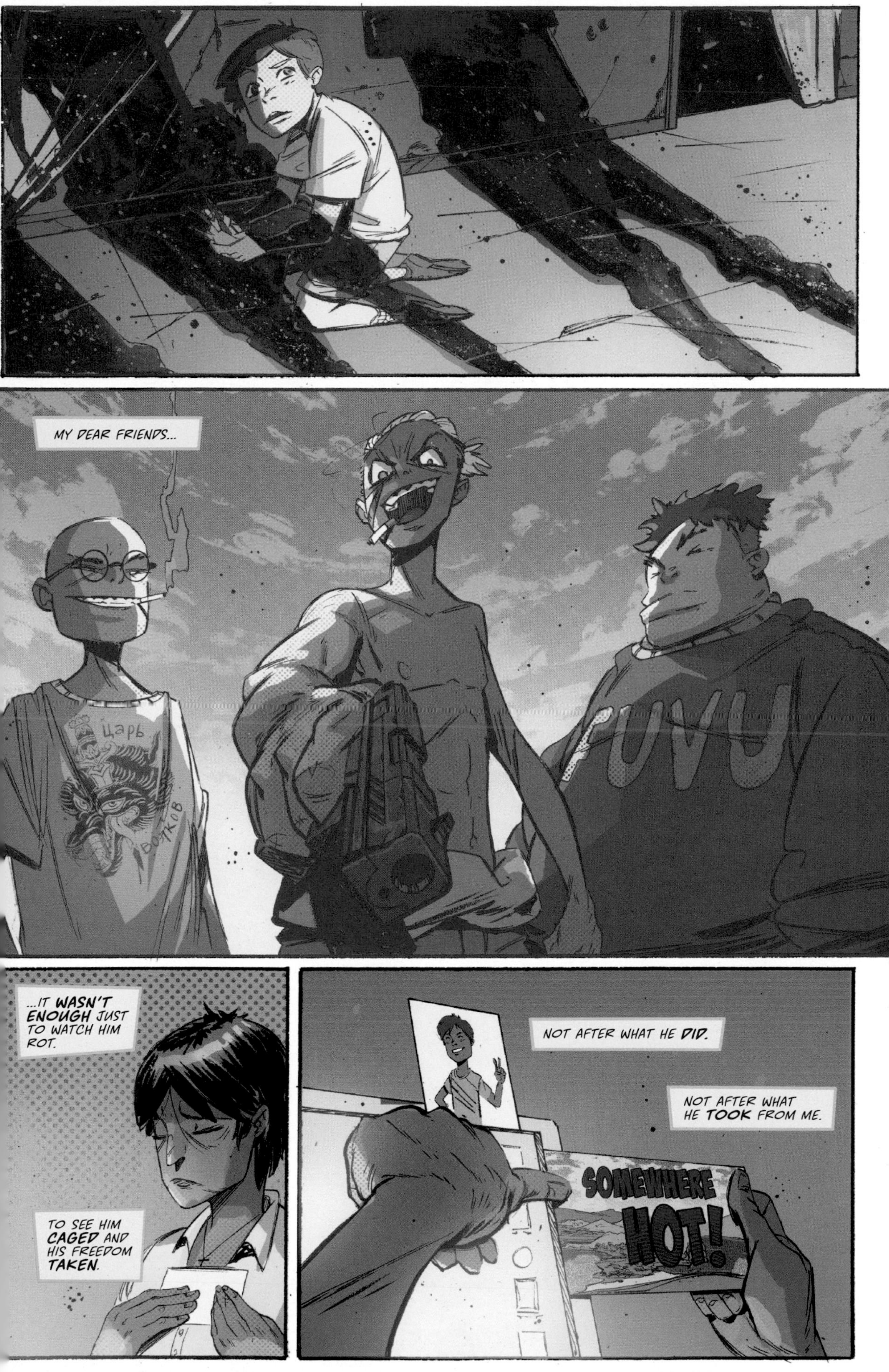
MY DEAR FRIENDS...
Царь
...IT **WASN'T ENOUGH** JUST TO WATCH HIM ROT.
TO SEE HIM **CAGED** AND HIS FREEDOM **TAKEN**.
NOT AFTER WHAT HE **DID**.
NOT AFTER WHAT HE **TOOK** FROM ME.
SOMEWHERE HOT!

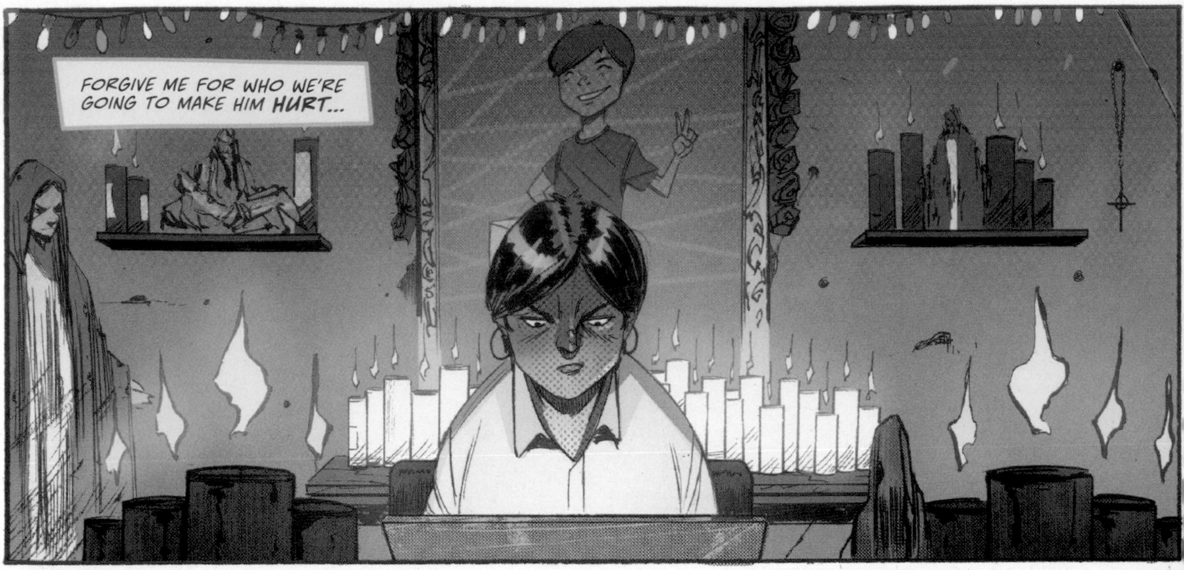
FORGIVE ME FOR WHO WE'RE GOING TO MAKE HIM HURT...

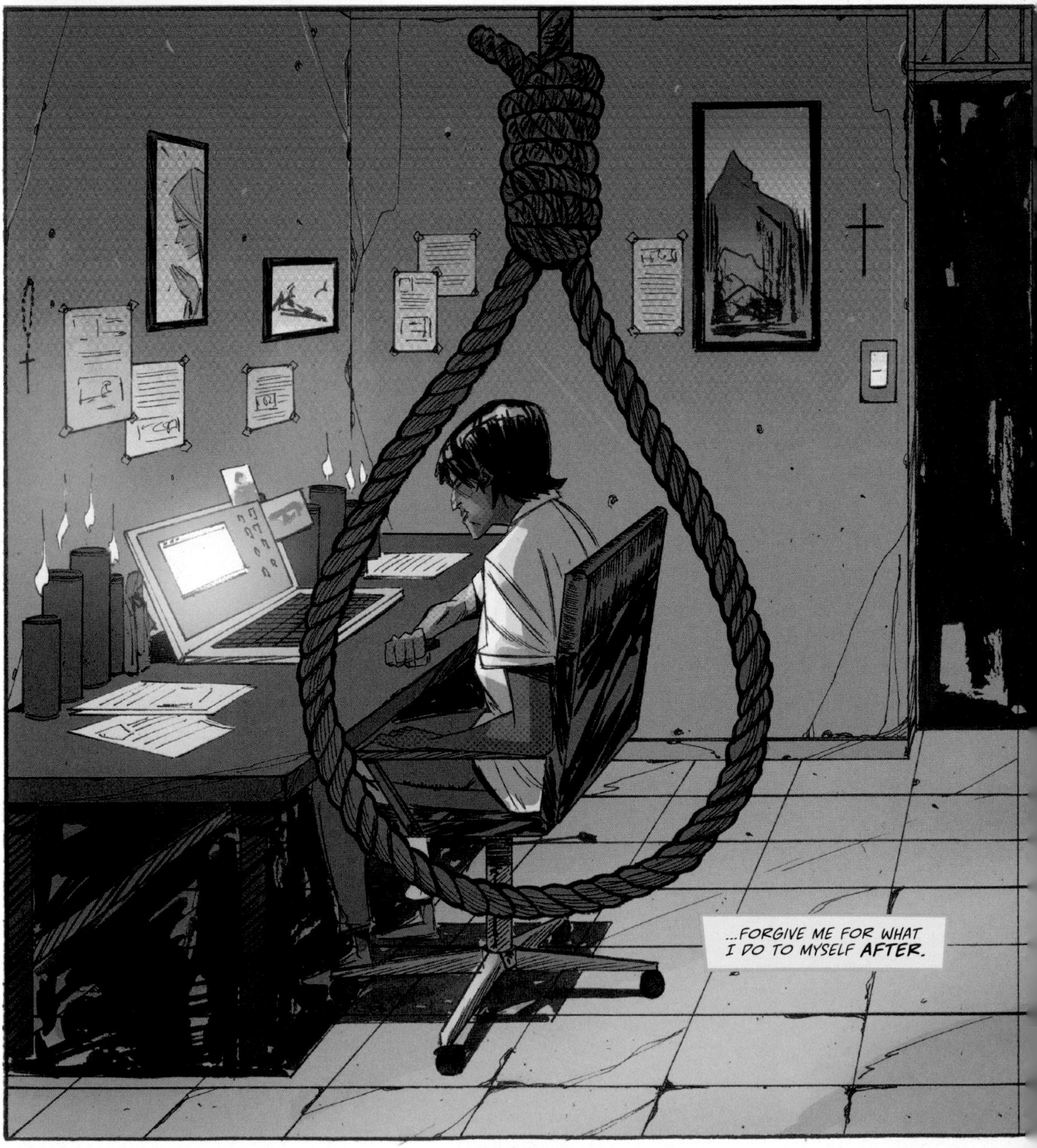
...FORGIVE ME FOR WHAT I DO TO MYSELF AFTER.

THREE

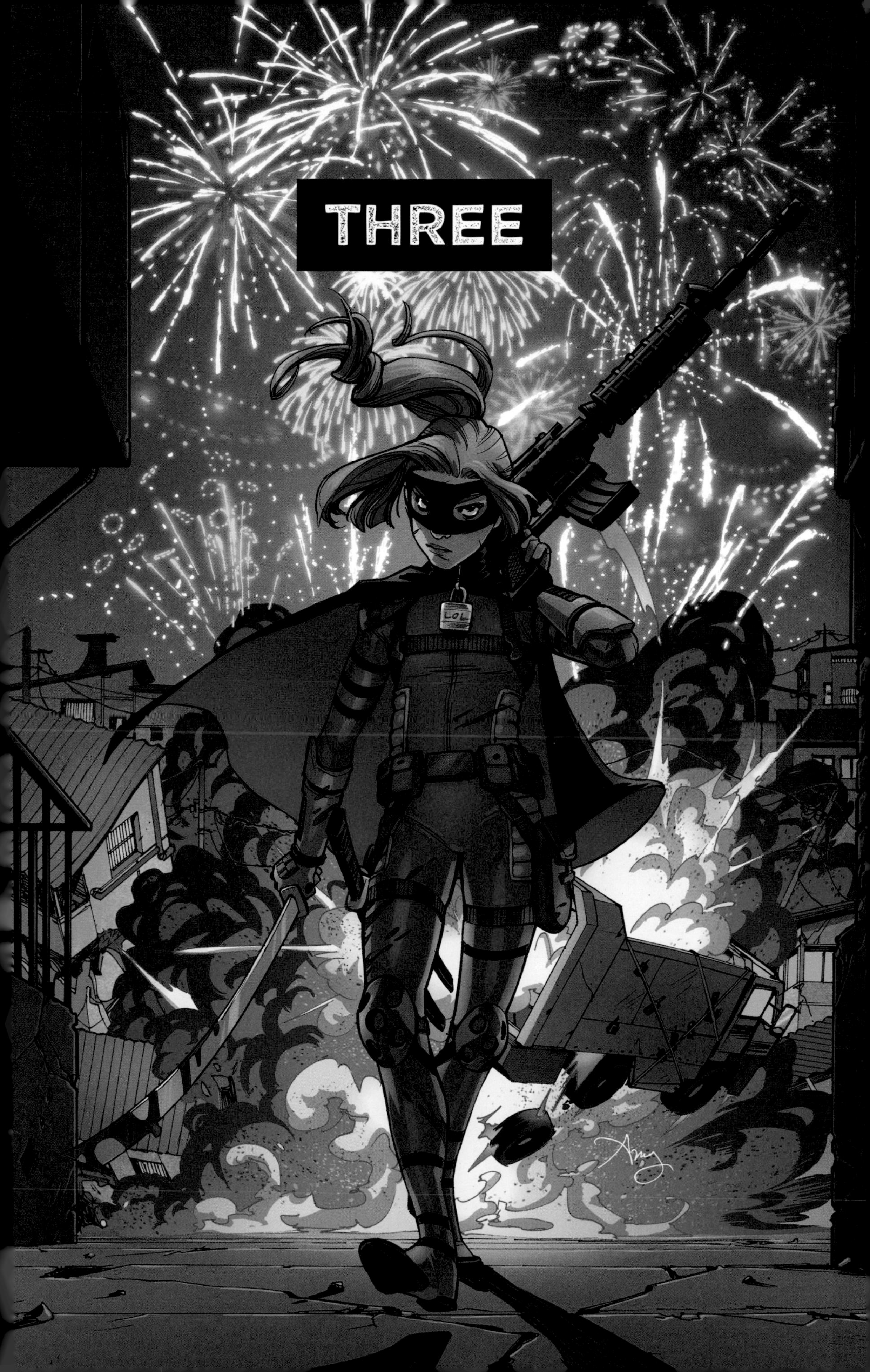
LOL

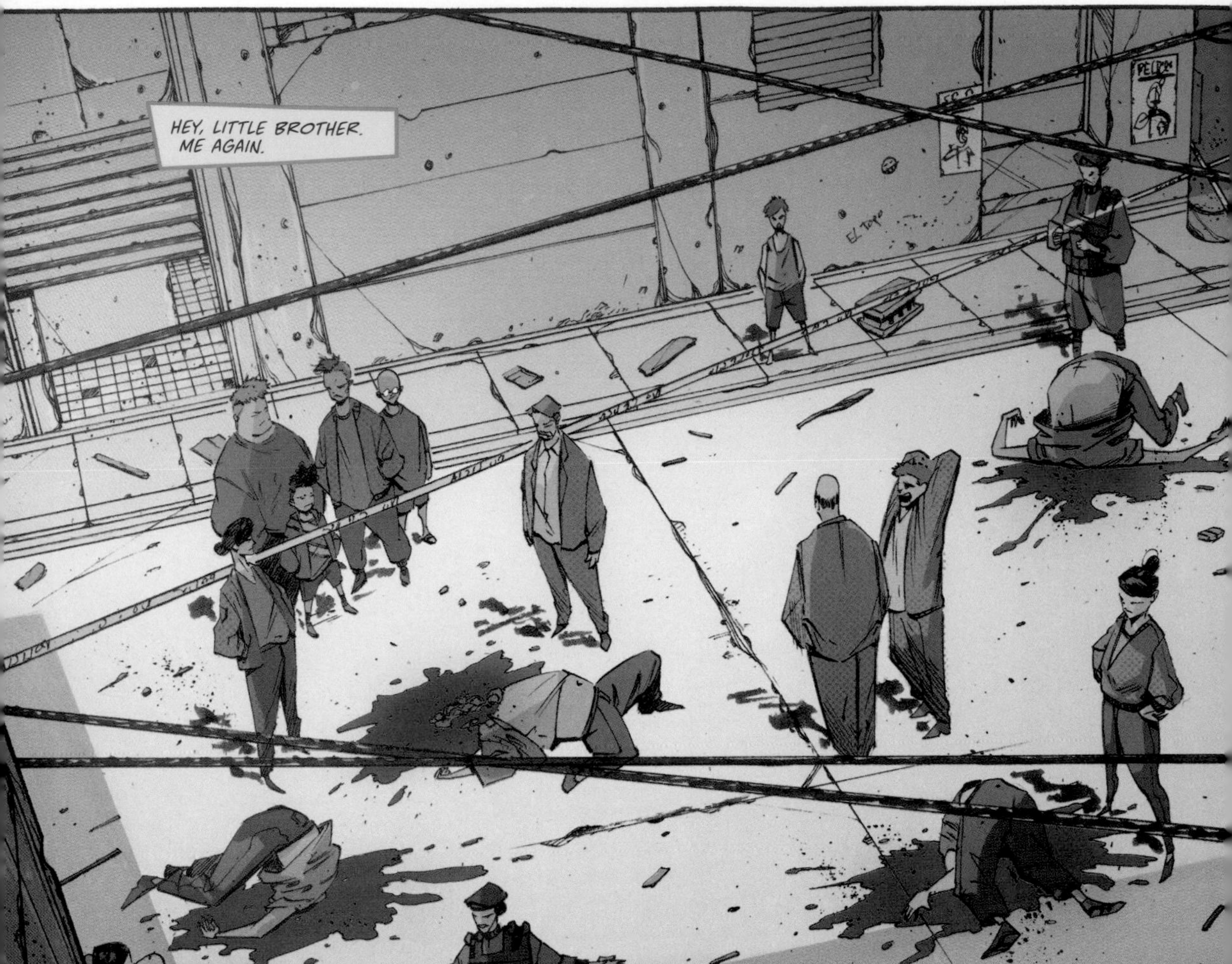
HEY, LITTLE BROTHER. ME AGAIN.
I KNOW WHAT I'M ASKING FOR LOOKS LIKE A TRAP, BUT YOU HAVE TO TRUST ME.
IT'S ALL GOING TO BE FINE.

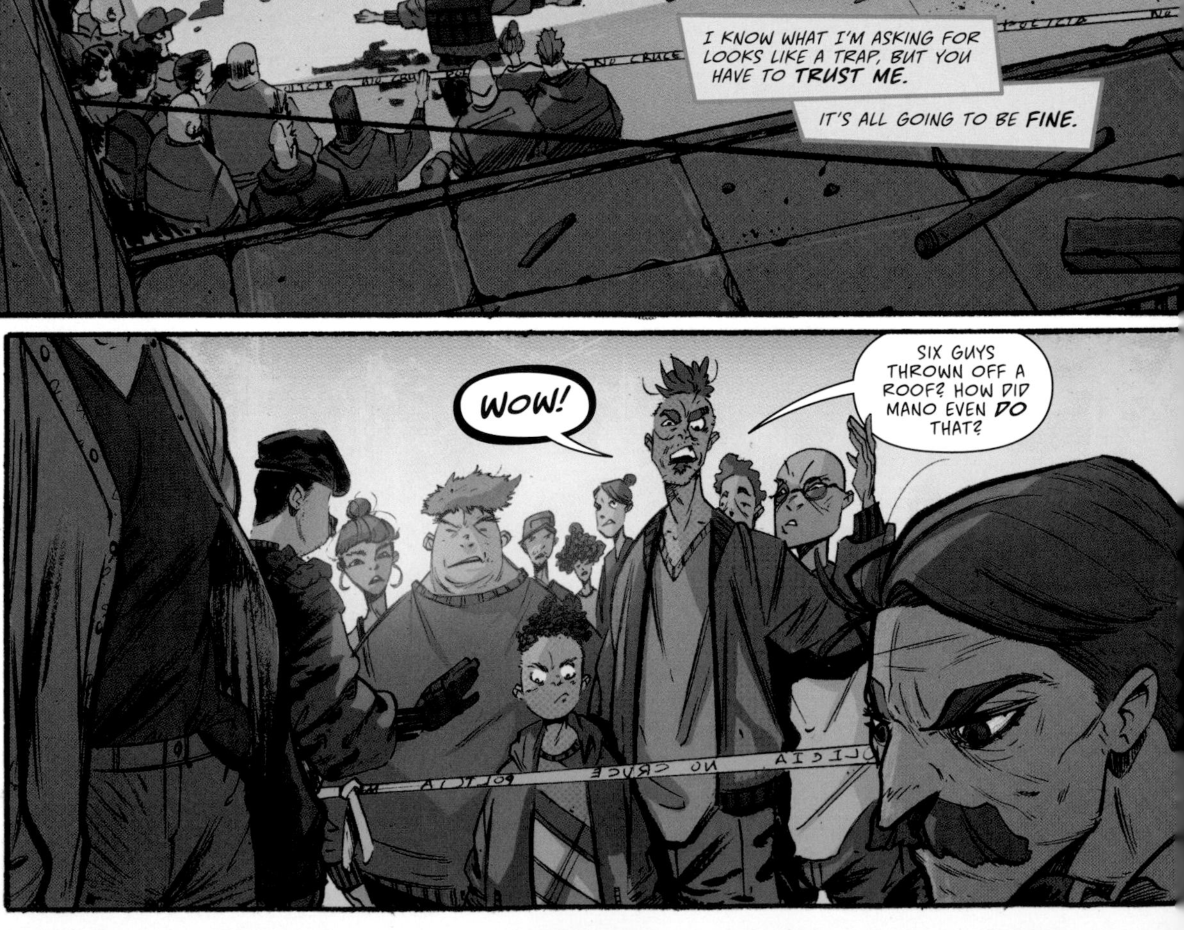
WOW!
SIX GUYS THROWN OFF A ROOF? HOW DID MANO EVEN DO THAT?

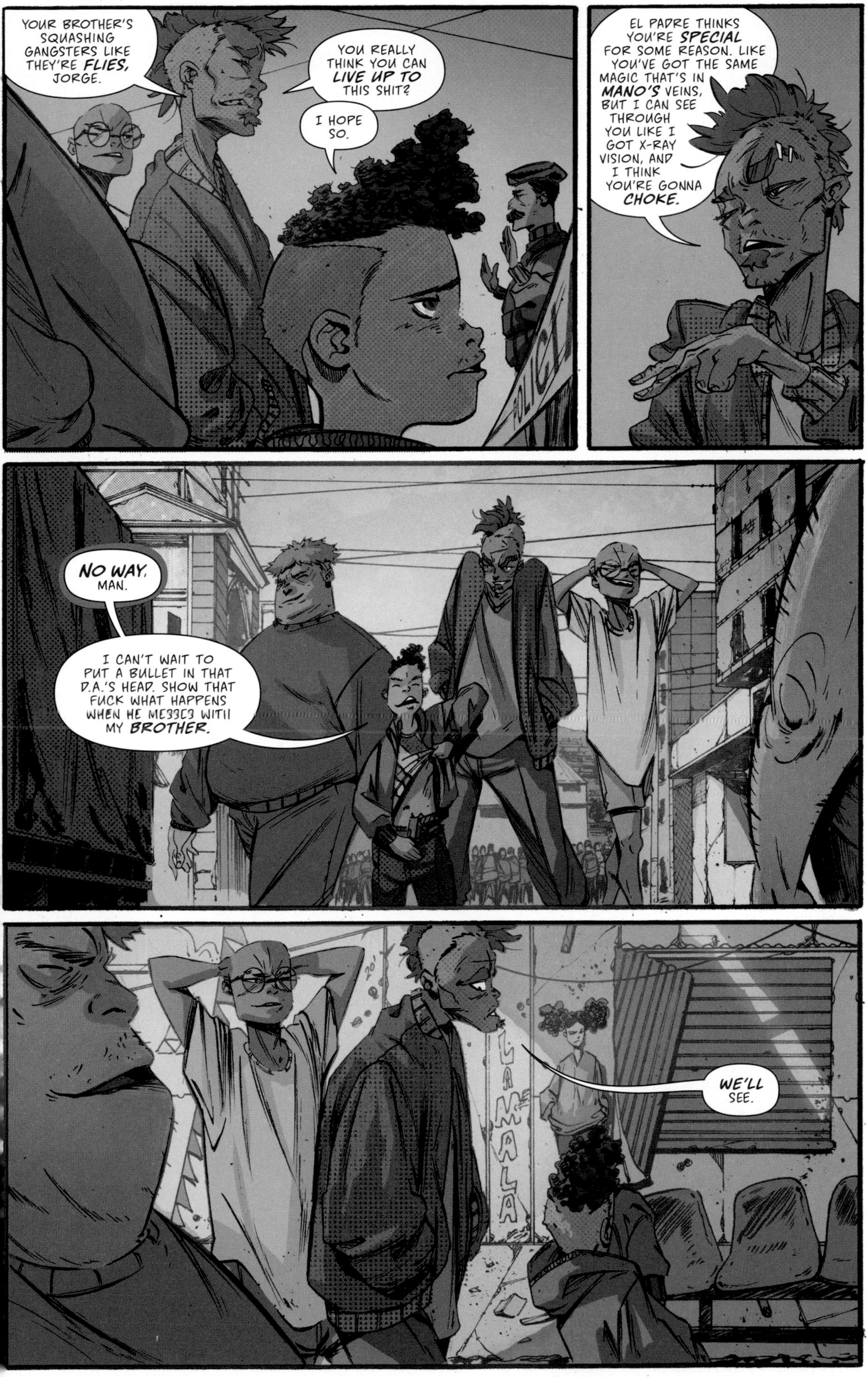
YOUR BROTHER'S SQUASHING GANGSTERS LIKE THEY'RE FLIES, JORGE.
YOU REALLY THINK YOU CAN LIVE UP TO THIS SHIT?
I HOPE SO.
EL PADRE THINKS YOU'RE SPECIAL FOR SOME REASON. LIKE YOU'VE GOT THE SAME MAGIC THAT'S IN MANO'S VEINS, BUT I CAN SEE THROUGH YOU LIKE I GOT X-RAY VISION, AND I THINK YOU'RE GONNA CHOKE.
NO WAY, MAN.
I CAN'T WAIT TO PUT A BULLET IN THAT D.A.'S HEAD. SHOW THAT FUCK WHAT HAPPENS WHEN HE MESSES WITH MY BROTHER.
WE'LL SEE.

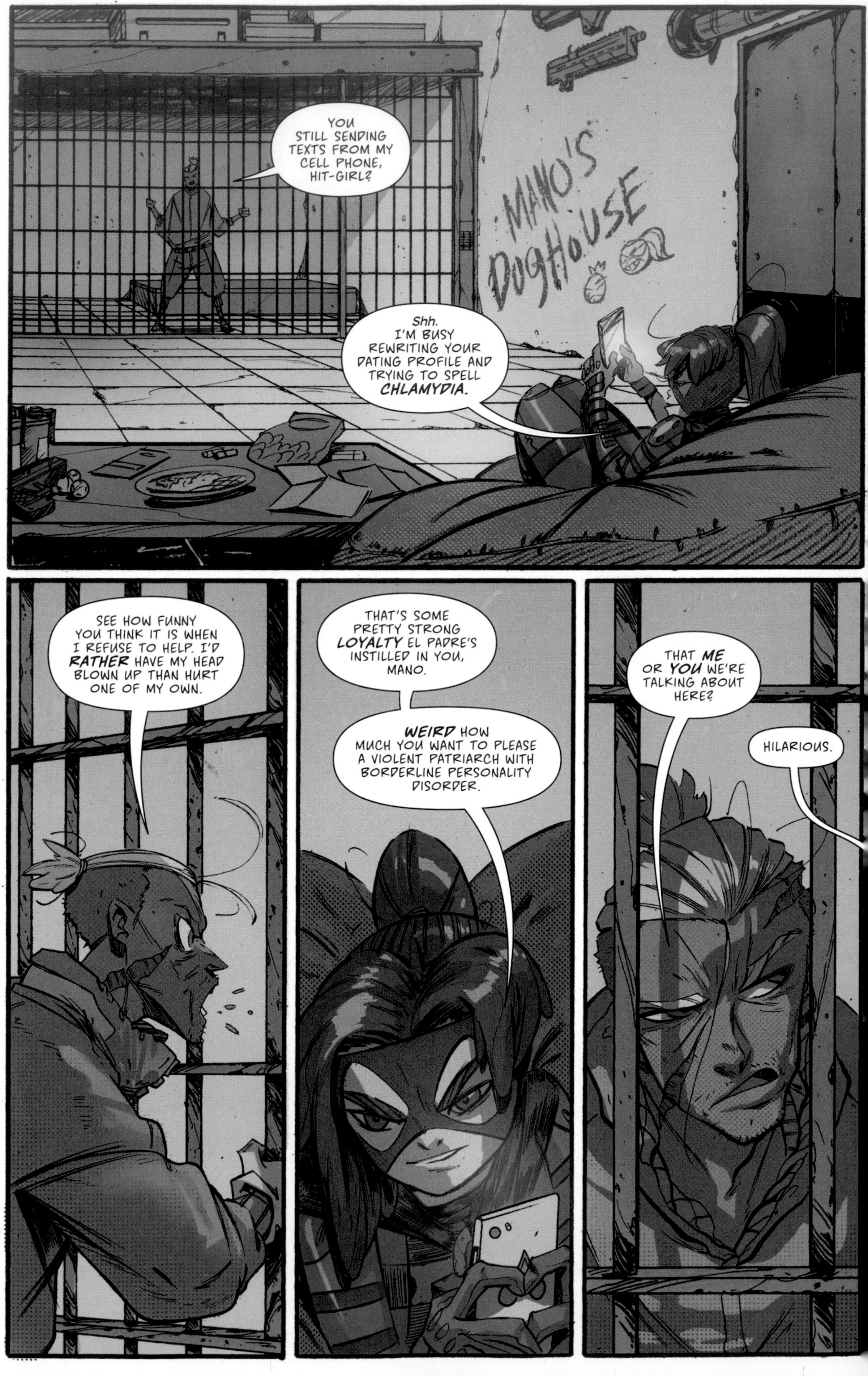

YOU STILL SENDING TEXTS FROM MY CELL PHONE, HIT-GIRL?
MANO'S DOGHOUSE
Shh. I'M BUSY REWRITING YOUR DATING PROFILE AND TRYING TO SPELL CHLAMYDIA.
SEE HOW FUNNY YOU THINK IT IS WHEN I REFUSE TO HELP. I'D RATHER HAVE MY HEAD BLOWN UP THAN HURT ONE OF MY OWN.
THAT'S SOME PRETTY STRONG LOYALTY EL PADRE'S INSTILLED IN YOU, MANO.
WEIRD HOW MUCH YOU WANT TO PLEASE A VIOLENT PATRIARCH WITH BORDERLINE PERSONALITY DISORDER.
THAT ME OR YOU WE'RE TALKING ABOUT HERE?
HILARIOUS.

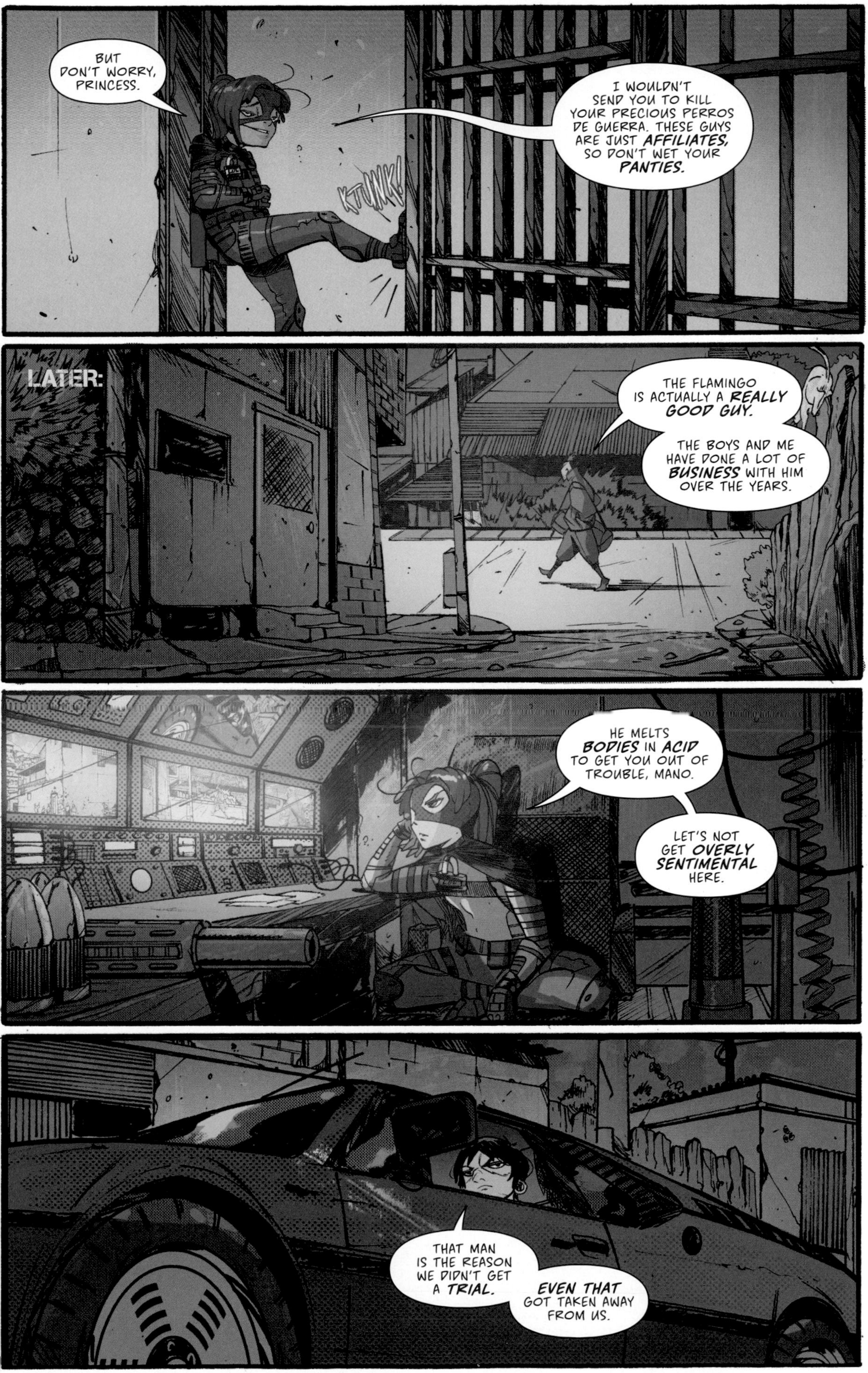
BUT DON'T WORRY, PRINCESS.
I WOULDN'T SEND YOU TO KILL YOUR PRECIOUS PERROS DE GUERRA. THESE GUYS ARE JUST AFFILIATES, SO DON'T WET YOUR PANTIES.
KTUNK!
LATER:
THE FLAMINGO IS ACTUALLY A REALLY GOOD GUY.
THE BOYS AND ME HAVE DONE A LOT OF BUSINESS WITH HIM OVER THE YEARS.
HE MELTS BODIES IN ACID TO GET YOU OUT OF TROUBLE, MANO.
LET'S NOT GET OVERLY SENTIMENTAL HERE.
THAT MAN IS THE REASON WE DIDN'T GET A TRIAL.
EVEN THAT GOT TAKEN AWAY FROM US.

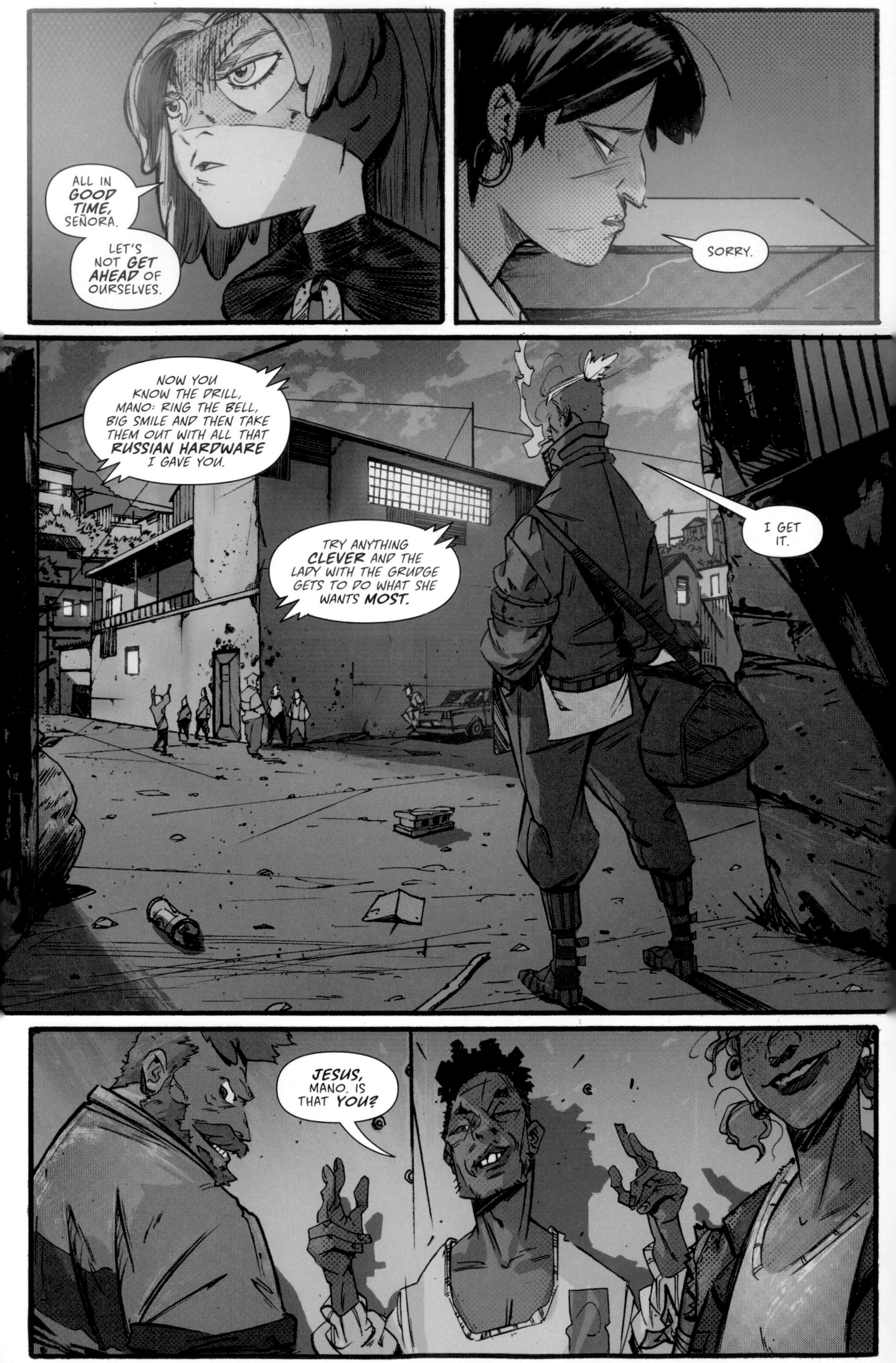
ALL IN GOOD TIME, SEÑORA.
LET'S NOT GET AHEAD OF OURSELVES.
SORRY.
NOW YOU KNOW THE DRILL, MANO: RING THE BELL, BIG SMILE AND THEN TAKE THEM OUT WITH ALL THAT RUSSIAN HARDWARE I GAVE YOU.
TRY ANYTHING CLEVER AND THE LADY WITH THE GRUDGE GETS TO DO WHAT SHE WANTS MOST.
I GET IT.
JESUS, MANO. IS THAT YOU?

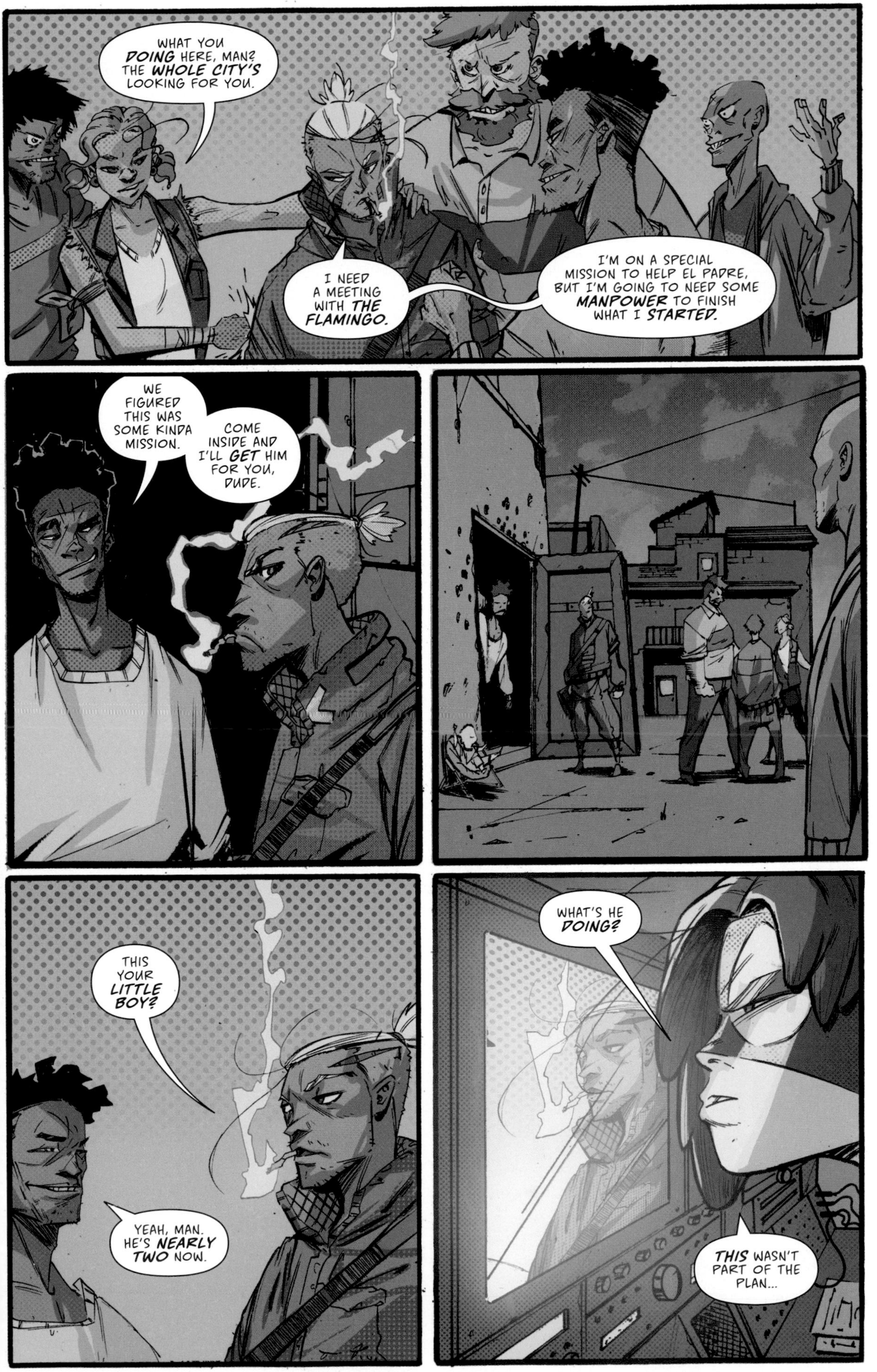
WHAT YOU DOING HERE, MAN? THE WHOLE CITY'S LOOKING FOR YOU.
I NEED A MEETING WITH THE FLAMINGO.
I'M ON A SPECIAL MISSION TO HELP EL PADRE, BUT I'M GOING TO NEED SOME MANPOWER TO FINISH WHAT I STARTED.
WE FIGURED THIS WAS SOME KINDA MISSION.
COME INSIDE AND I'LL GET HIM FOR YOU, DUDE.
THIS YOUR LITTLE BOY?
YEAH, MAN. HE'S NEARLY TWO NOW.
WHAT'S HE DOING?
THIS WASN'T PART OF THE PLAN...

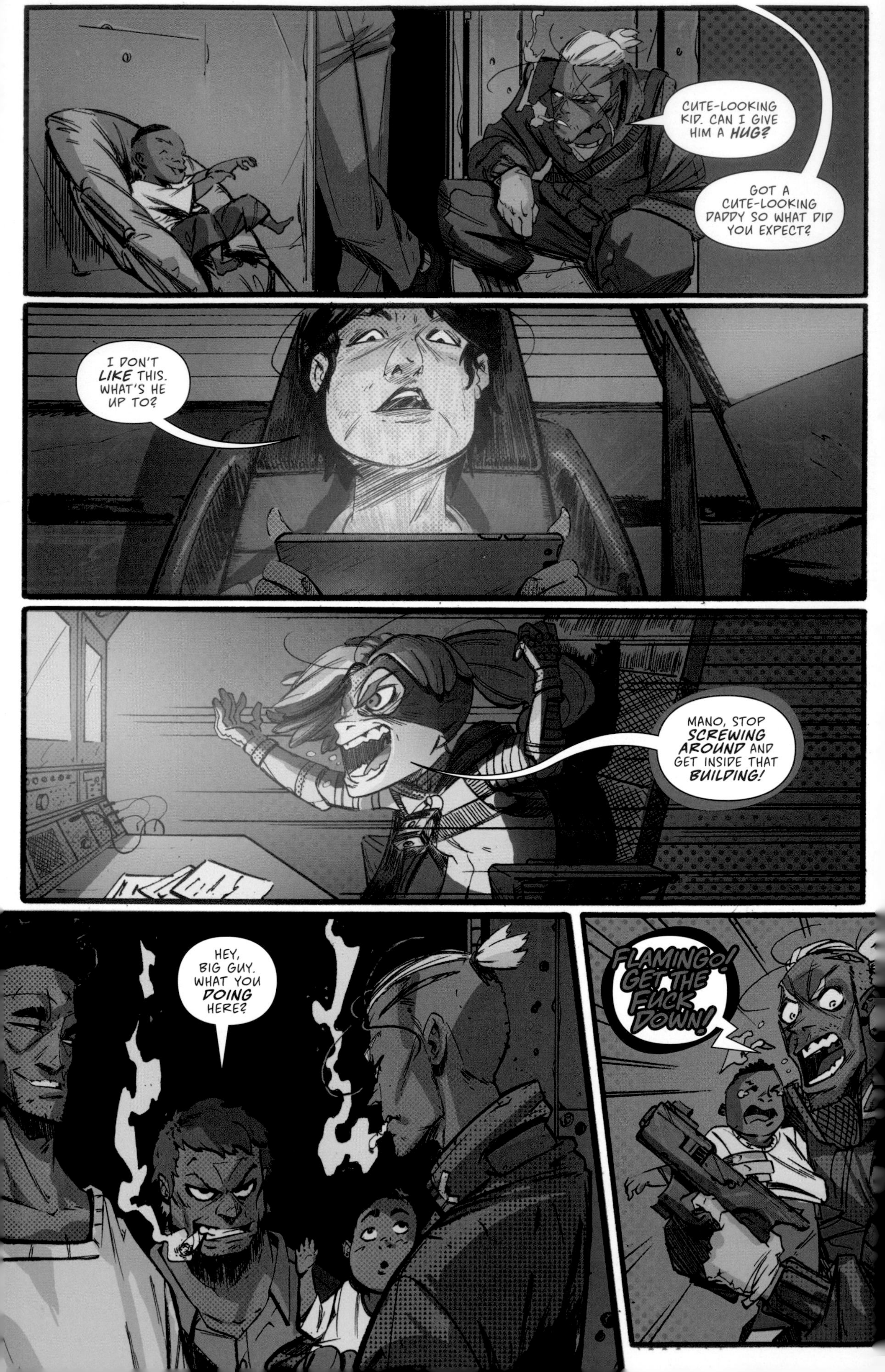

CUTE-LOOKING KID. CAN I GIVE HIM A HUG?
GOT A CUTE-LOOKING DADDY SO WHAT DID YOU EXPECT?
I DON'T LIKE THIS. WHAT'S HE UP TO?
MANO, STOP SCREWING AROUND AND GET INSIDE THAT BUILDING!
HEY, BIG GUY. WHAT YOU DOING HERE?
FLAMINGO! GET THE FUCK DOWN!

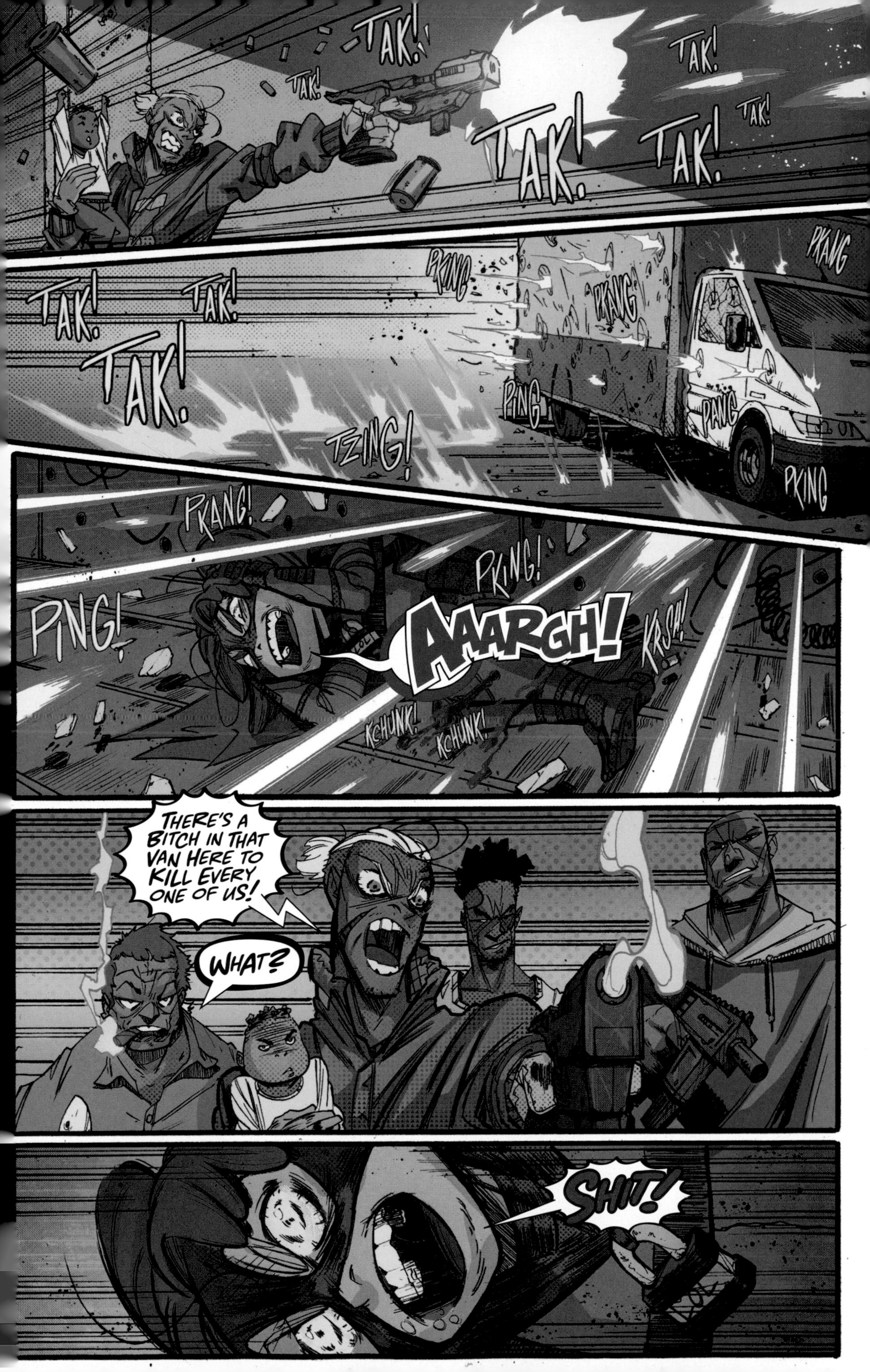
TAK!
TAK!
TAK!
TAK!
TAK!
TAK!
TAK!
TAK!
TAK!
TAK!
PKING
PKANG
PKANG
PING
PANG
TZING!
PKING
PRANG!
PKING!
PING!
AAARGH!
KRSH!
KCHUNK!
KCHUNK!
THERE'S A BITCH IN THAT VAN HERE TO KILL EVERY ONE OF US!
WHAT?
SHIT!

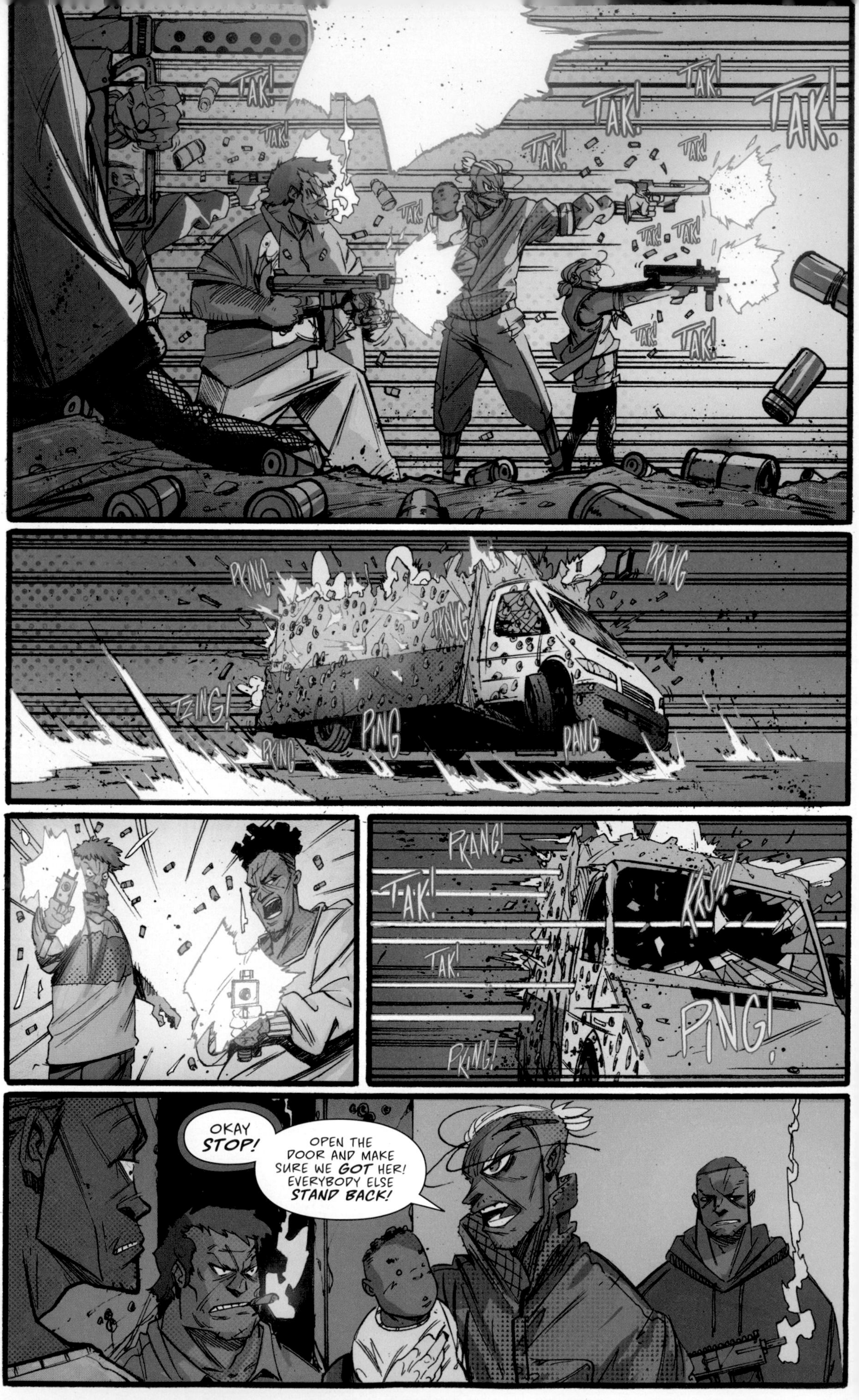

TAK!
TAK!
TAK!
TAK!
TAK!
TAK!
TAK!
TAK!
TAK!
TAK!
TAK!
TAK!
TAK!
PKING
PKANG
PKANG
TZING!
PKING
PING
PANG
PKANG!
TAK!
TAK!
KRSH!
PING!
PKING!
OKAY STOP!
OPEN THE DOOR AND MAKE SURE WE GOT HER! EVERYBODY ELSE STAND BACK!

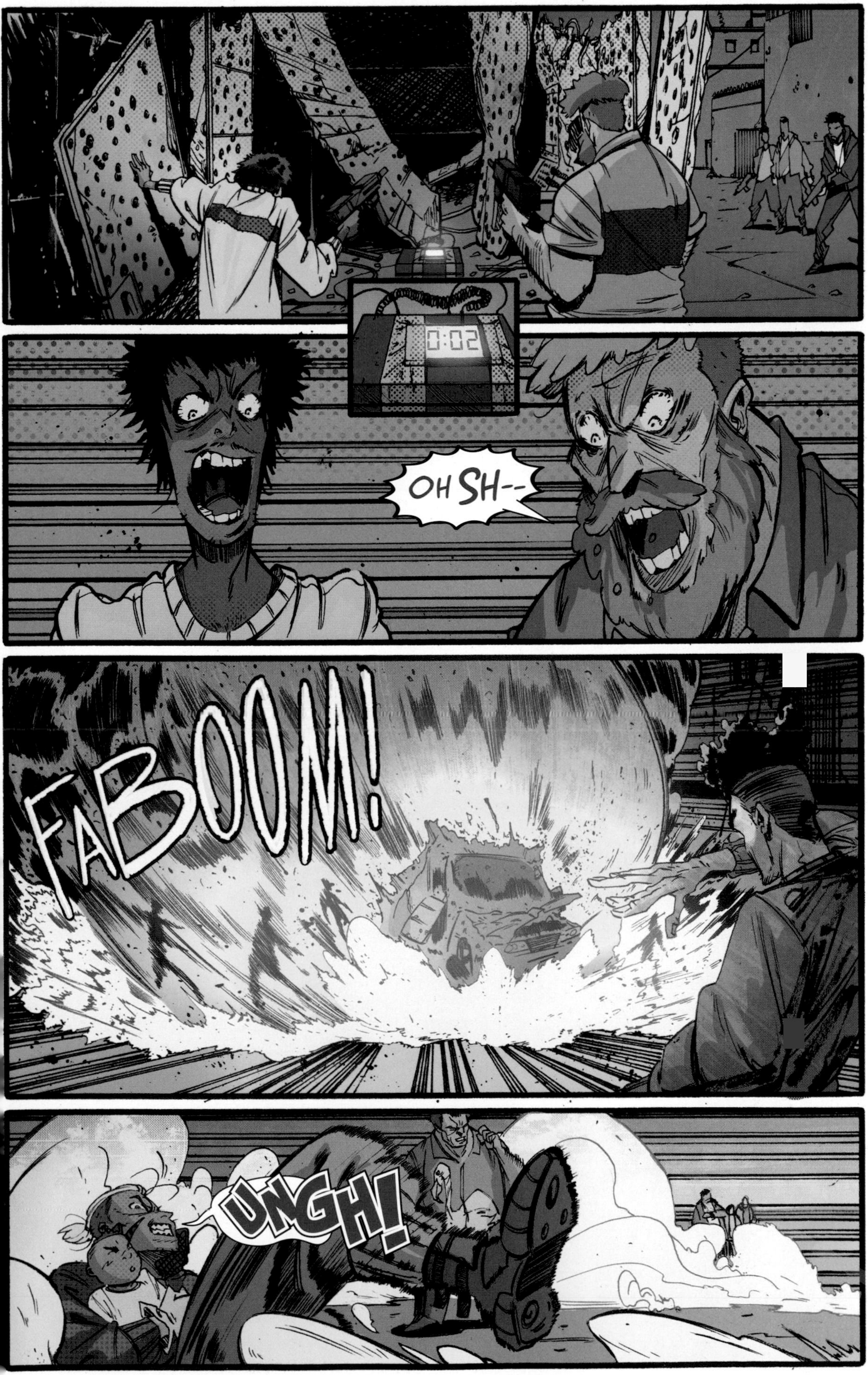
0:02
OH SH--
FABOOM!
UNGH!

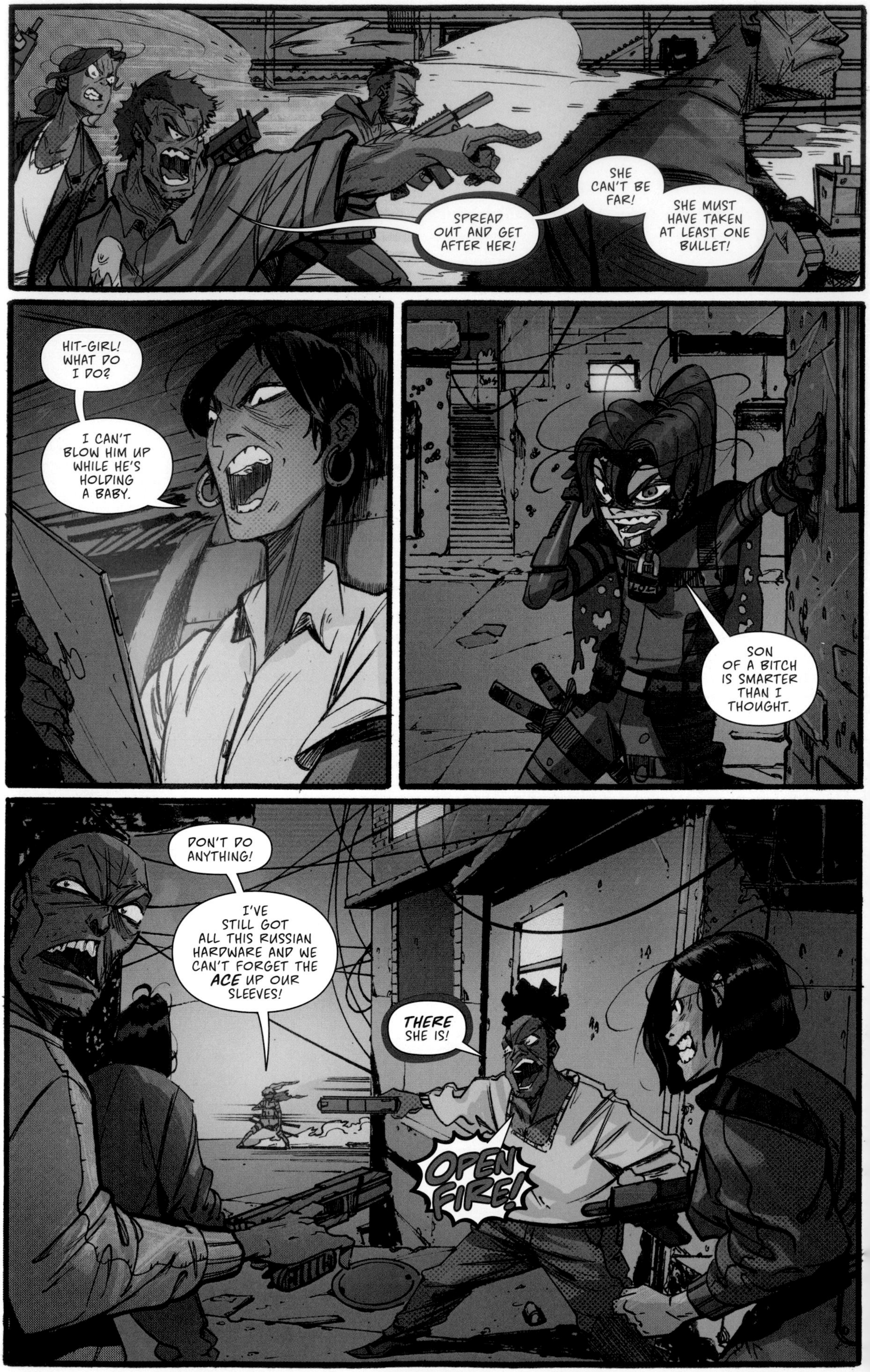
SPREAD OUT AND GET AFTER HER!
SHE CAN'T BE FAR!
SHE MUST HAVE TAKEN AT LEAST ONE BULLET!
HIT-GIRL! WHAT DO I DO?
I CAN'T BLOW HIM UP WHILE HE'S HOLDING A BABY.
SON OF A BITCH IS SMARTER THAN I THOUGHT.
DON'T DO ANYTHING!
I'VE STILL GOT ALL THIS RUSSIAN HARDWARE AND WE CAN'T FORGET THE ACE UP OUR SLEEVES!
THERE SHE IS!
OPEN FIRE!

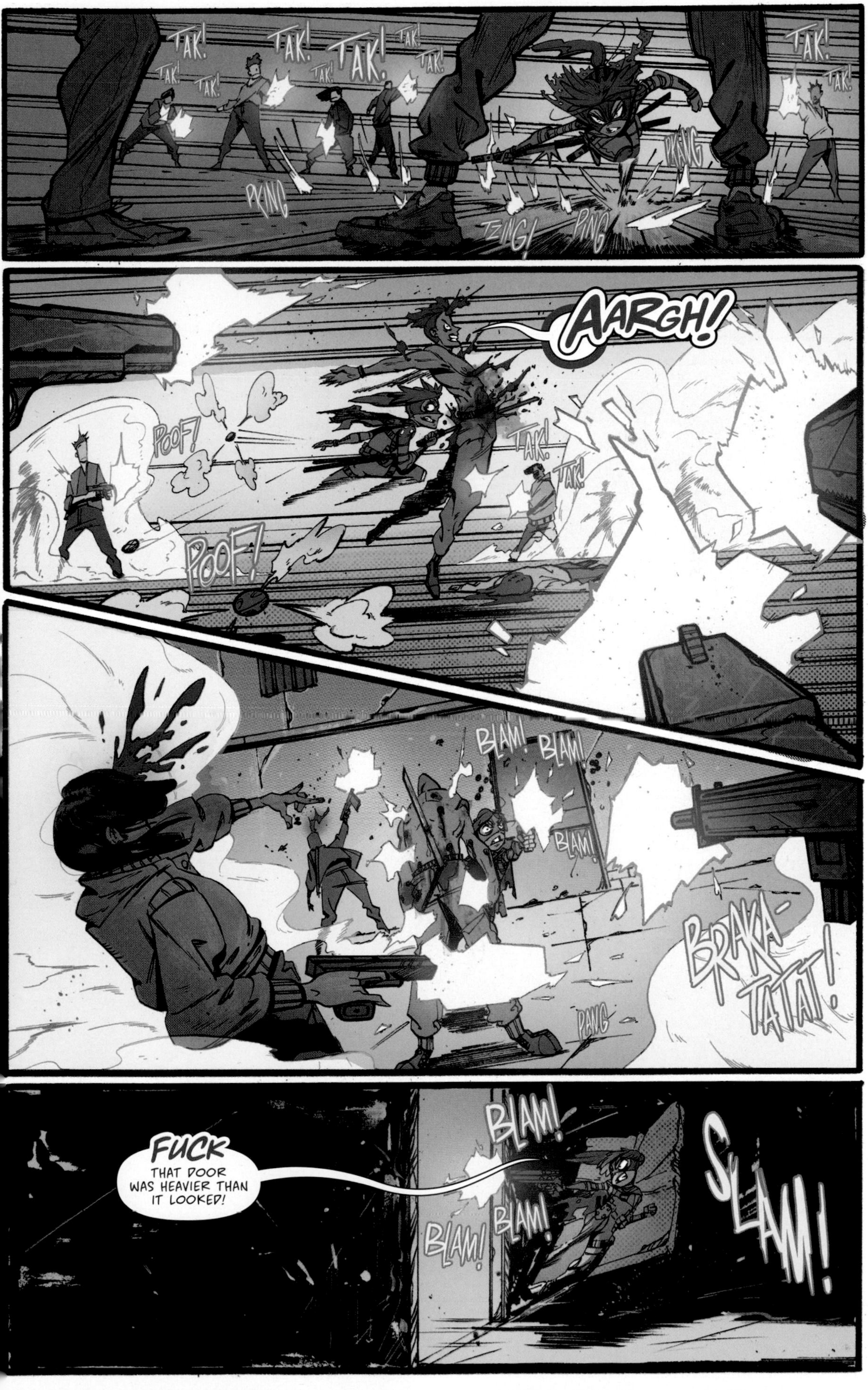
TAK!
TAK!
TAK!
TAK!
TAK!
TAK!
TAK!
TAK!
TAK!
TAK!
PKING
PKING
TZING!
PING
AARGH!
POOF!
POOF!
TAK!
TAK!
BLAM!
BLAM!
BLAM!
BRAKA-TATAT!
PANG
FUCK THAT DOOR WAS HEAVIER THAN IT LOOKED!
BLAM!
BLAM!
BLAM!
SLAM!

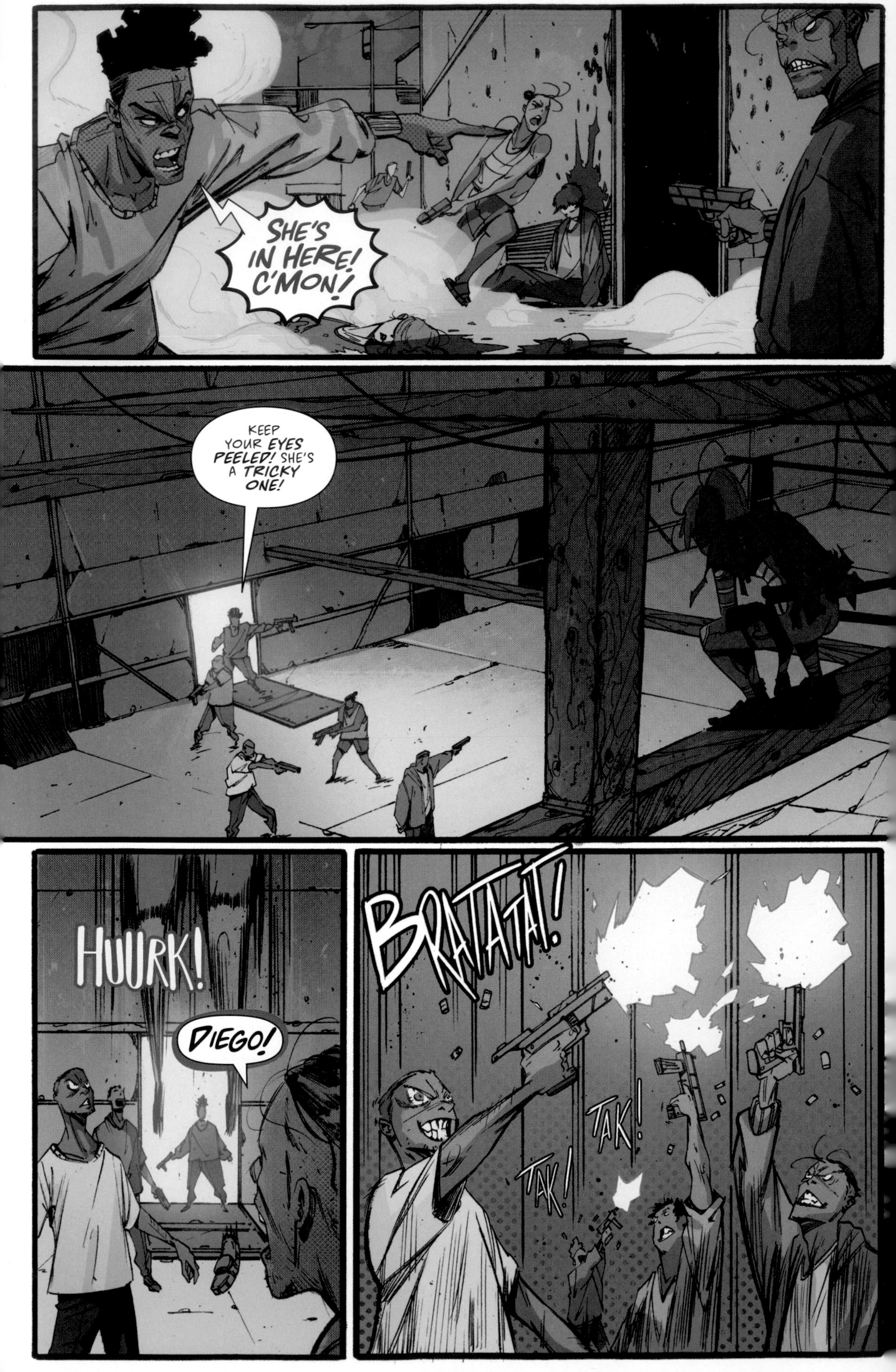
SHE'S IN HERE! C'MON!
KEEP YOUR EYES PEELED! SHE'S A TRICKY ONE!
HUURK!
DIEGO!
BRATATAT!
TAK!
TAK!

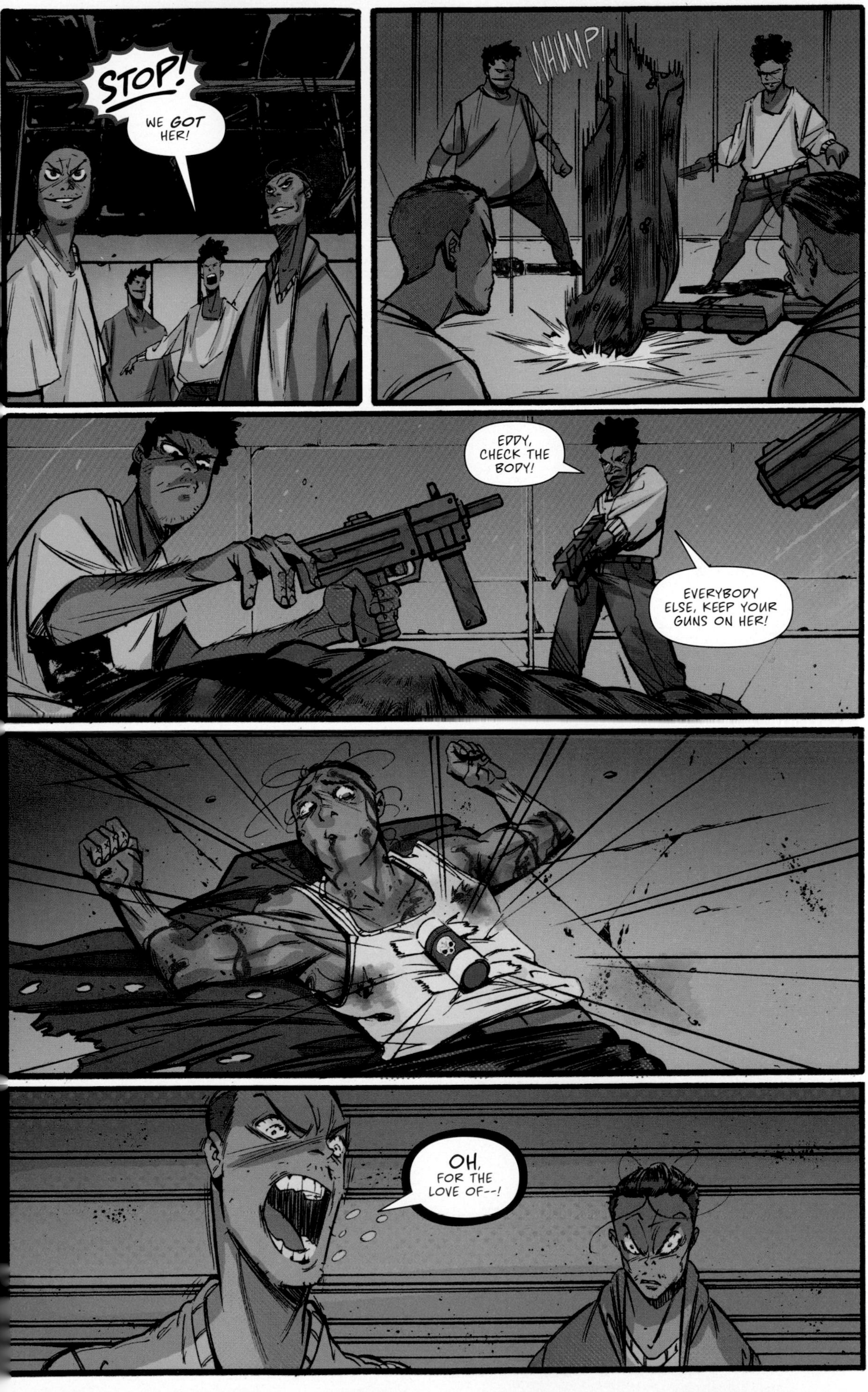
STOP!
WE GOT HER!
WHUMP!
EDDY, CHECK THE BODY!
EVERYBODY ELSE, KEEP YOUR GUNS ON HER!
OH, FOR THE LOVE OF--!

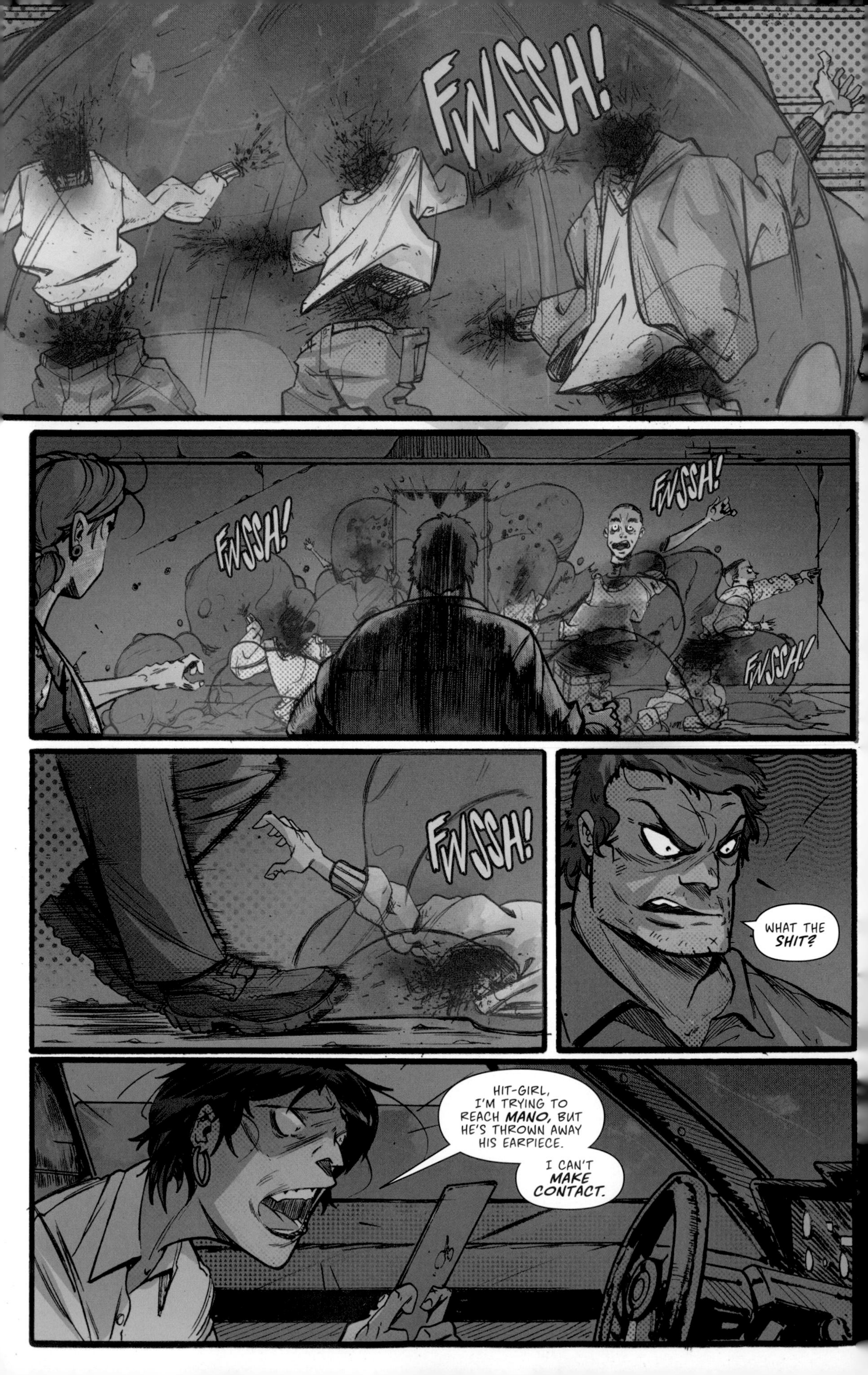
FWSSH!
FWSSH!
FWSSH!
FWSSH!
FWSSH!
WHAT THE SHIT?
HIT-GIRL, I'M TRYING TO REACH MANO, BUT HE'S THROWN AWAY HIS EARPIECE.
I CAN'T MAKE CONTACT.

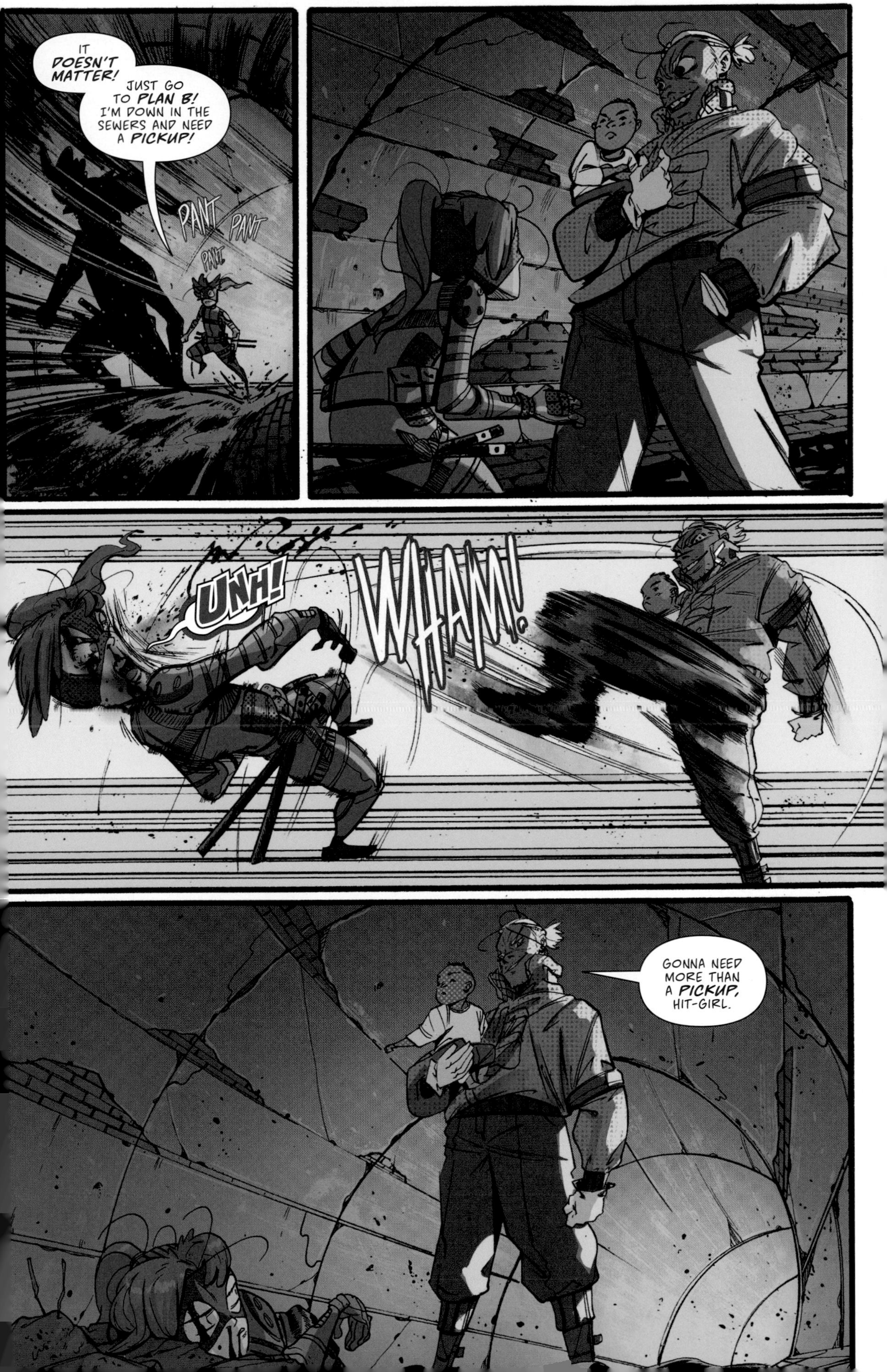
IT DOESN'T MATTER!
JUST GO TO PLAN B! I'M DOWN IN THE SEWERS AND NEED A PICKUP!
PANT PANT
PANT
UNH!
WHAM!
GONNA NEED MORE THAN A PICKUP, HIT-GIRL.

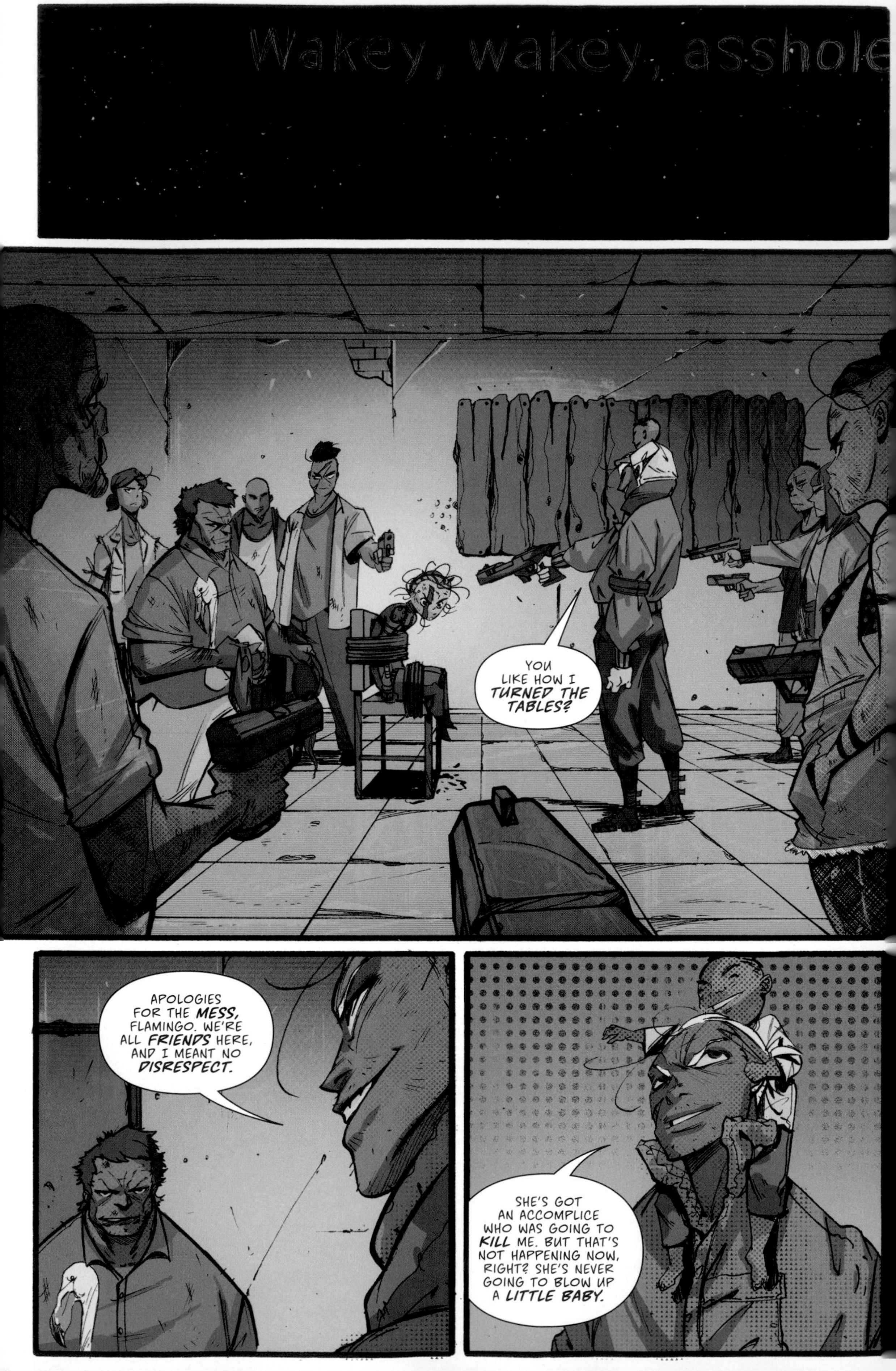
Wakey, wakey, asshole
YOU LIKE HOW I TURNED THE TABLES?
APOLOGIES FOR THE MESS, FLAMINGO. WE'RE ALL FRIENDS HERE, AND I MEANT NO DISRESPECT.
SHE'S GOT AN ACCOMPLICE WHO WAS GOING TO KILL ME. BUT THAT'S NOT HAPPENING NOW, RIGHT? SHE'S NEVER GOING TO BLOW UP A LITTLE BABY.

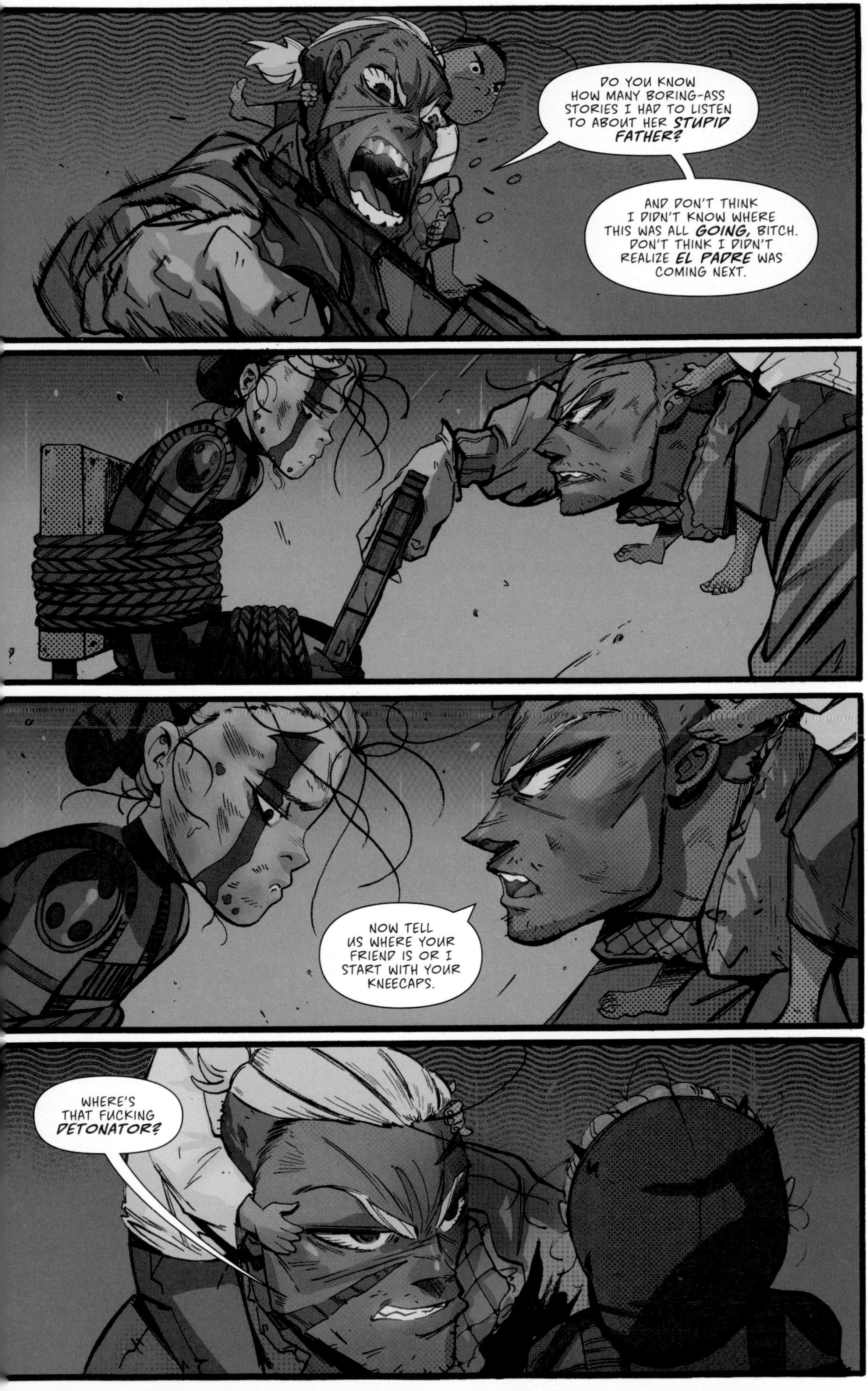
DO YOU KNOW HOW MANY BORING-ASS STORIES I HAD TO LISTEN TO ABOUT HER STUPID FATHER?
AND DON'T THINK I DIDN'T KNOW WHERE THIS WAS ALL GOING, BITCH. DON'T THINK I DIDN'T REALIZE EL PADRE WAS COMING NEXT.
NOW TELL US WHERE YOUR FRIEND IS OR I START WITH YOUR KNEECAPS.
WHERE'S THAT FUCKING DETONATOR?

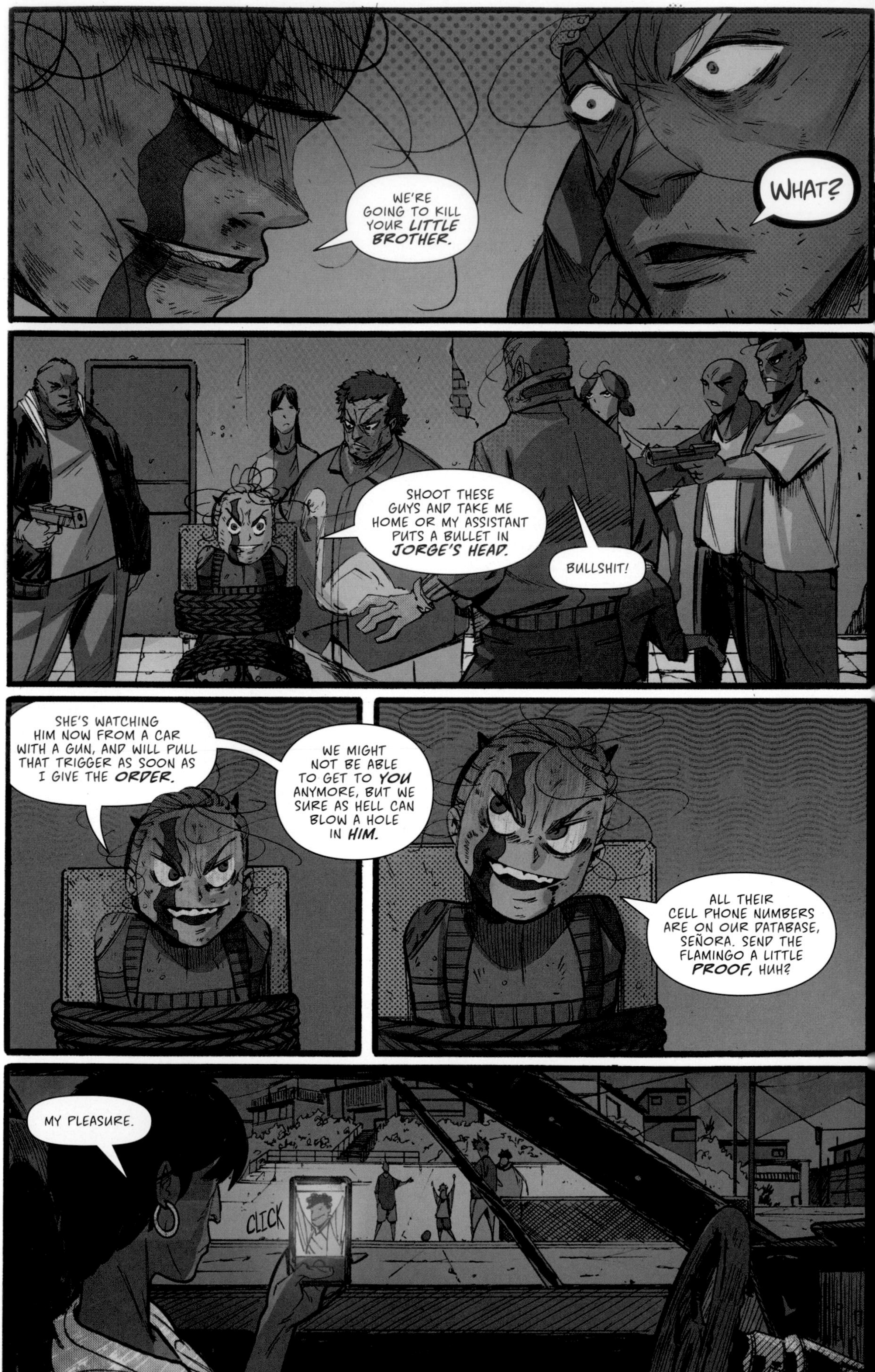
WE'RE GOING TO KILL YOUR LITTLE BROTHER.
WHAT?
SHOOT THESE GUYS AND TAKE ME HOME OR MY ASSISTANT PUTS A BULLET IN JORGE'S HEAD.
BULLSHIT!
SHE'S WATCHING HIM NOW FROM A CAR WITH A GUN, AND WILL PULL THAT TRIGGER AS SOON AS I GIVE THE ORDER.
WE MIGHT NOT BE ABLE TO GET TO YOU ANYMORE, BUT WE SURE AS HELL CAN BLOW A HOLE IN HIM.
ALL THEIR CELL PHONE NUMBERS ARE ON OUR DATABASE, SEÑORA. SEND THE FLAMINGO A LITTLE PROOF, HUH?
MY PLEASURE.
CLICK

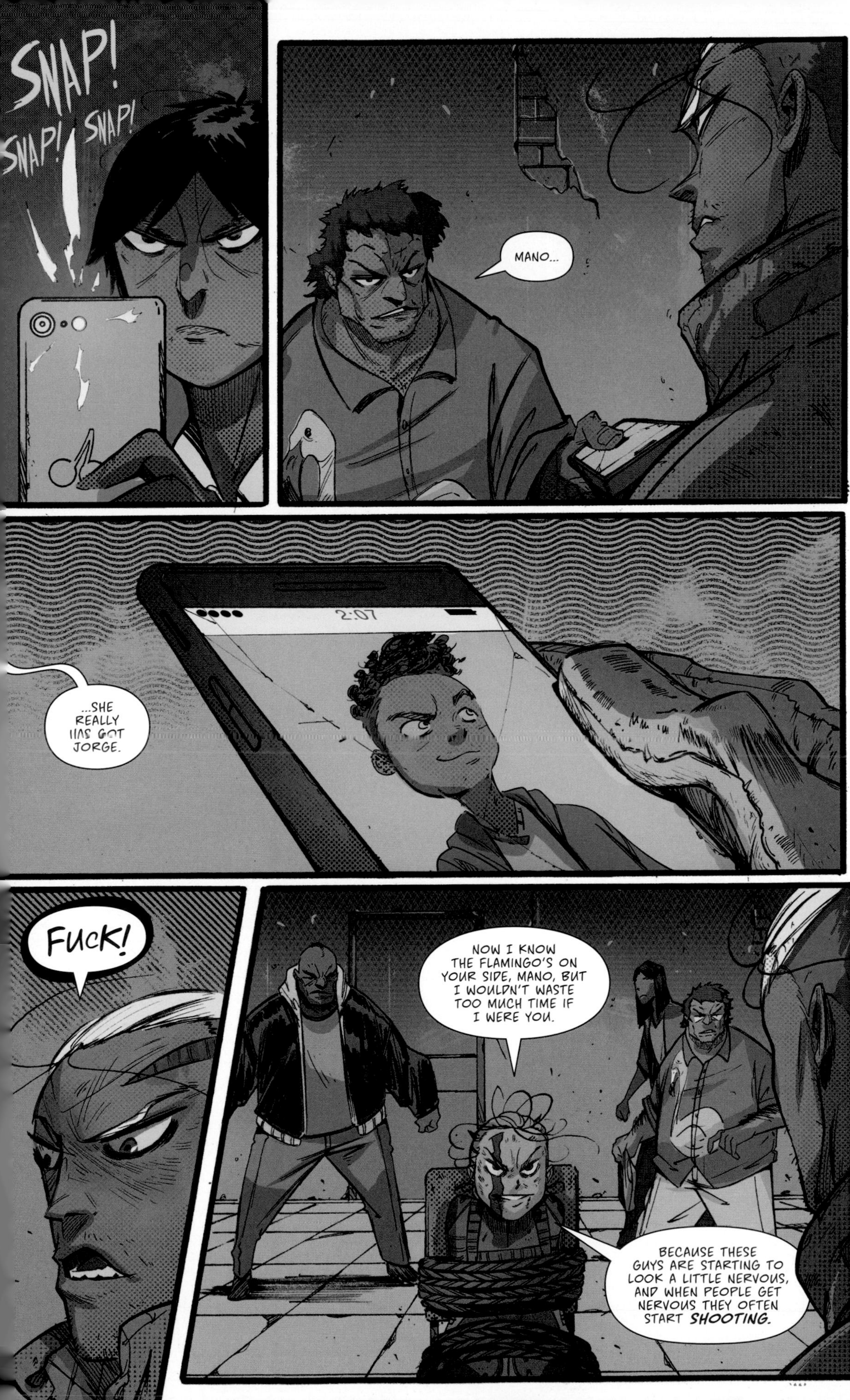
SNAP!
SNAP! SNAP!
MANO...
...SHE REALLY HAS GOT JORGE.
FUCK!
NOW I KNOW THE FLAMINGO'S ON YOUR SIDE, MANO, BUT I WOULDN'T WASTE TOO MUCH TIME IF I WERE YOU.
BECAUSE THESE GUYS ARE STARTING TO LOOK A LITTLE NERVOUS, AND WHEN PEOPLE GET NERVOUS THEY OFTEN START SHOOTING.

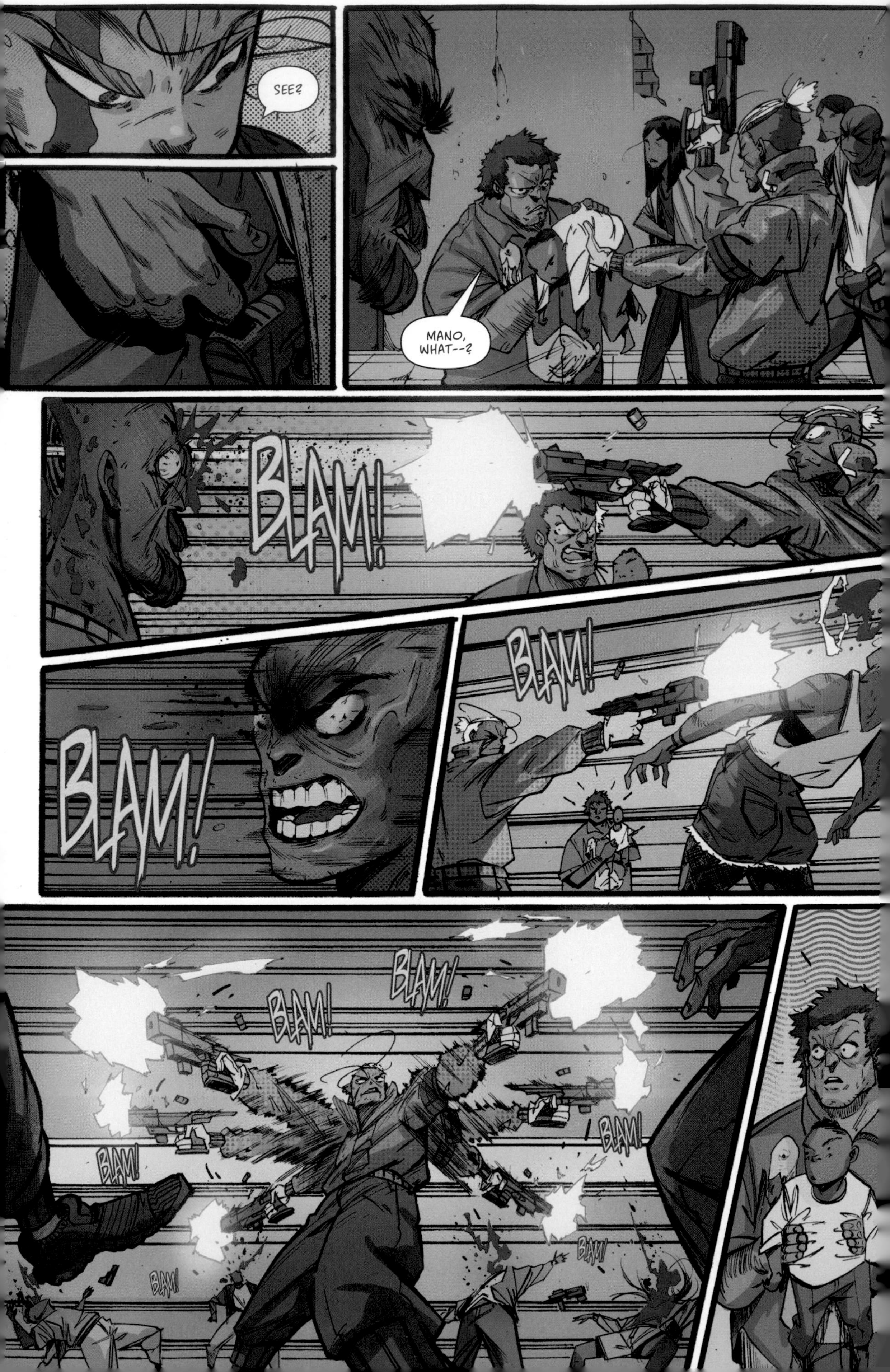
SEE?
MANO, WHAT--?
BLAM!
BLAM!
BLAM!
BLAM!
BLAM!
BLAM!
BLAM!
BLAM!
BLAM!

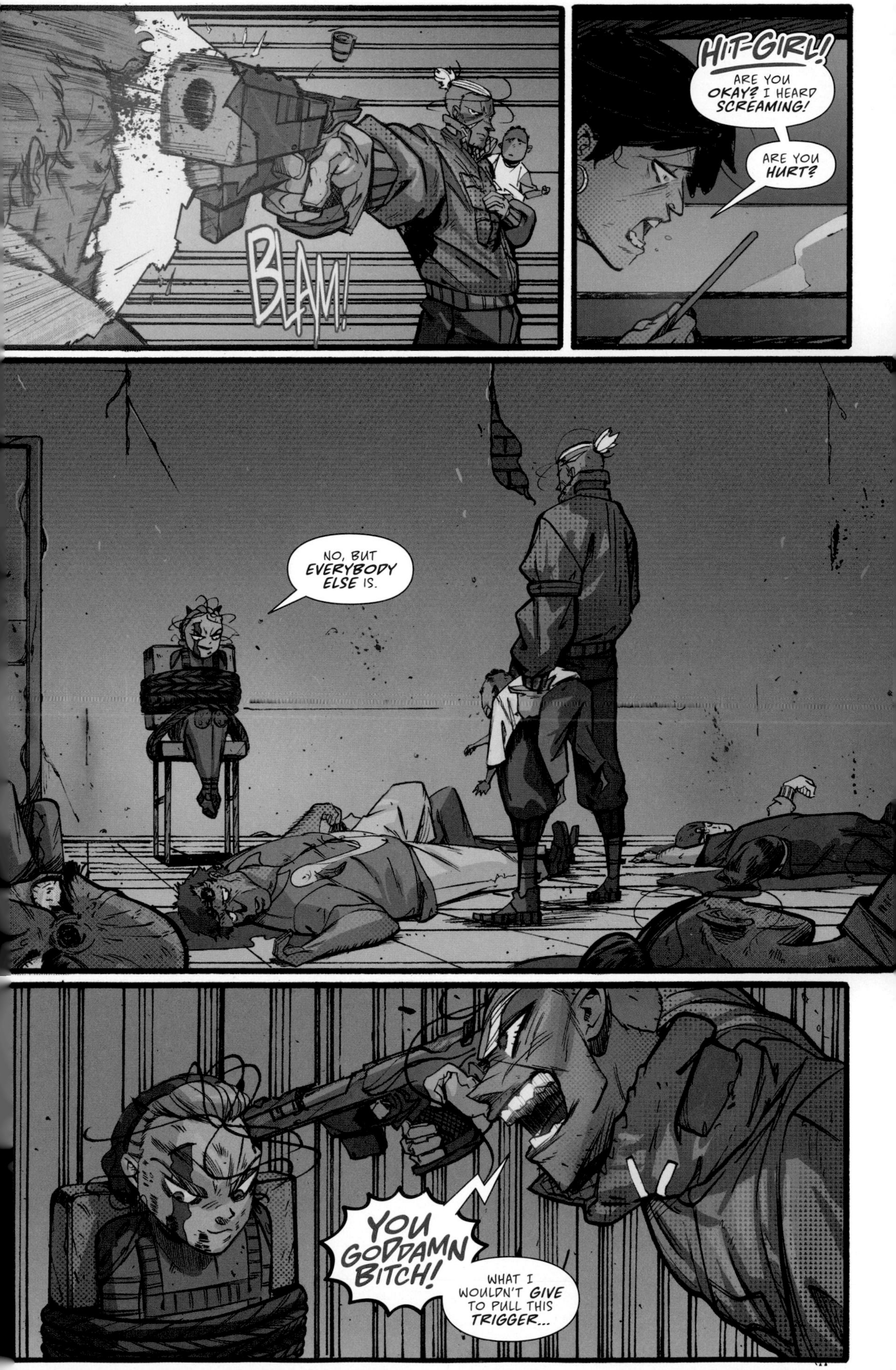
BLAM!
HIT-GIRL!
ARE YOU OKAY? I HEARD SCREAMING!
ARE YOU HURT?
NO, BUT EVERYBODY ELSE IS.
YOU GODDAMN BITCH!
WHAT I WOULDN'T GIVE TO PULL THIS TRIGGER...

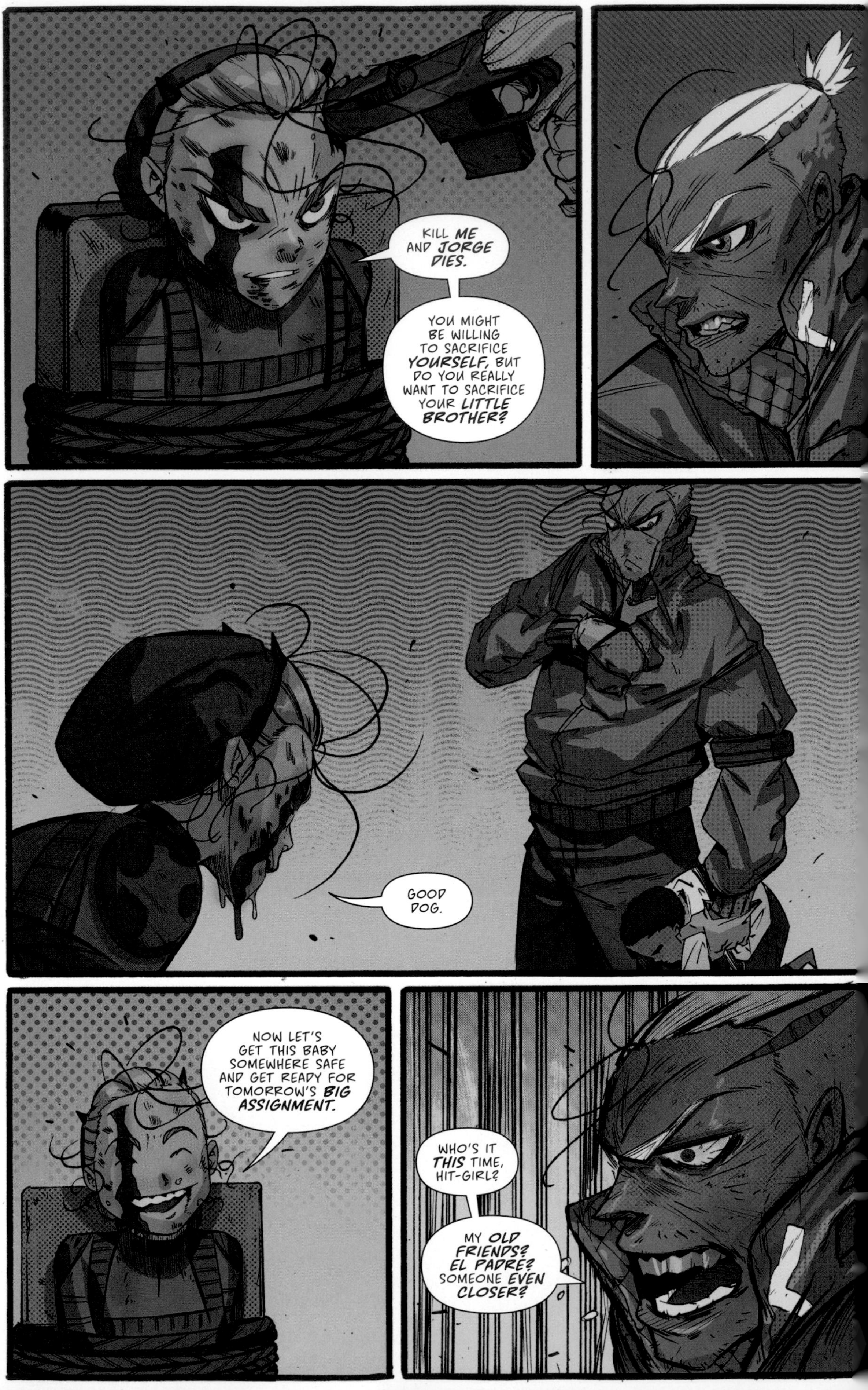
KILL ME AND JORGE DIES.
YOU MIGHT BE WILLING TO SACRIFICE YOURSELF, BUT DO YOU REALLY WANT TO SACRIFICE YOUR LITTLE BROTHER?
GOOD DOG.
NOW LET'S GET THIS BABY SOMEWHERE SAFE AND GET READY FOR TOMORROW'S BIG ASSIGNMENT.
WHO'S IT THIS TIME, HIT-GIRL?
MY OLD FRIENDS? EL PADRÉ? SOMEONE EVEN CLOSER?

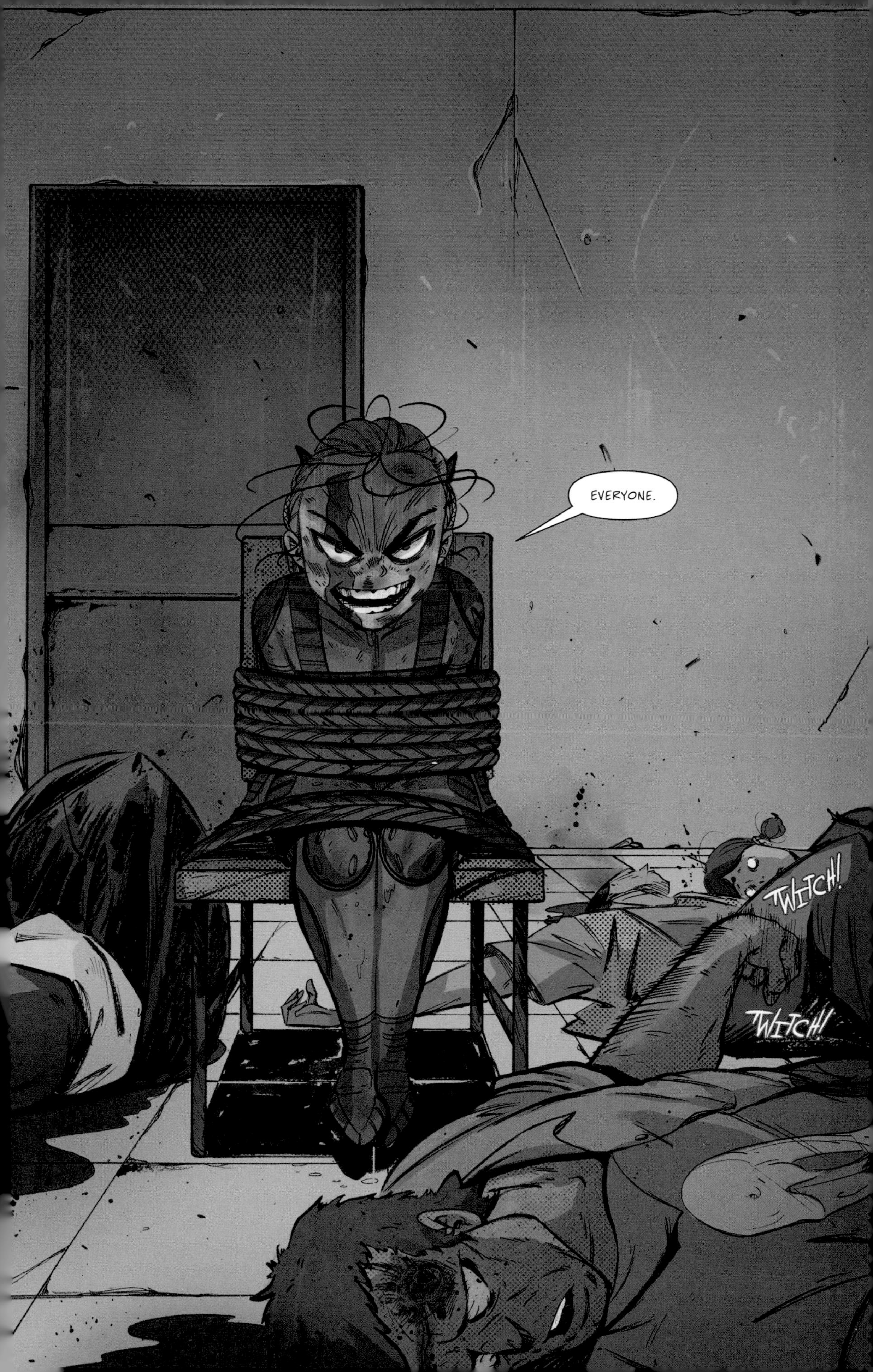
EVERYONE.
TWITCH!
TWITCH!

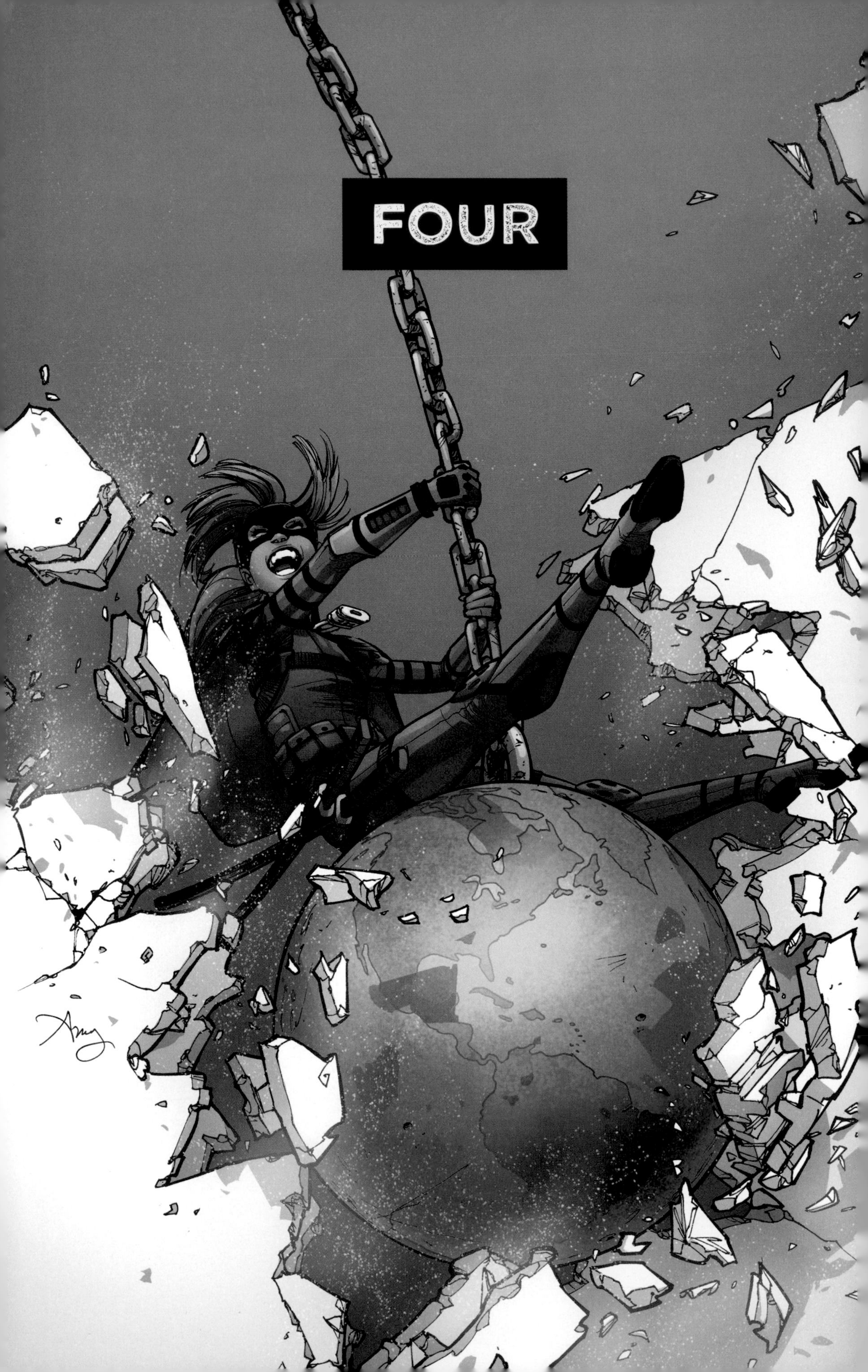
FOUR

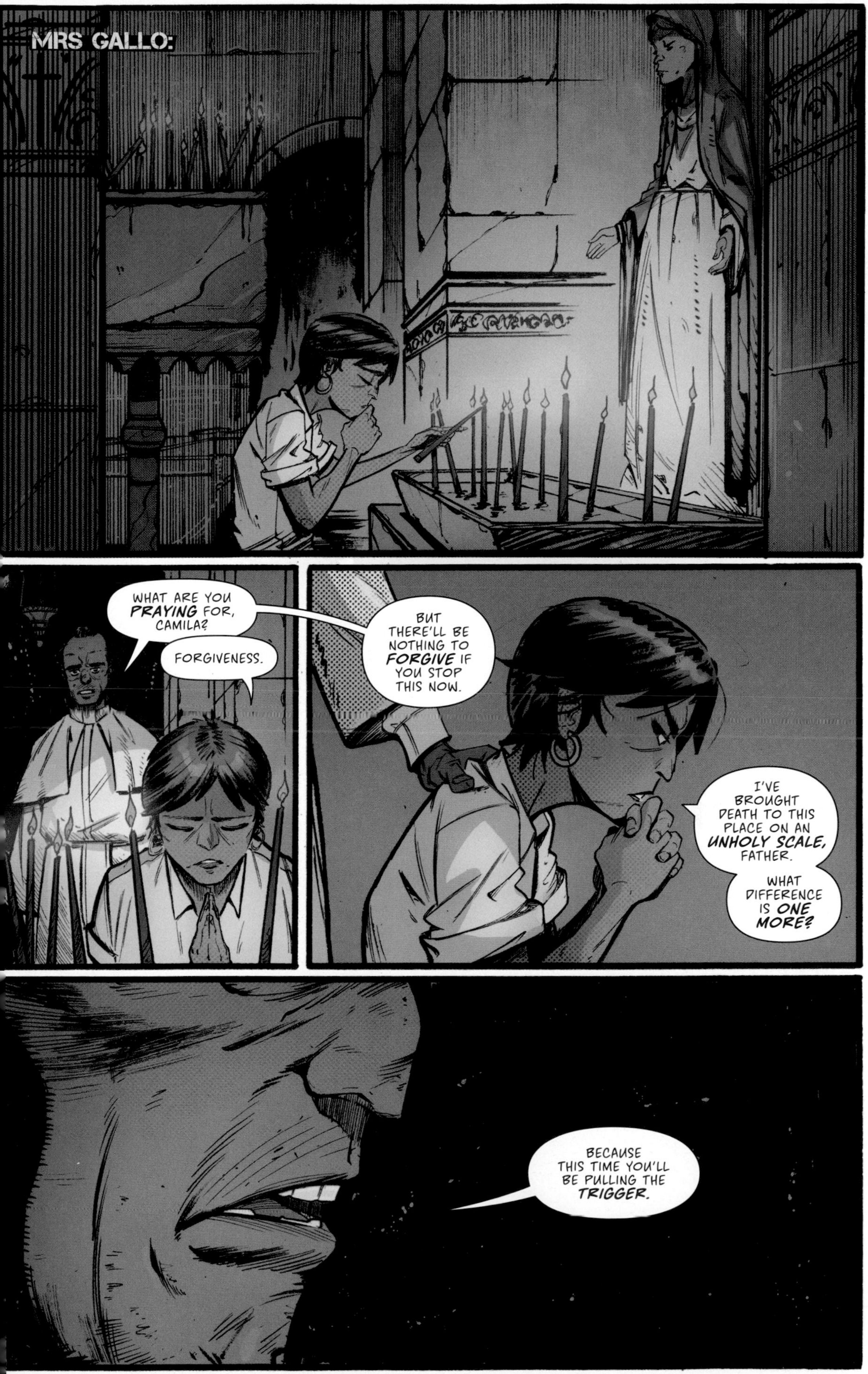
MRS GALLO:
WHAT ARE YOU PRAYING FOR, CAMILA?
FORGIVENESS.
BUT THERE'LL BE NOTHING TO FORGIVE IF YOU STOP THIS NOW.
I'VE BROUGHT DEATH TO THIS PLACE ON AN UNHOLY SCALE, FATHER.
WHAT DIFFERENCE IS ONE MORE?
BECAUSE THIS TIME YOU'LL BE PULLING THE TRIGGER.

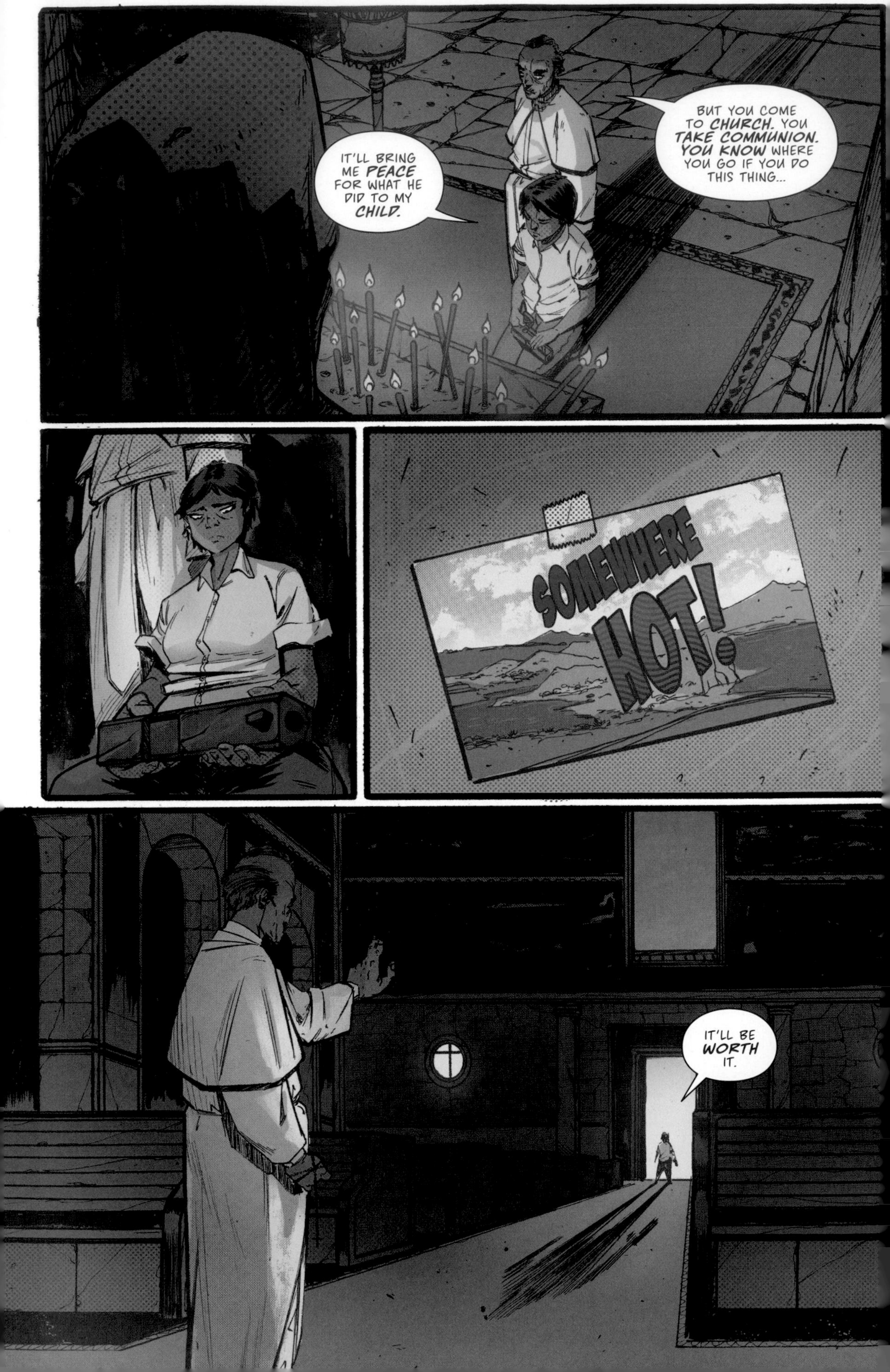
IT'LL BRING ME PEACE FOR WHAT HE DID TO MY CHILD.
BUT YOU COME TO CHURCH. YOU TAKE COMMUNION. YOU KNOW WHERE YOU GO IF YOU DO THIS THING...
SOMEWHERE HOT!
IT'LL BE WORTH IT.

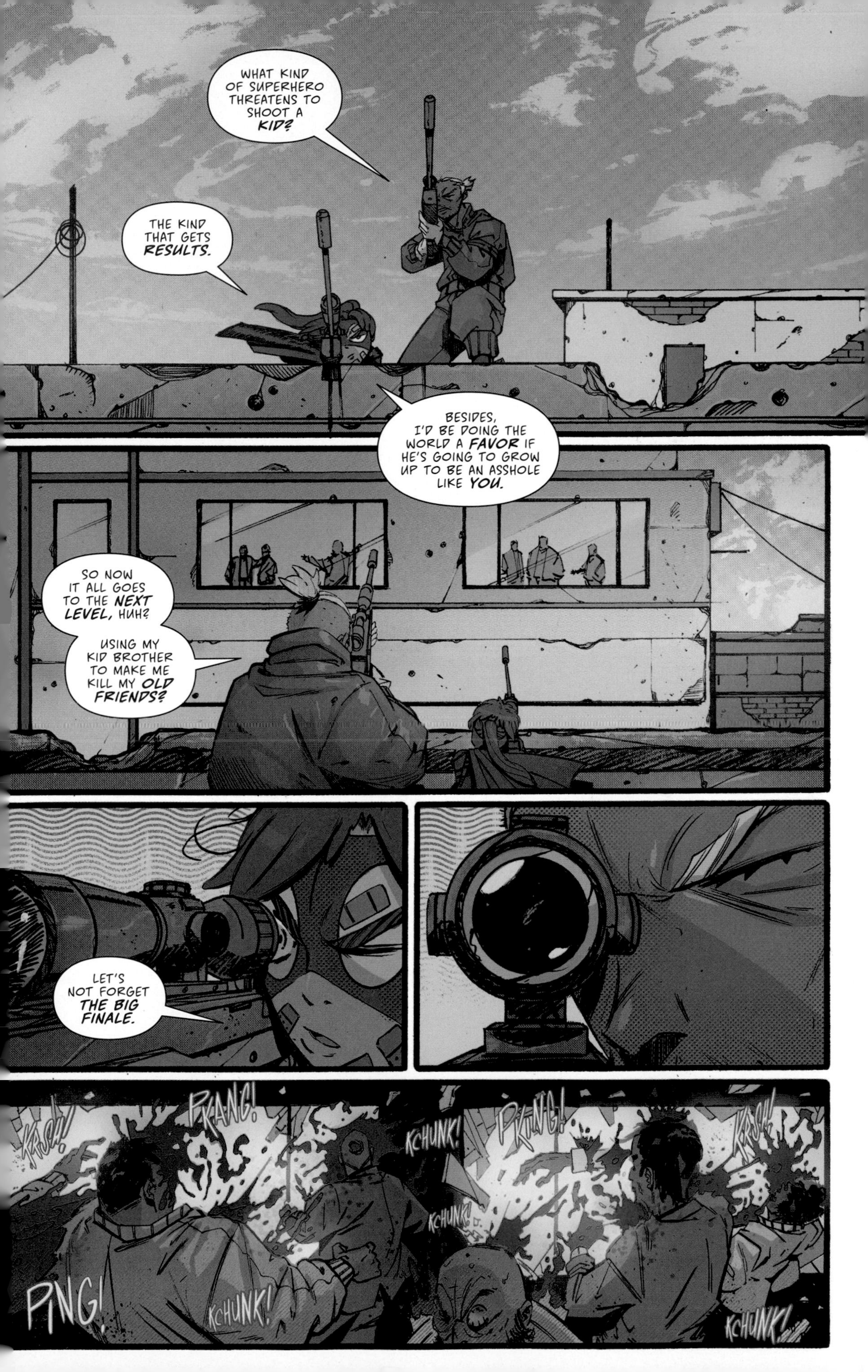
WHAT KIND OF SUPERHERO THREATENS TO SHOOT A KID?
THE KIND THAT GETS RESULTS.
BESIDES, I'D BE DOING THE WORLD A FAVOR IF HE'S GOING TO GROW UP TO BE AN ASSHOLE LIKE YOU.
SO NOW IT ALL GOES TO THE NEXT LEVEL, HUH?
USING MY KID BROTHER TO MAKE ME KILL MY OLD FRIENDS?
LET'S NOT FORGET THE BIG FINALE.
PKANG!
KCHUNK!
PKING!
KCHUNK!
PING!
KCHUNK!
KCHUNK!

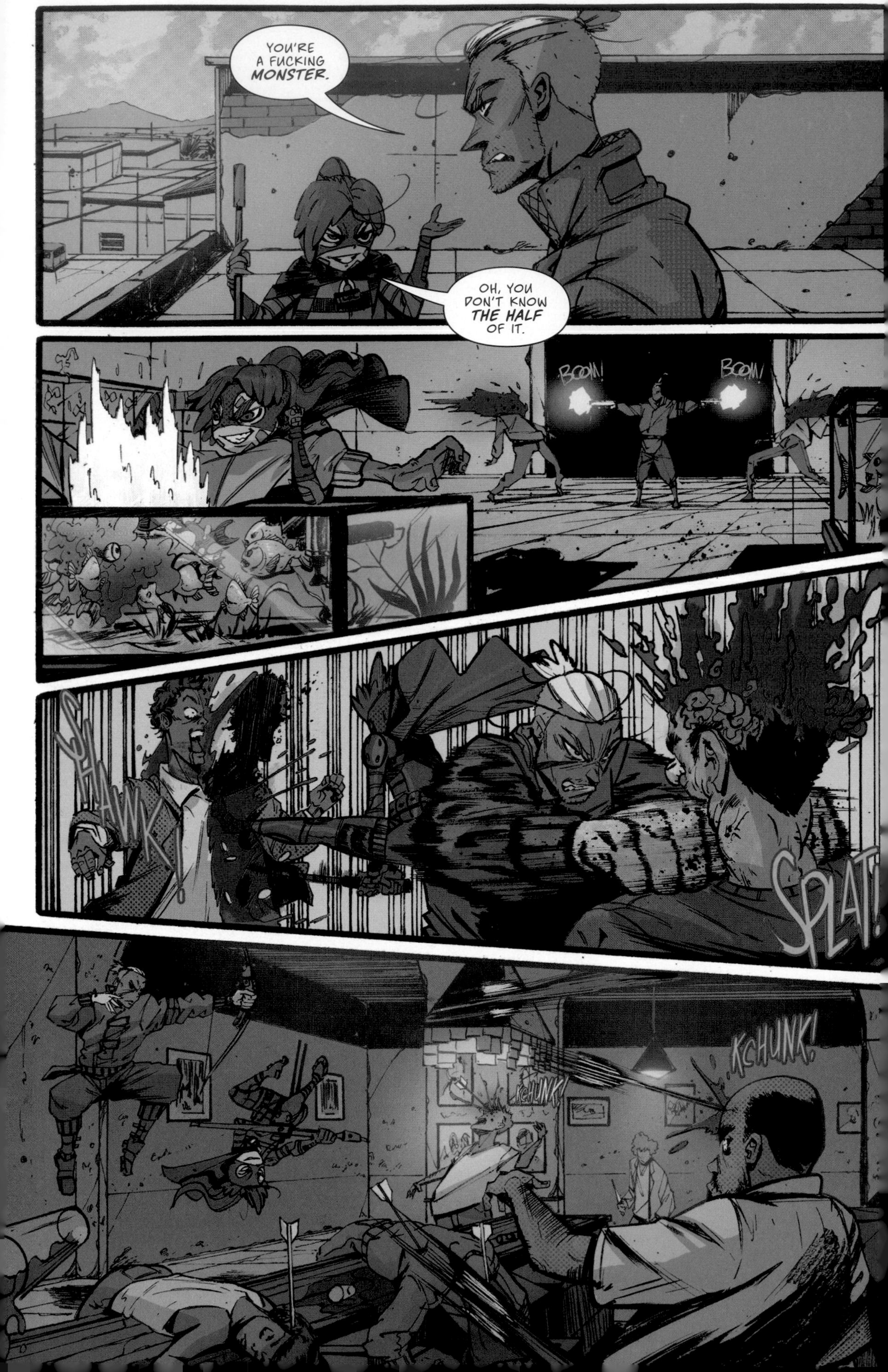
YOU'RE A FUCKING MONSTER.
OH, YOU DON'T KNOW THE HALF OF IT.
BOOM!
BOOM!
SHAWK!
SPLAT!
KCHUNK!
KCHUNK!

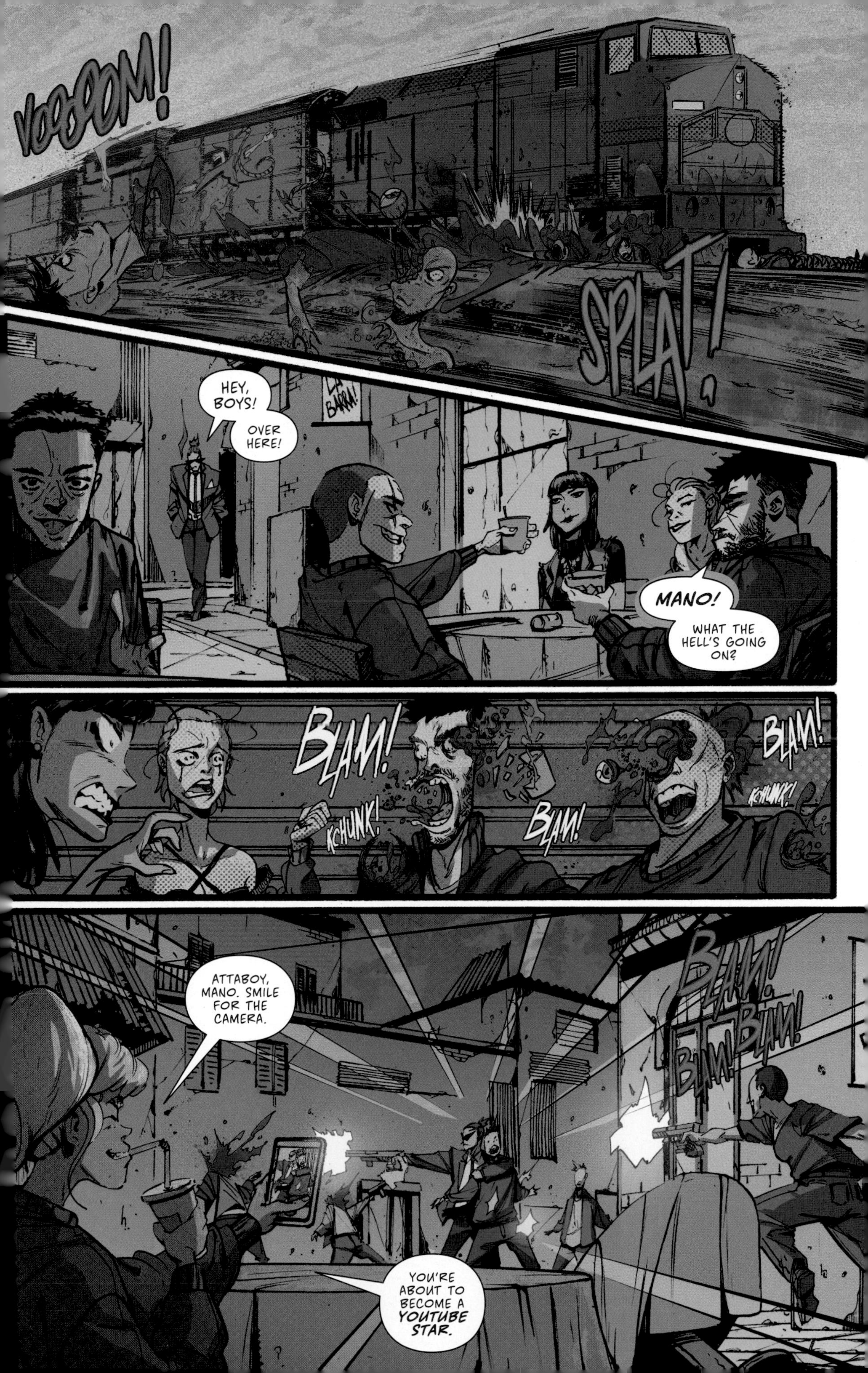
VOOOOOM!
SPLAT!
LA BARRA!
HEY, BOYS!
OVER HERE!
MANO!
WHAT THE HELL'S GOING ON?
BLAM!
BLAM!
KCHUNK!
BLAM!
KCHUNK!
ATTABOY, MANO. SMILE FOR THE CAMERA.
BLAM!
BLAM!
BLAM!
BLAM!
YOU'RE ABOUT TO BECOME A YOUTUBE STAR.

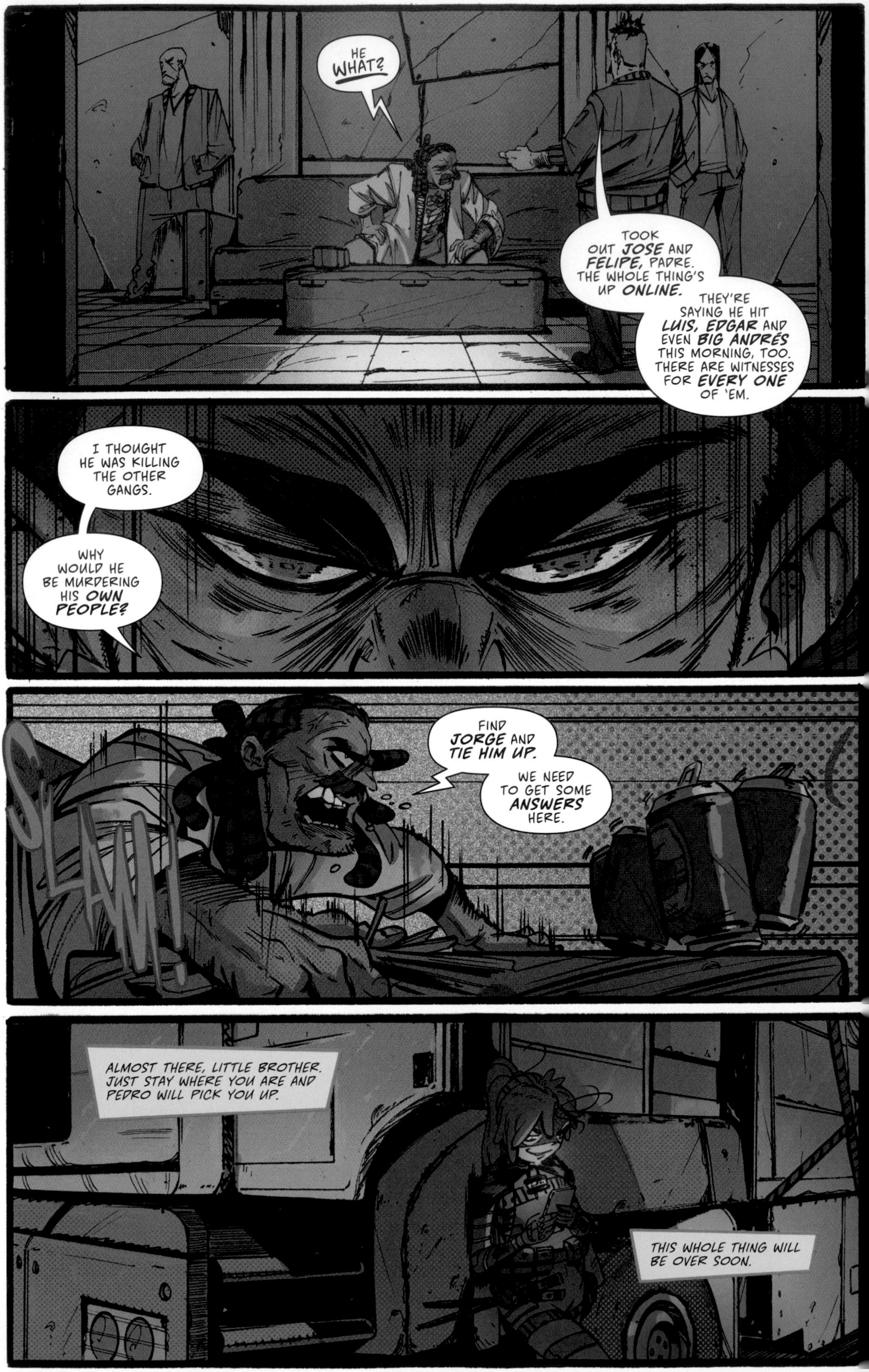
HE WHAT?
TOOK OUT JOSE AND FELIPE, PADRE. THE WHOLE THING'S UP ONLINE.
THEY'RE SAYING HE HIT LUIS, EDGAR AND EVEN BIG ANDRÉS THIS MORNING, TOO. THERE ARE WITNESSES FOR EVERY ONE OF 'EM.
I THOUGHT HE WAS KILLING THE OTHER GANGS.
WHY WOULD HE BE MURDERING HIS OWN PEOPLE?
SLAM!
FIND JORGE AND TIE HIM UP.
WE NEED TO GET SOME ANSWERS HERE.
ALMOST THERE, LITTLE BROTHER. JUST STAY WHERE YOU ARE AND PEDRO WILL PICK YOU UP.
THIS WHOLE THING WILL BE OVER SOON.

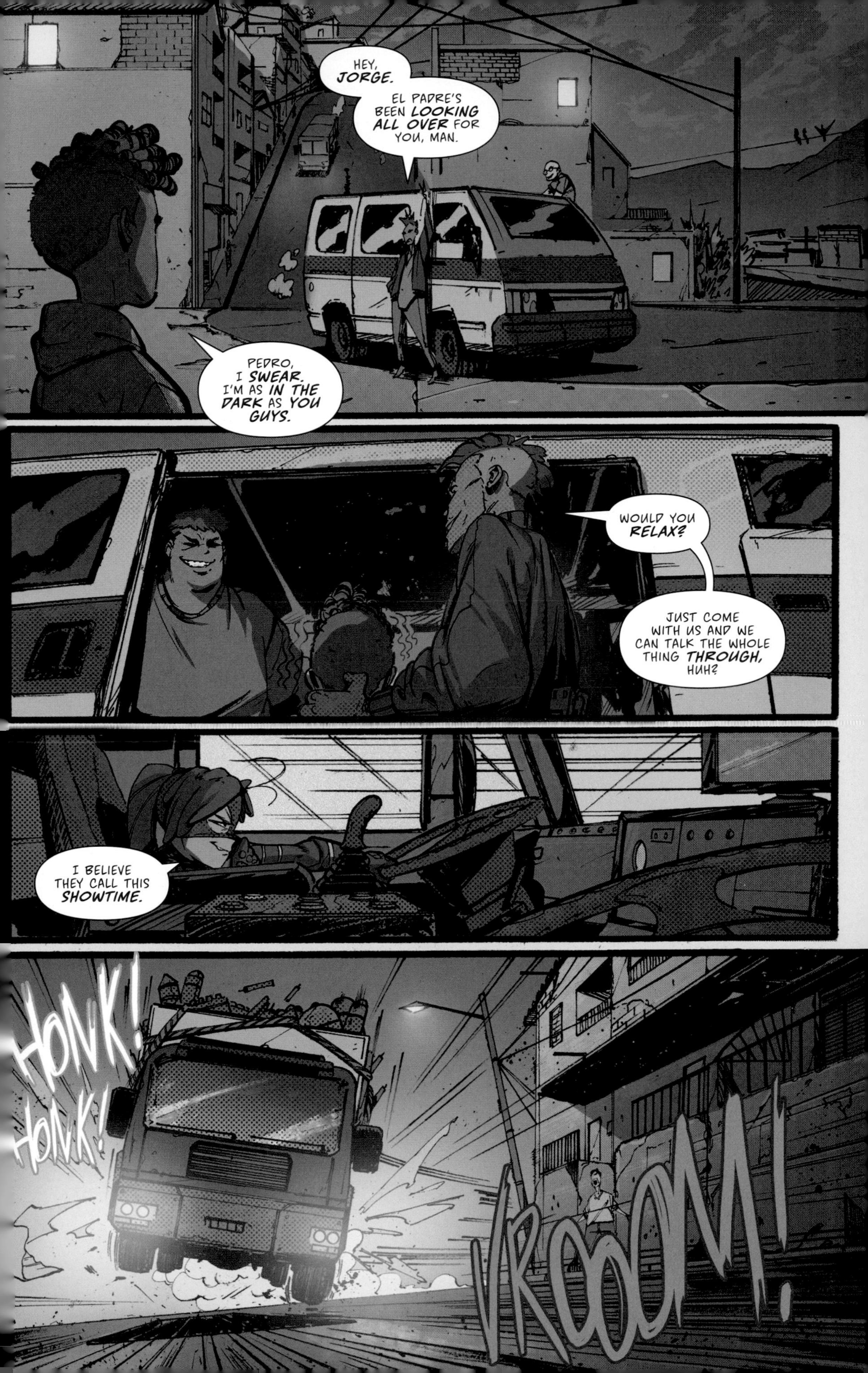
HEY, JORGE.
EL PADRE'S BEEN LOOKING ALL OVER FOR YOU, MAN.
PEDRO, I SWEAR. I'M AS IN THE DARK AS YOU GUYS.
WOULD YOU RELAX?
JUST COME WITH US AND WE CAN TALK THE WHOLE THING THROUGH, HUH?
I BELIEVE THEY CALL THIS SHOWTIME.
HONK!
HONK!
VROOOM!

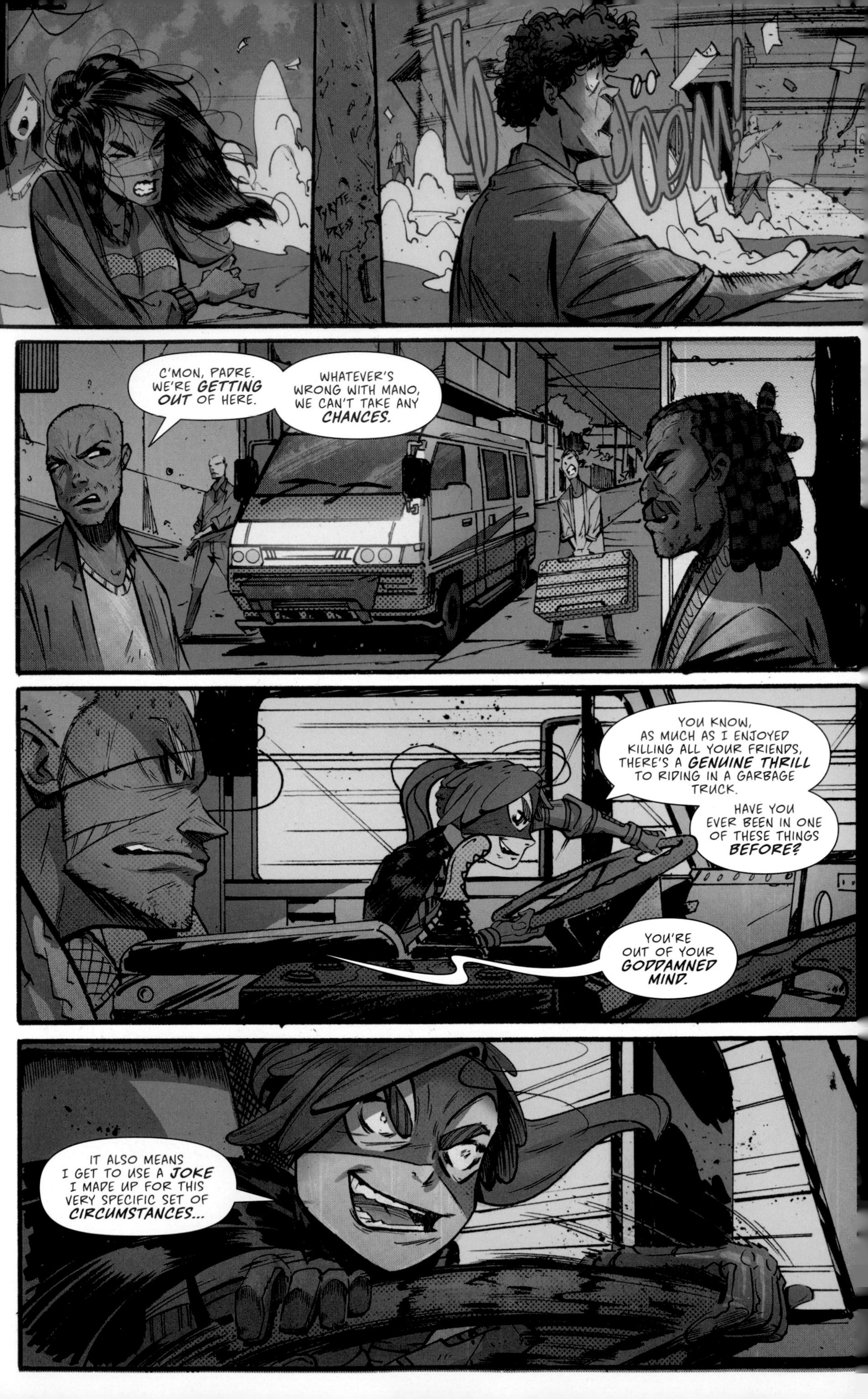
VOOOM!
TYRYTE DRESS
C'MON, PADRE. WE'RE GETTING OUT OF HERE.
WHATEVER'S WRONG WITH MANO, WE CAN'T TAKE ANY CHANCES.
YOU KNOW, AS MUCH AS I ENJOYED KILLING ALL YOUR FRIENDS, THERE'S A GENUINE THRILL TO RIDING IN A GARBAGE TRUCK.
HAVE YOU EVER BEEN IN ONE OF THESE THINGS BEFORE?
YOU'RE OUT OF YOUR GODDAMNED MIND.
IT ALSO MEANS I GET TO USE A JOKE I MADE UP FOR THIS VERY SPECIFIC SET OF CIRCUMSTANCES...

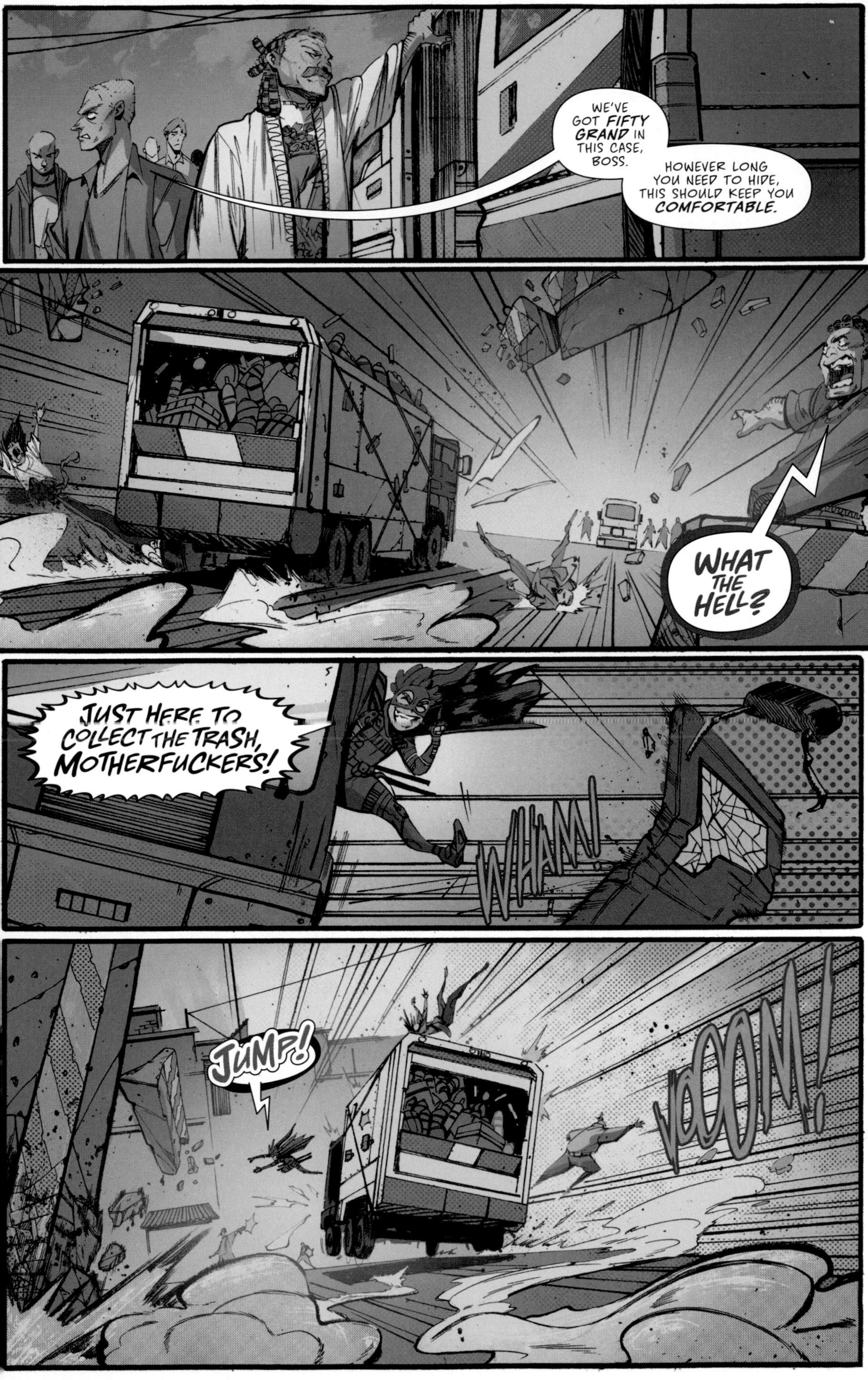
WE'VE GOT FIFTY GRAND IN THIS CASE, BOSS.
HOWEVER LONG YOU NEED TO HIDE, THIS SHOULD KEEP YOU COMFORTABLE.
WHAT THE HELL?
JUST HERE TO COLLECT THE TRASH, MOTHERFUCKERS!
WHAM!
JUMP!
VOOOM!

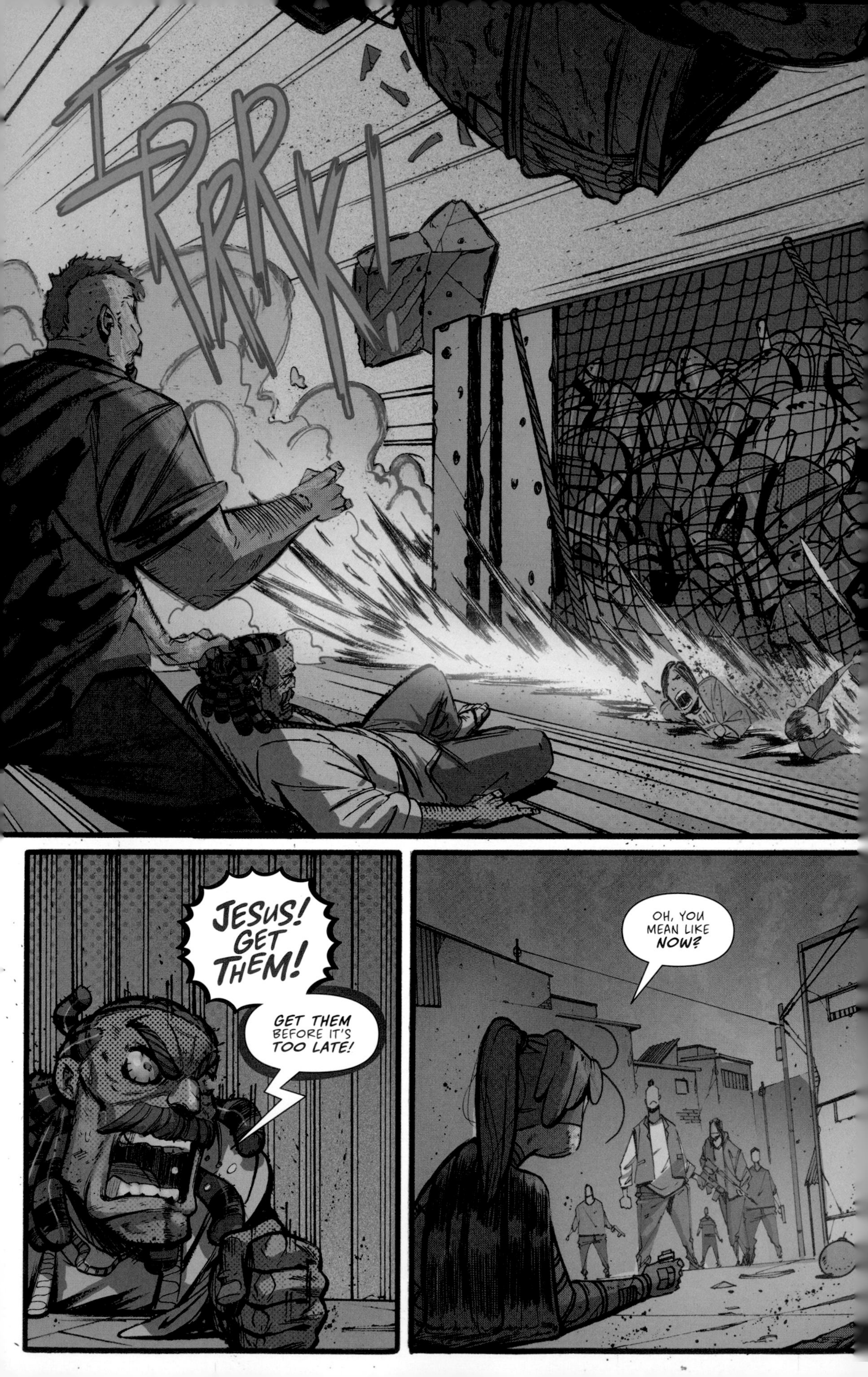
KRRKK!
JESUS! GET THEM!
GET THEM BEFORE IT'S TOO LATE!
OH, YOU MEAN LIKE NOW?

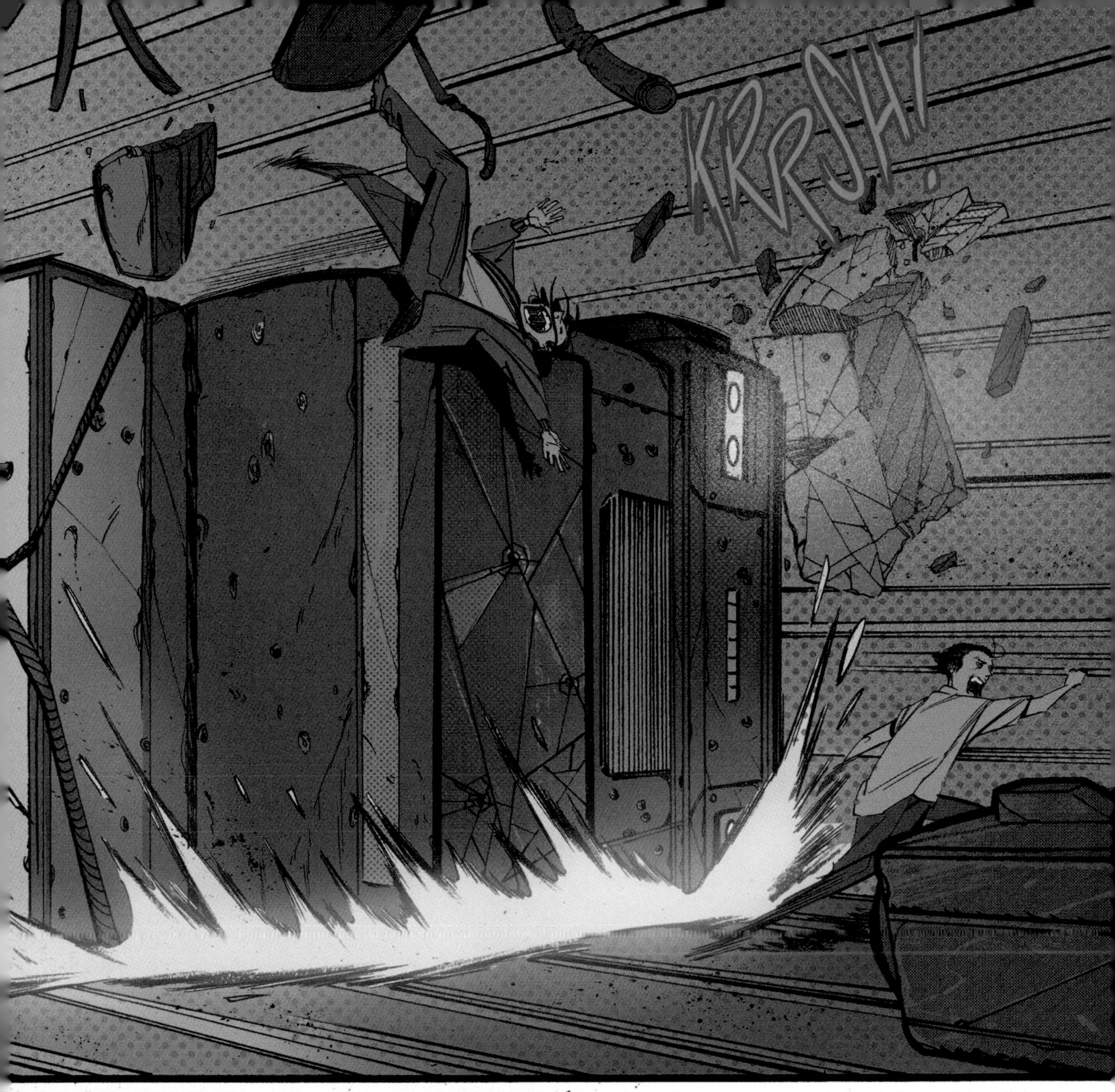
KRRSH!

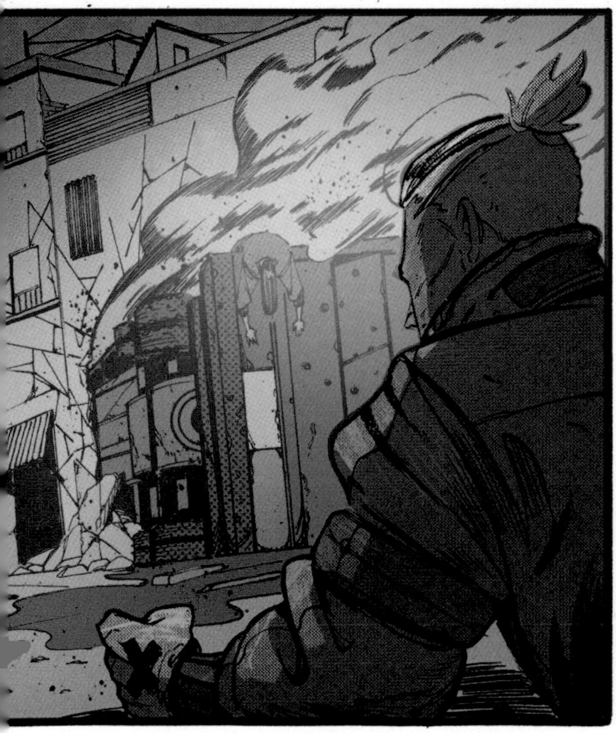

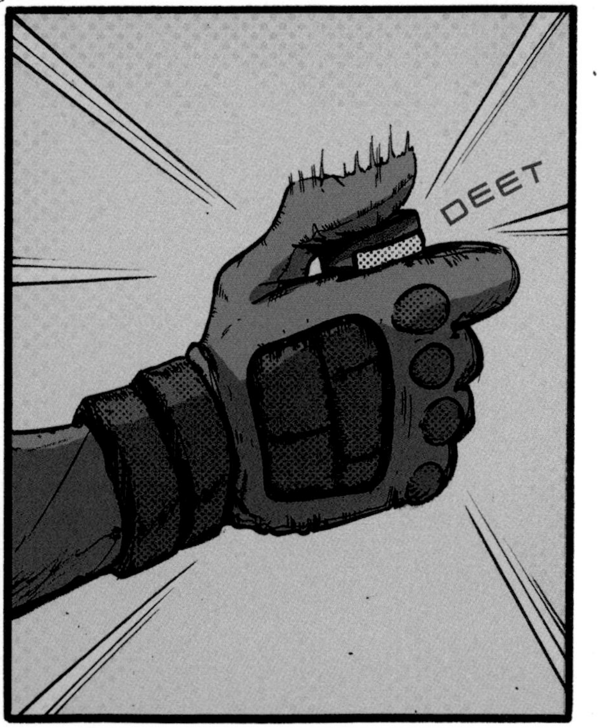
DEET

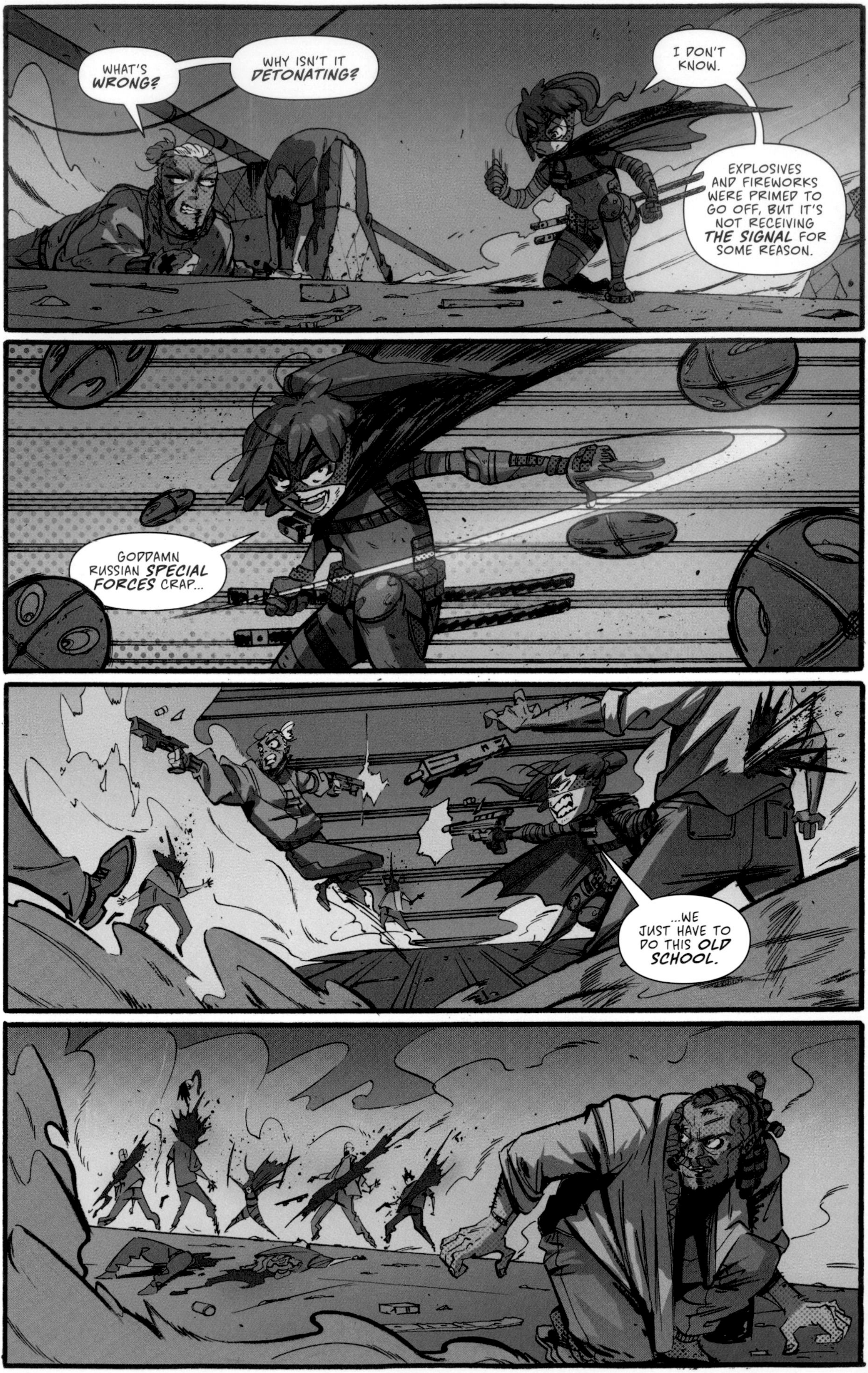
WHAT'S WRONG?
WHY ISN'T IT DETONATING?
I DON'T KNOW.
EXPLOSIVES AND FIREWORKS WERE PRIMED TO GO OFF, BUT IT'S NOT RECEIVING THE SIGNAL FOR SOME REASON.
GODDAMN RUSSIAN SPECIAL FORCES CRAP...
...WE JUST HAVE TO DO THIS OLD SCHOOL.

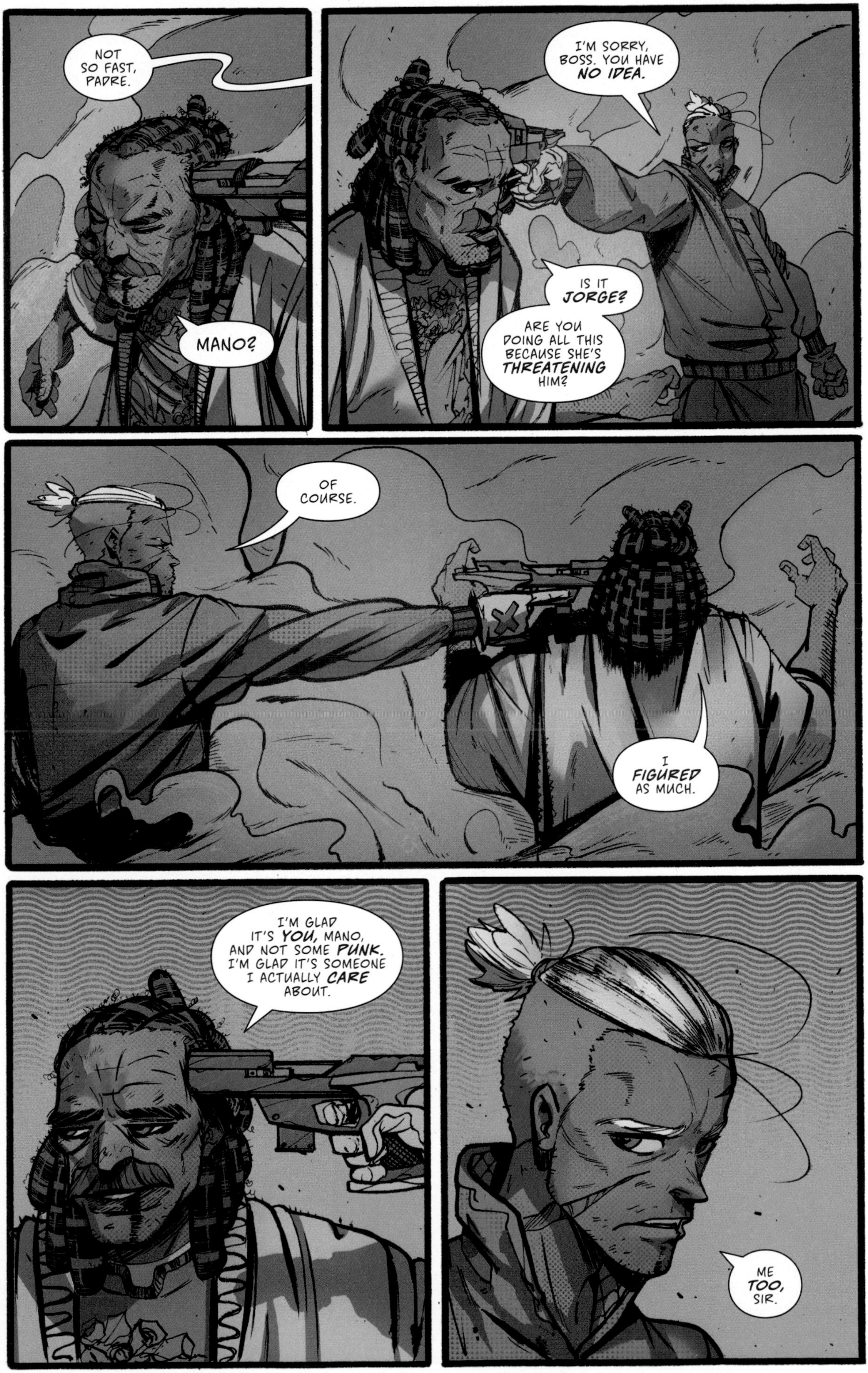
NOT SO FAST, PADRE.
MANO?
I'M SORRY, BOSS. YOU HAVE NO IDEA.
IS IT JORGE?
ARE YOU DOING ALL THIS BECAUSE SHE'S THREATENING HIM?
OF COURSE.
I FIGURED AS MUCH.
I'M GLAD IT'S YOU, MANO, AND NOT SOME PUNK. I'M GLAD IT'S SOMEONE I ACTUALLY CARE ABOUT.
ME TOO, SIR.

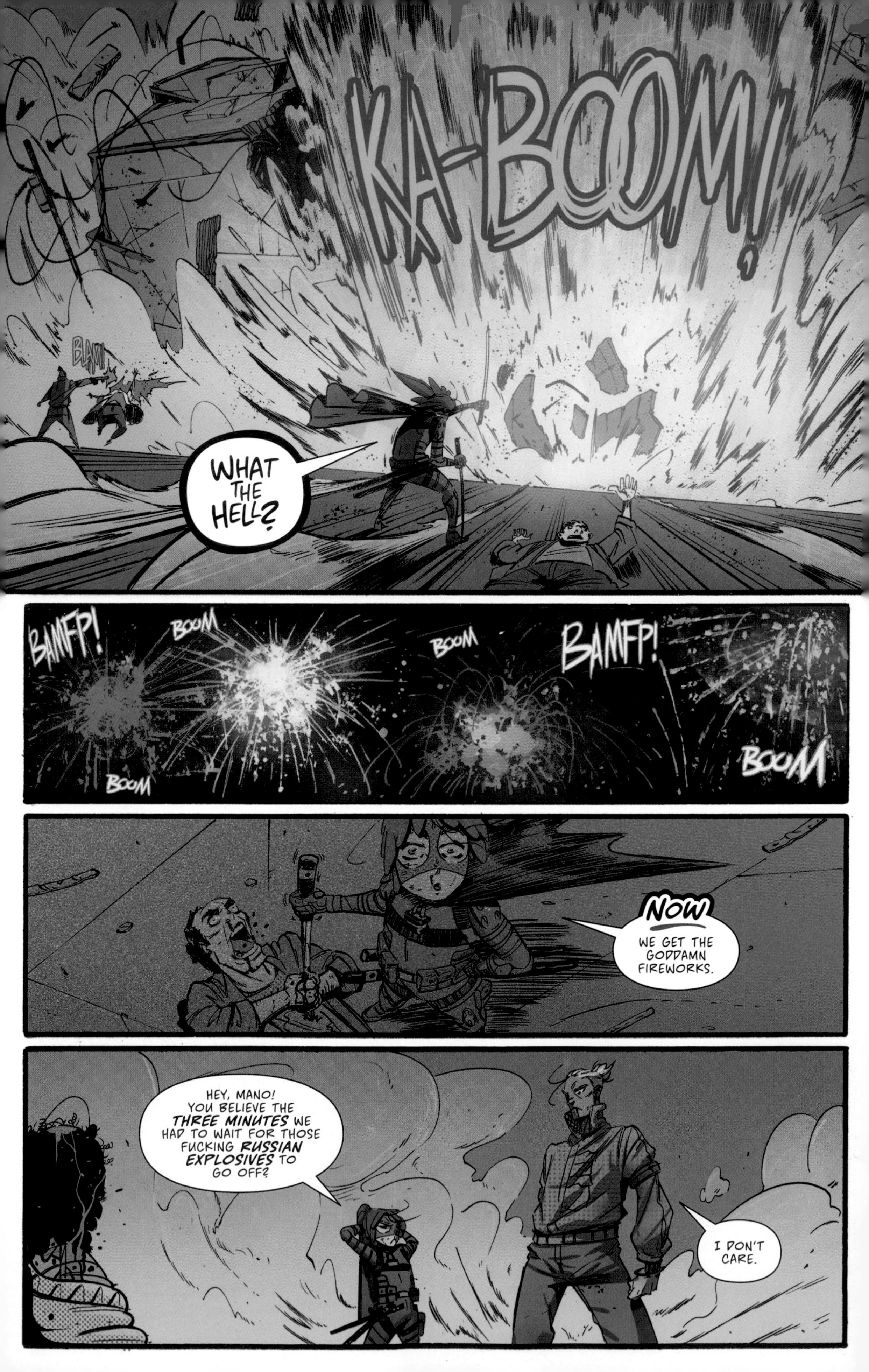
KA-BOOM!
BLAM!
WHAT THE HELL?
BAMFP!
BOOM
BOOM
BOOM
BAMFP!
BOOM
NOW WE GET THE GODDAMN FIREWORKS.
HEY, MANO! YOU BELIEVE THE THREE MINUTES WE HAD TO WAIT FOR THOSE FUCKING RUSSIAN EXPLOSIVES TO GO OFF?
I DON'T CARE.

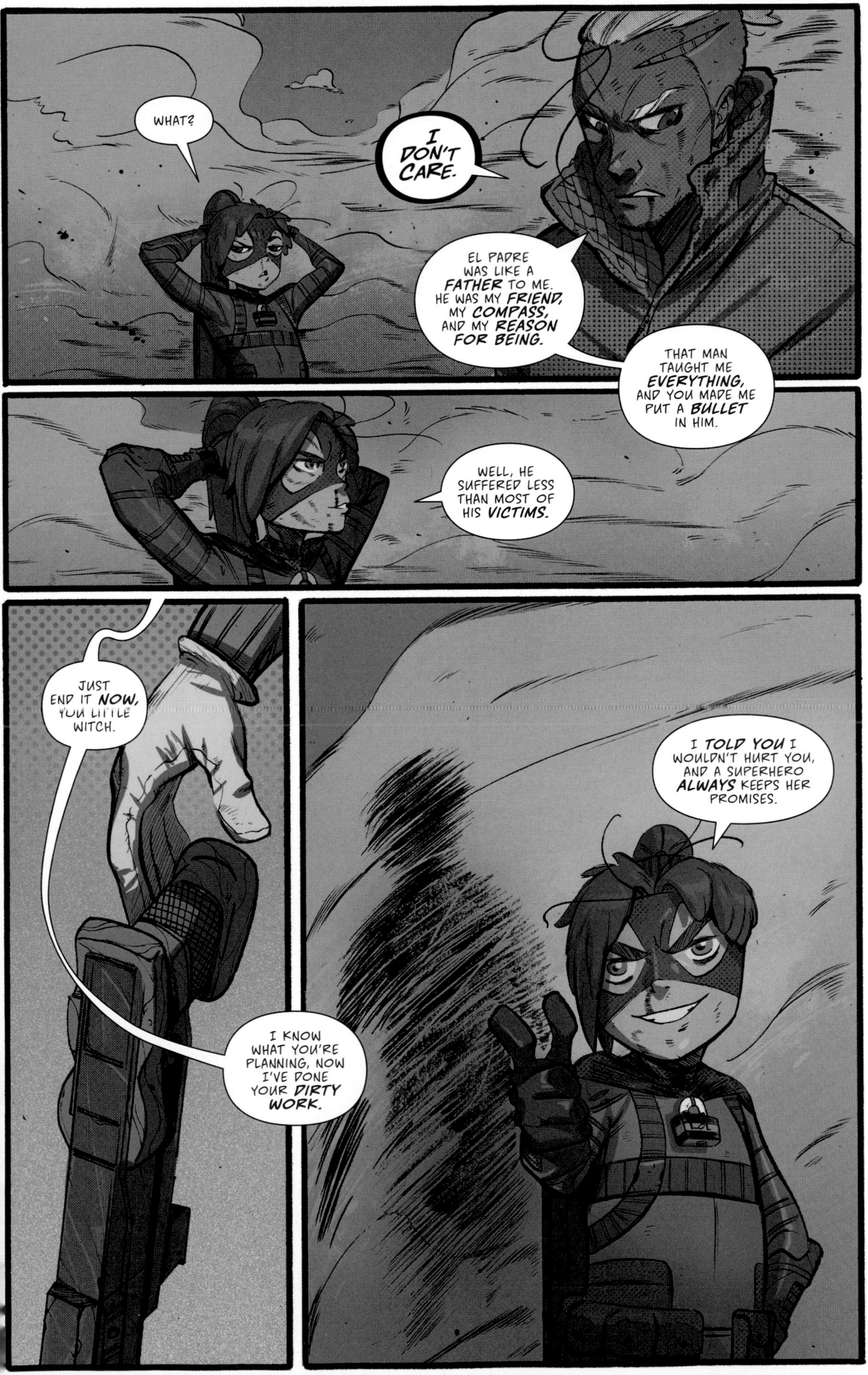
WHAT?
I DON'T CARE.
EL PADRE WAS LIKE A FATHER TO ME. HE WAS MY FRIEND, MY COMPASS, AND MY REASON FOR BEING.
THAT MAN TAUGHT ME EVERYTHING, AND YOU MADE ME PUT A BULLET IN HIM.
WELL, HE SUFFERED LESS THAN MOST OF HIS VICTIMS.
JUST END IT NOW, YOU LITTLE WITCH.
I KNOW WHAT YOU'RE PLANNING, NOW I'VE DONE YOUR DIRTY WORK.
I TOLD YOU I WOULDN'T HURT YOU, AND A SUPERHERO ALWAYS KEEPS HER PROMISES.

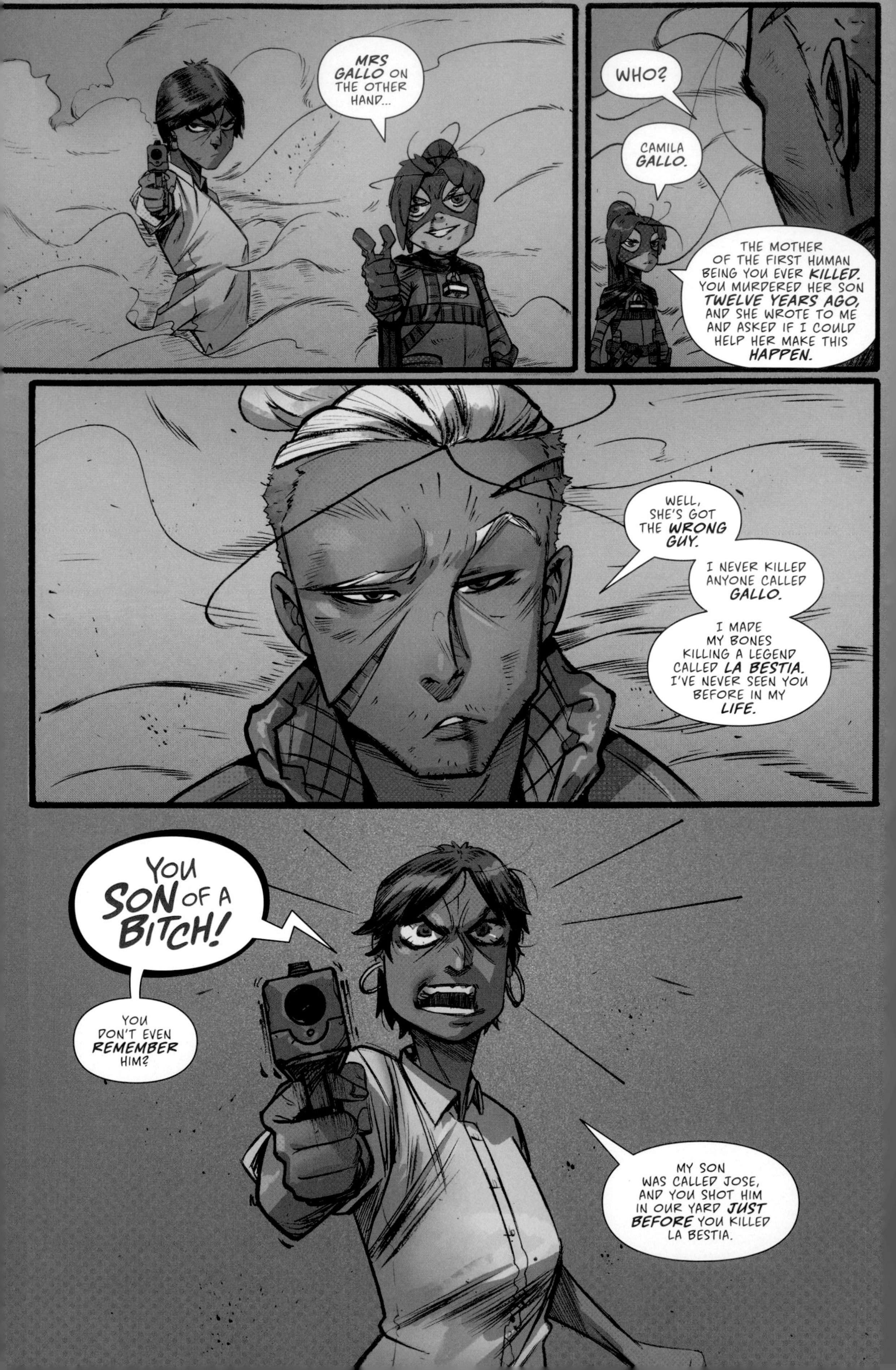
MRS GALLO ON THE OTHER HAND...
WHO?
CAMILA GALLO.
THE MOTHER OF THE FIRST HUMAN BEING YOU EVER KILLED. YOU MURDERED HER SON TWELVE YEARS AGO, AND SHE WROTE TO ME AND ASKED IF I COULD HELP HER MAKE THIS HAPPEN.
WELL, SHE'S GOT THE WRONG GUY.
I NEVER KILLED ANYONE CALLED GALLO.
I MADE MY BONES KILLING A LEGEND CALLED LA BESTIA. I'VE NEVER SEEN YOU BEFORE IN MY LIFE.
YOU SON OF A BITCH!
YOU DON'T EVEN REMEMBER HIM?
MY SON WAS CALLED JOSE, AND YOU SHOT HIM IN OUR YARD JUST BEFORE YOU KILLED LA BESTIA.

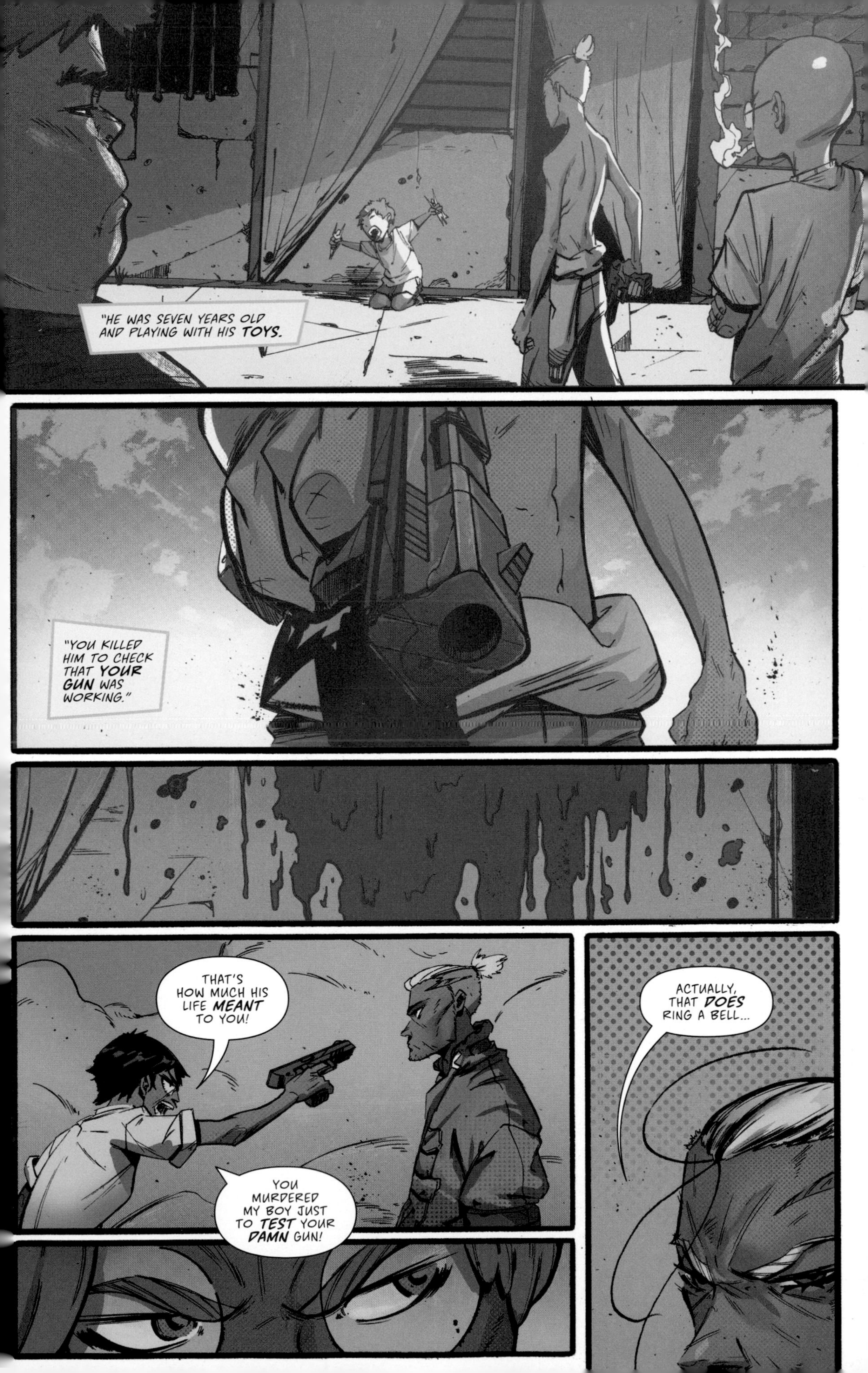
"HE WAS SEVEN YEARS OLD AND PLAYING WITH HIS TOYS.
"YOU KILLED HIM TO CHECK THAT YOUR GUN WAS WORKING."
THAT'S HOW MUCH HIS LIFE MEANT TO YOU!
YOU MURDERED MY BOY JUST TO TEST YOUR DAMN GUN!
ACTUALLY, THAT DOES RING A BELL...

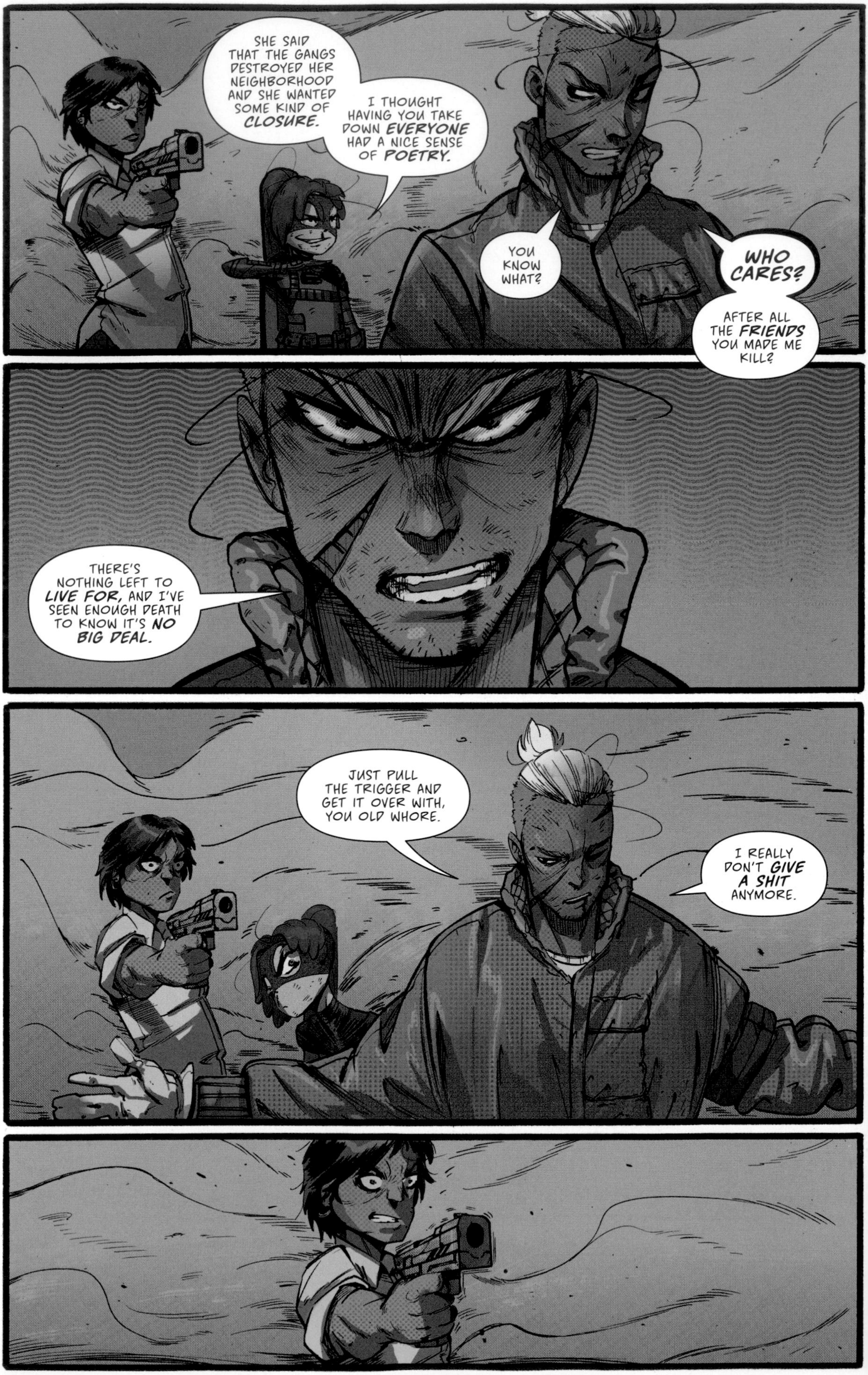
SHE SAID THAT THE GANGS DESTROYED HER NEIGHBORHOOD AND SHE WANTED SOME KIND OF CLOSURE.
I THOUGHT HAVING YOU TAKE DOWN EVERYONE HAD A NICE SENSE OF POETRY.
YOU KNOW WHAT?
WHO CARES?
AFTER ALL THE FRIENDS YOU MADE ME KILL?
THERE'S NOTHING LEFT TO LIVE FOR, AND I'VE SEEN ENOUGH DEATH TO KNOW IT'S NO BIG DEAL.
JUST PULL THE TRIGGER AND GET IT OVER WITH, YOU OLD WHORE.
I REALLY DON'T GIVE A SHIT ANYMORE.

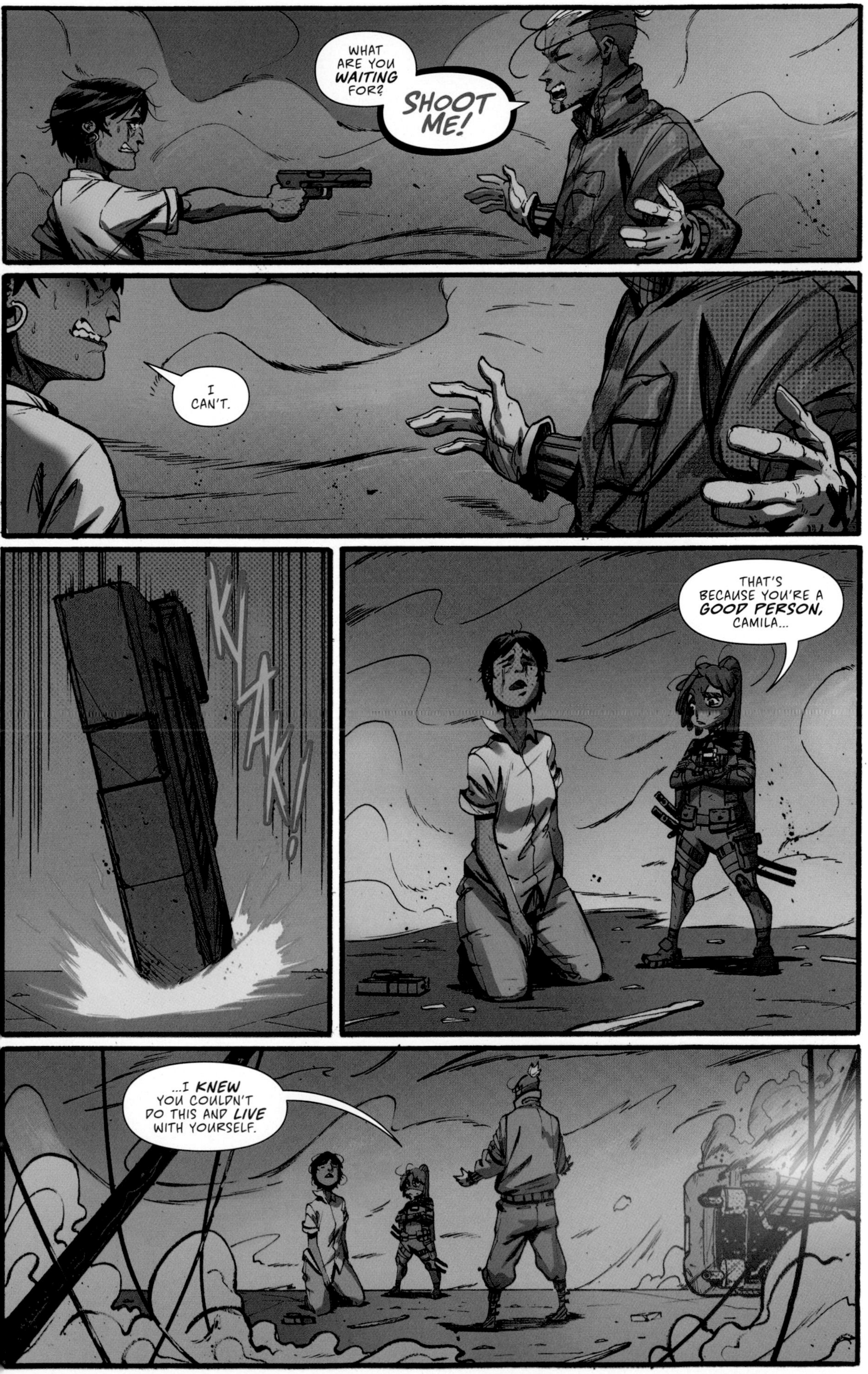
WHAT ARE YOU WAITING FOR?
SHOOT ME!
I CAN'T.
KLAK!
THAT'S BECAUSE YOU'RE A GOOD PERSON, CAMILA...
...I KNEW YOU COULDN'T DO THIS AND LIVE WITH YOURSELF.

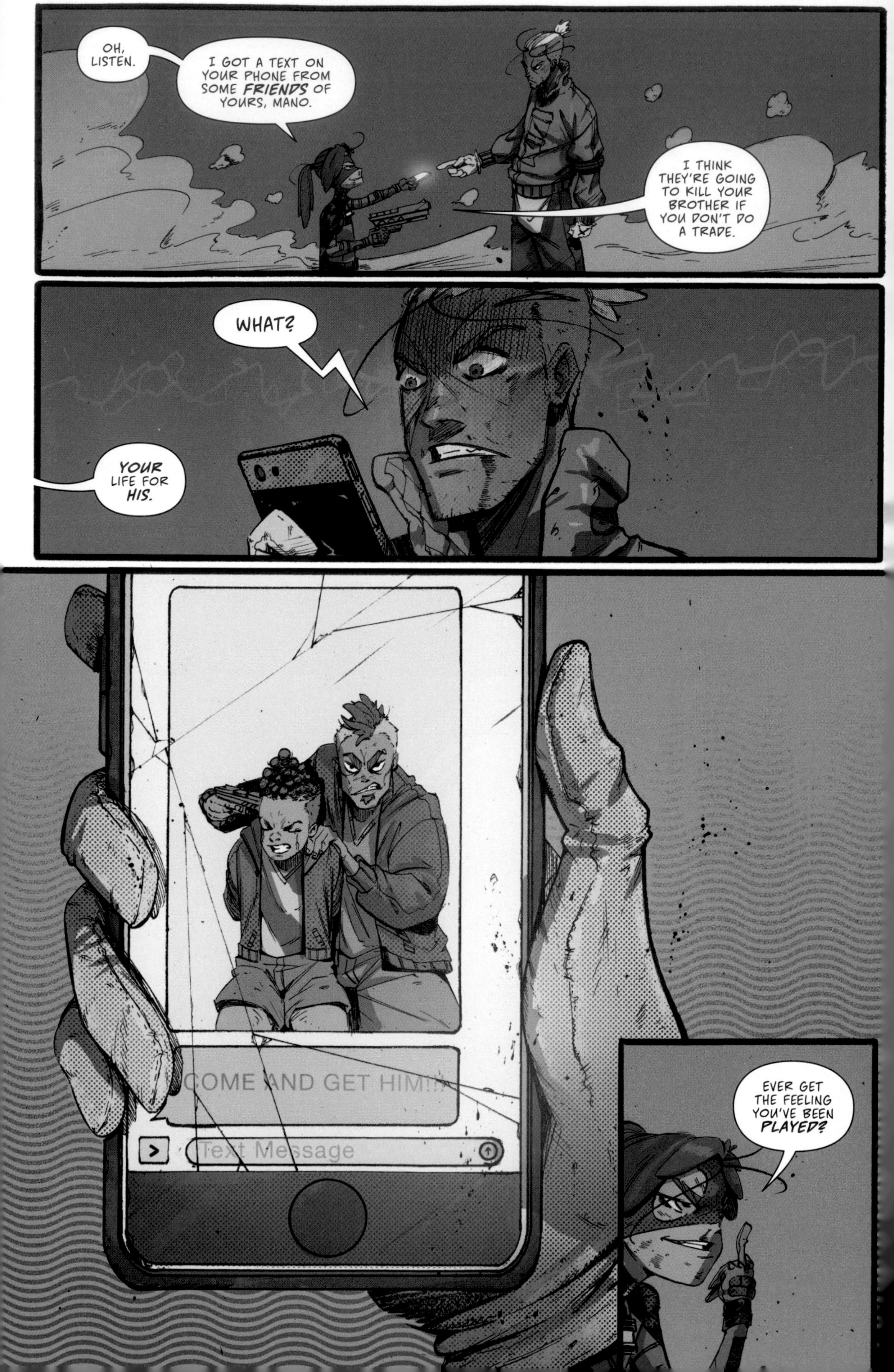
OH, LISTEN.
I GOT A TEXT ON YOUR PHONE FROM SOME FRIENDS OF YOURS, MANO.
I THINK THEY'RE GOING TO KILL YOUR BROTHER IF YOU DON'T DO A TRADE.
WHAT?
YOUR LIFE FOR HIS.
COME AND GET HIM!!!
Text Message
EVER GET THE FEELING YOU'VE BEEN PLAYED?

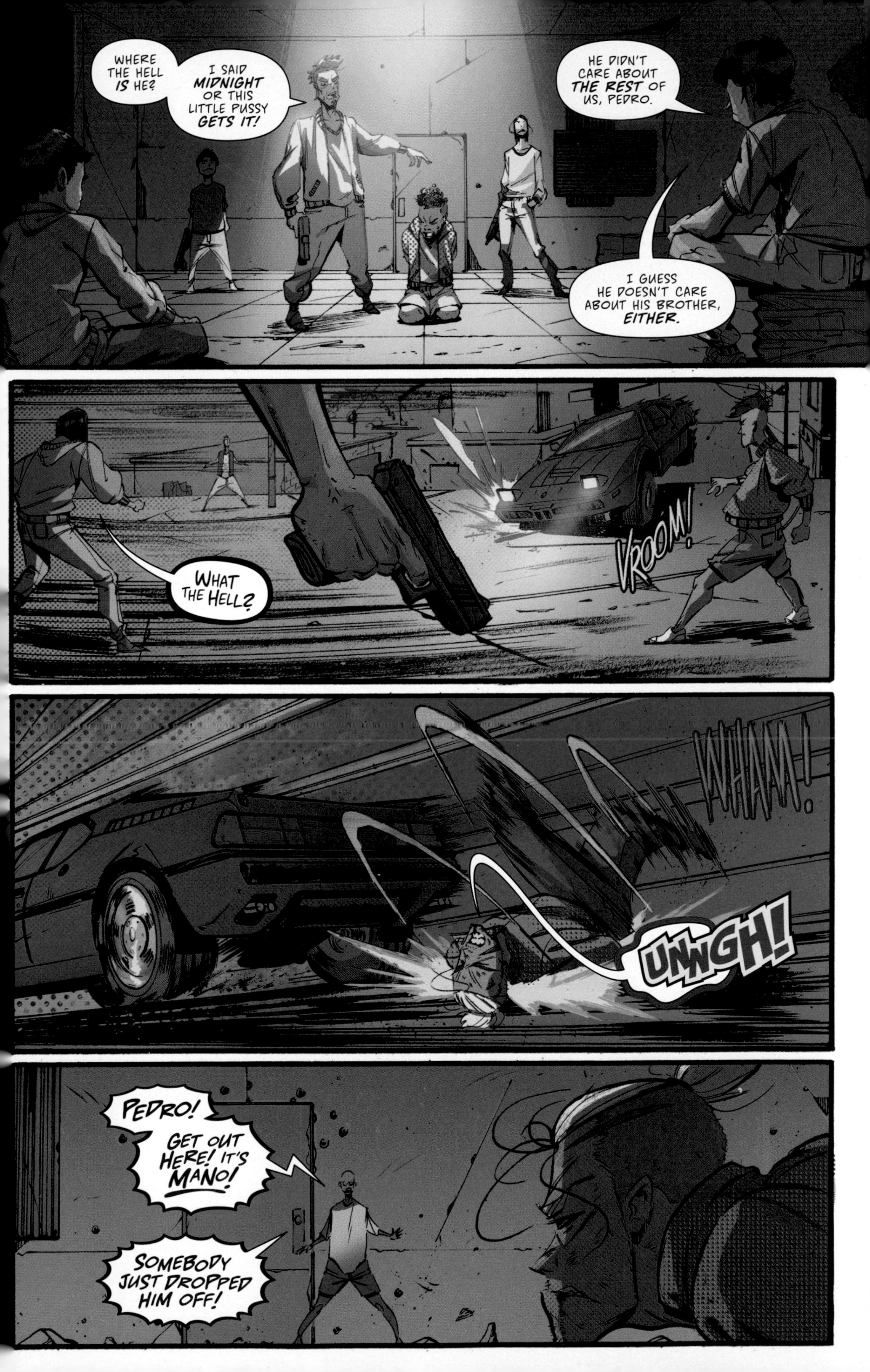
WHERE THE HELL IS HE?
I SAID MIDNIGHT OR THIS LITTLE PUSSY GETS IT!
HE DIDN'T CARE ABOUT THE REST OF US, PEDRO.
I GUESS HE DOESN'T CARE ABOUT HIS BROTHER, EITHER.
VROOM!
WHAT THE HELL?
WHAAM!
UNNGH!
PEDRO!
GET OUT HERE! IT'S MANO!
SOMEBODY JUST DROPPED HIM OFF!

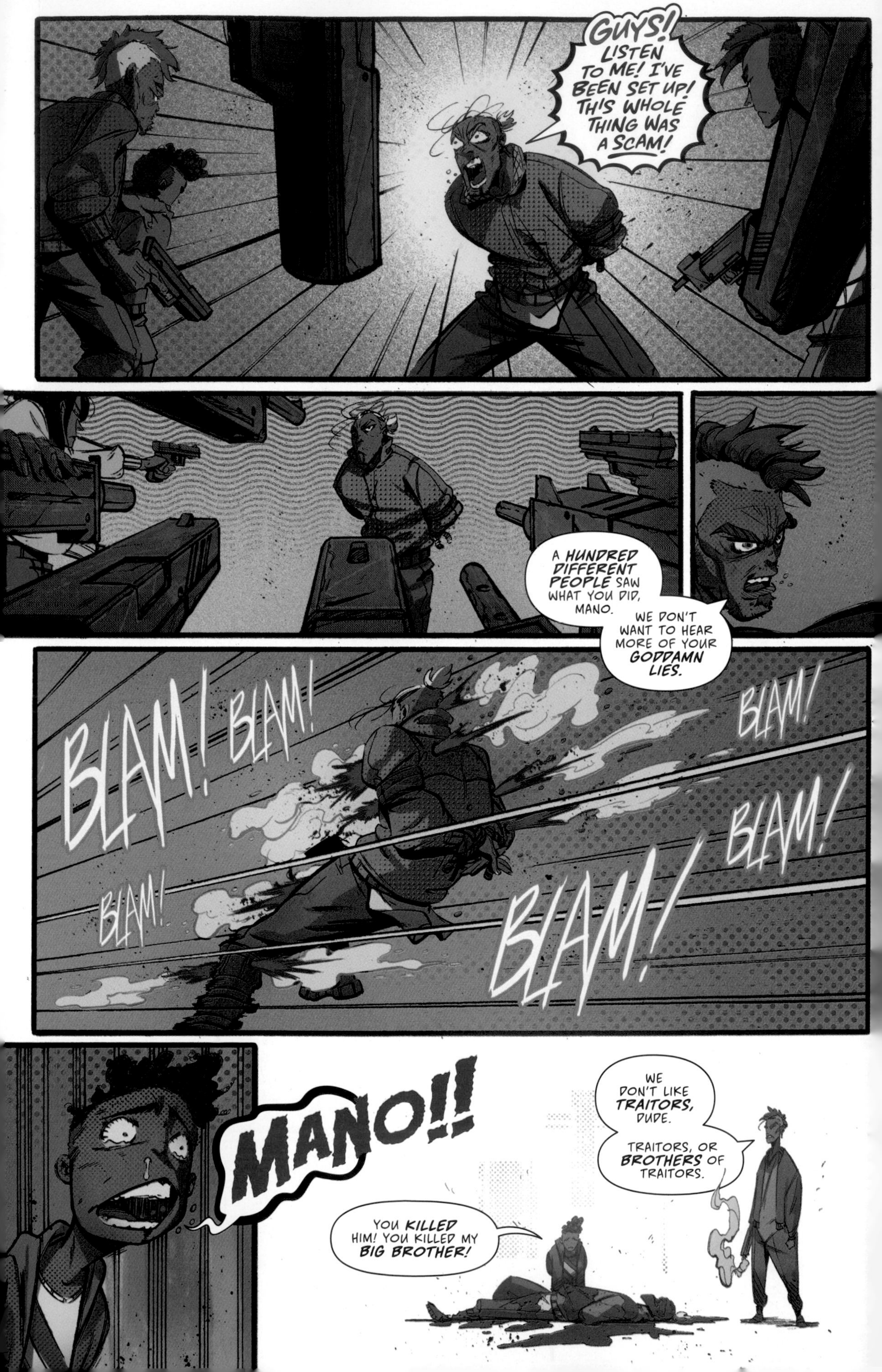
GUYS! LISTEN TO ME! I'VE BEEN SET UP! THIS WHOLE THING WAS A SCAM!
A HUNDRED DIFFERENT PEOPLE SAW WHAT YOU DID, MANO.
WE DON'T WANT TO HEAR MORE OF YOUR GODDAMN LIES.
BLAM! BLAM!
BLAM!
BLAM!
BLAM!
BLAM!
BLAM!
MANO!!
WE DON'T LIKE TRAITORS, DUDE.
TRAITORS, OR BROTHERS OF TRAITORS.
YOU KILLED HIM! YOU KILLED MY BIG BROTHER!

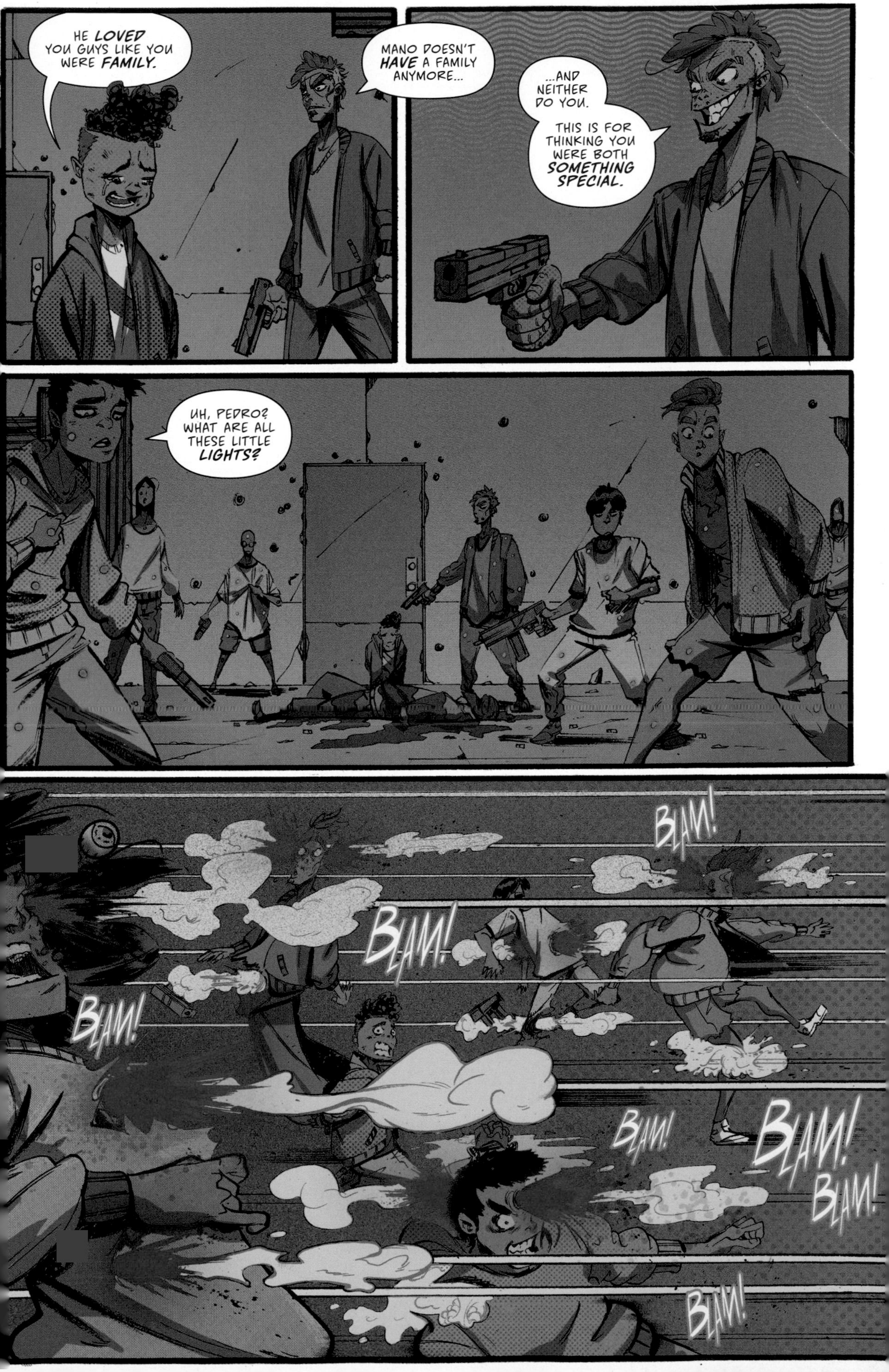
HE LOVED YOU GUYS LIKE YOU WERE FAMILY.
MANO DOESN'T HAVE A FAMILY ANYMORE...
...AND NEITHER DO YOU.
THIS IS FOR THINKING YOU WERE BOTH SOMETHING SPECIAL.
UH, PEDRO? WHAT ARE ALL THESE LITTLE LIGHTS?
BLAM!
BLAM!
BLAM!
BLAM!
BLAM!
BLAM!
BLAM!

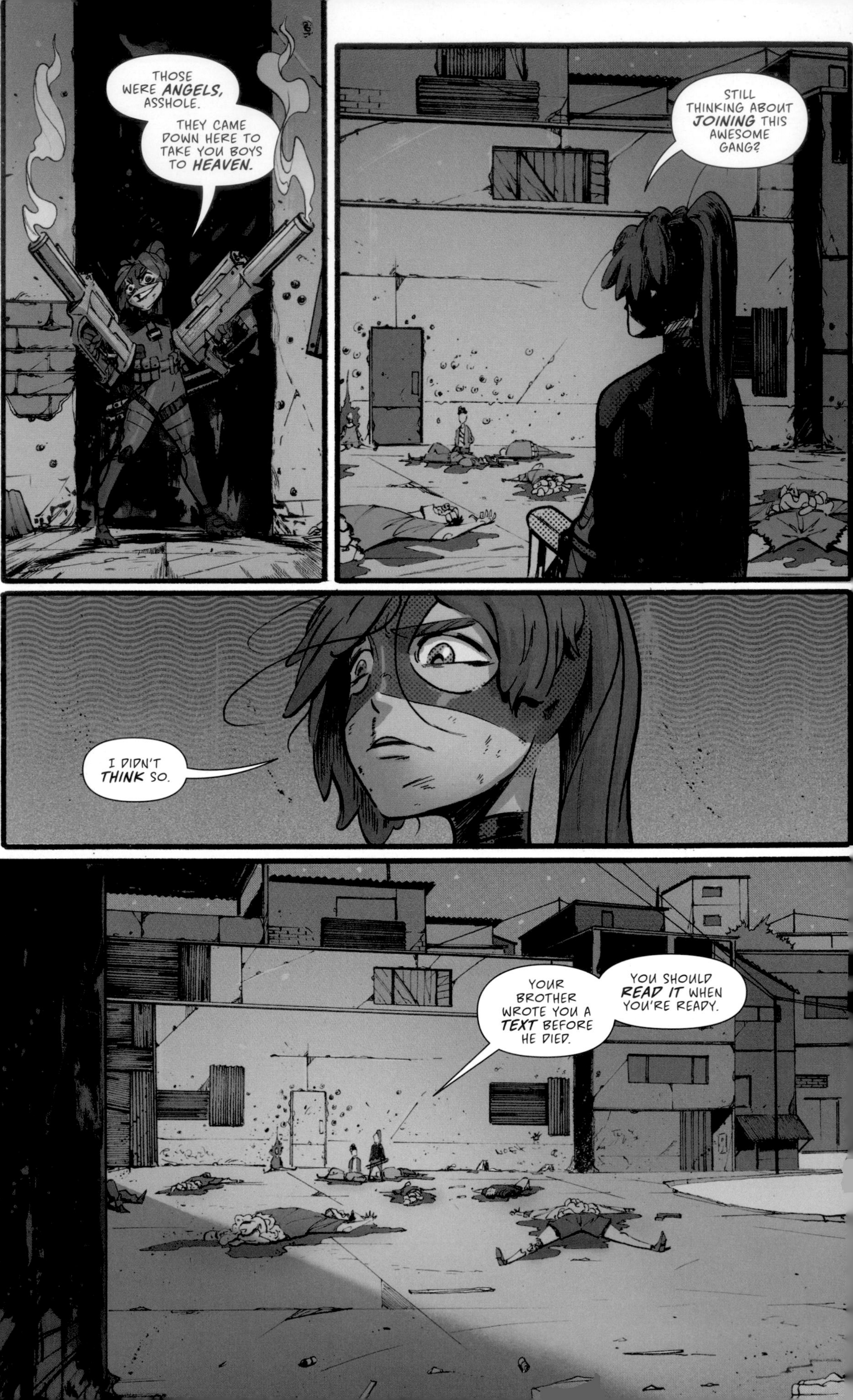
THOSE WERE ANGELS, ASSHOLE.
THEY CAME DOWN HERE TO TAKE YOU BOYS TO HEAVEN.
STILL THINKING ABOUT JOINING THIS AWESOME GANG?
I DIDN'T THINK SO.
YOUR BROTHER WROTE YOU A TEXT BEFORE HE DIED.
YOU SHOULD READ IT WHEN YOU'RE READY.

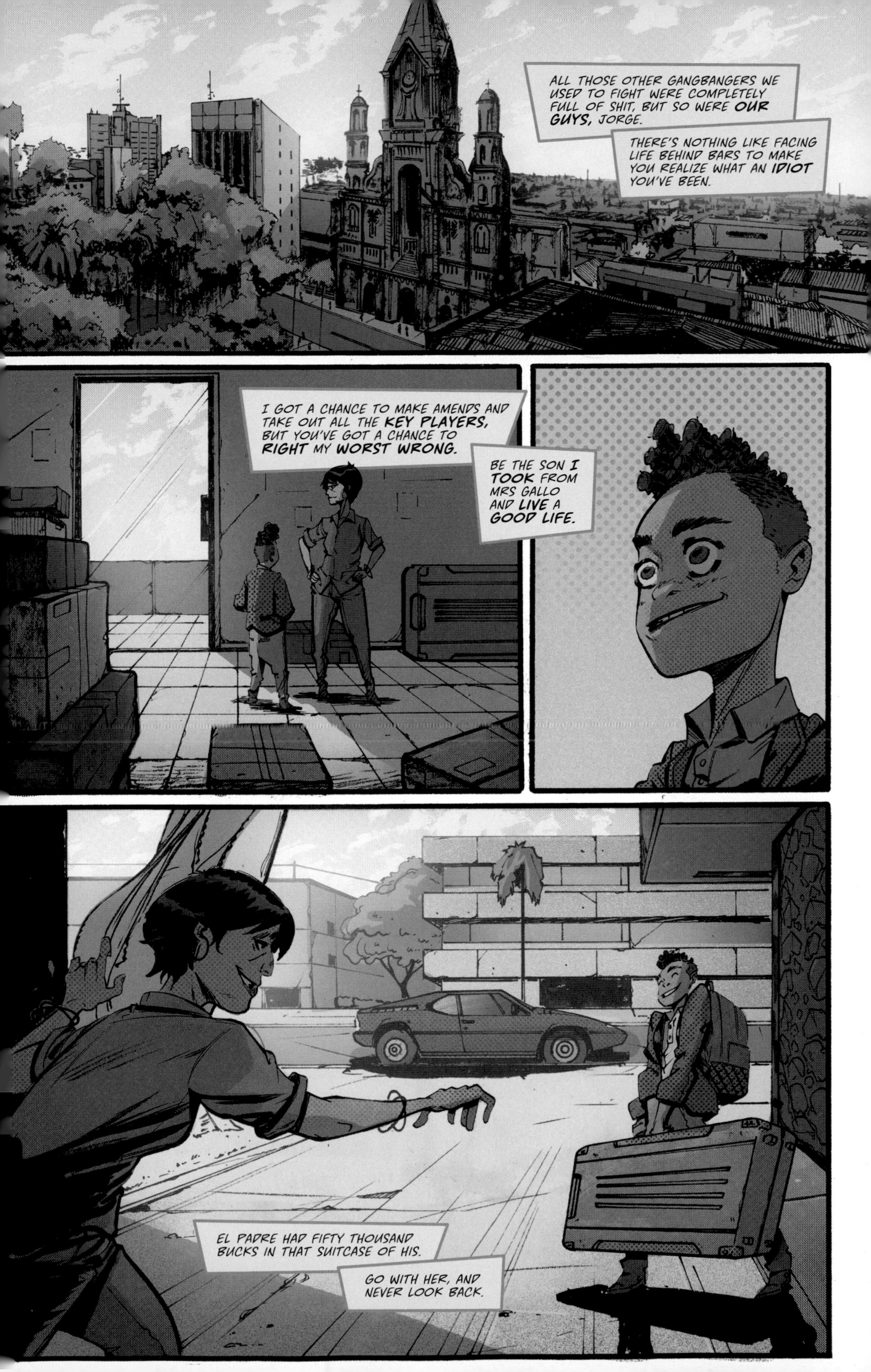

ALL THOSE OTHER GANGBANGERS WE USED TO FIGHT WERE COMPLETELY FULL OF SHIT, BUT SO WERE OUR GUYS, JORGE.
THERE'S NOTHING LIKE FACING LIFE BEHIND BARS TO MAKE YOU REALIZE WHAT AN IDIOT YOU'VE BEEN.
I GOT A CHANCE TO MAKE AMENDS AND TAKE OUT ALL THE KEY PLAYERS, BUT YOU'VE GOT A CHANCE TO RIGHT MY WORST WRONG.
BE THE SON I TOOK FROM MRS GALLO AND LIVE A GOOD LIFE.
EL PADRE HAD FIFTY THOUSAND BUCKS IN THAT SUITCASE OF HIS.
GO WITH HER, AND NEVER LOOK BACK.

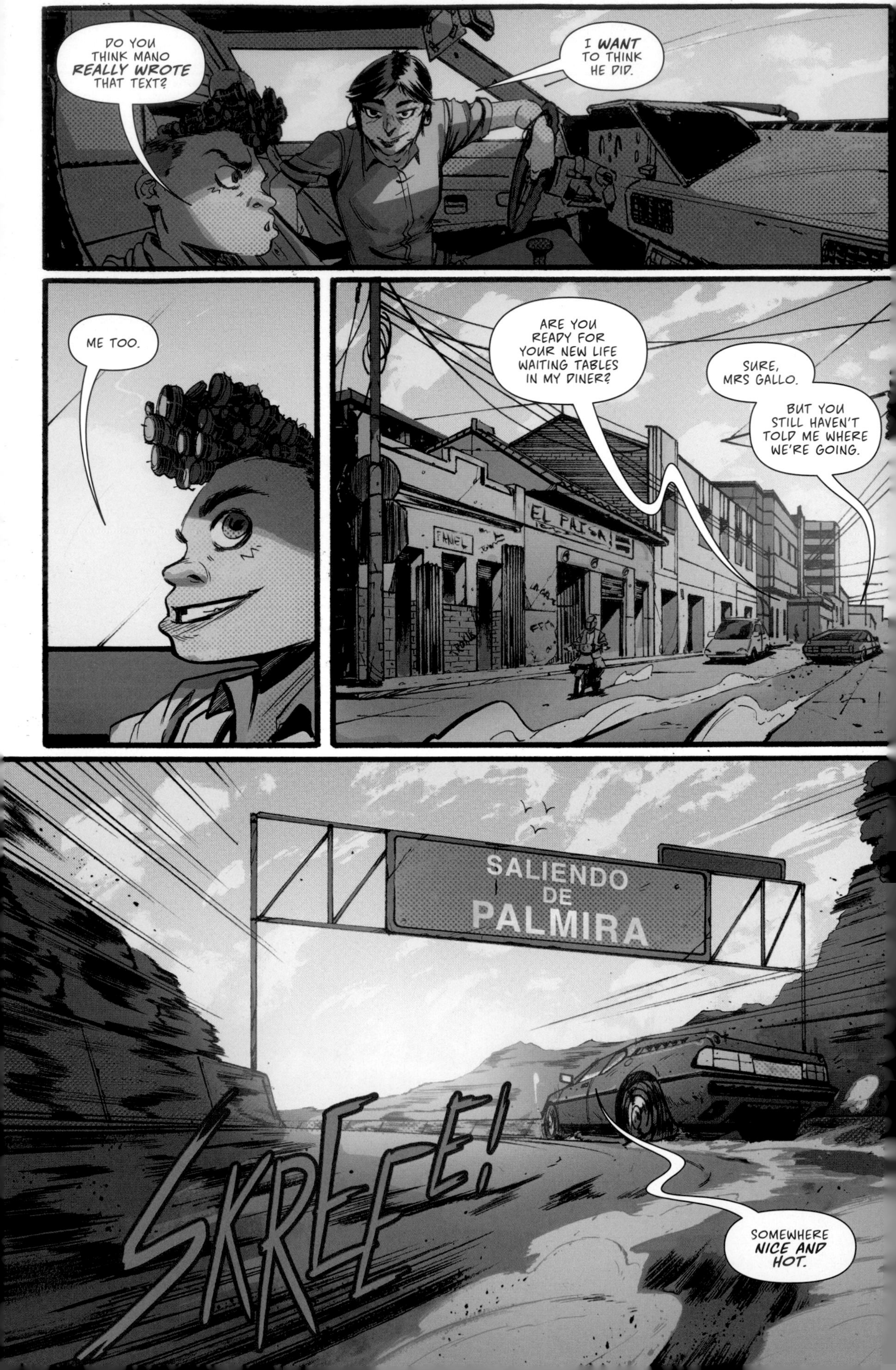
DO YOU THINK MANO REALLY WROTE THAT TEXT?
I WANT TO THINK HE DID.
ME TOO.
ARE YOU READY FOR YOUR NEW LIFE WAITING TABLES IN MY DINER?
SURE, MRS GALLO.
BUT YOU STILL HAVEN'T TOLD ME WHERE WE'RE GOING.
SALIENDO DE PALMIRA
SKREEE!
SOMEWHERE NICE AND HOT.

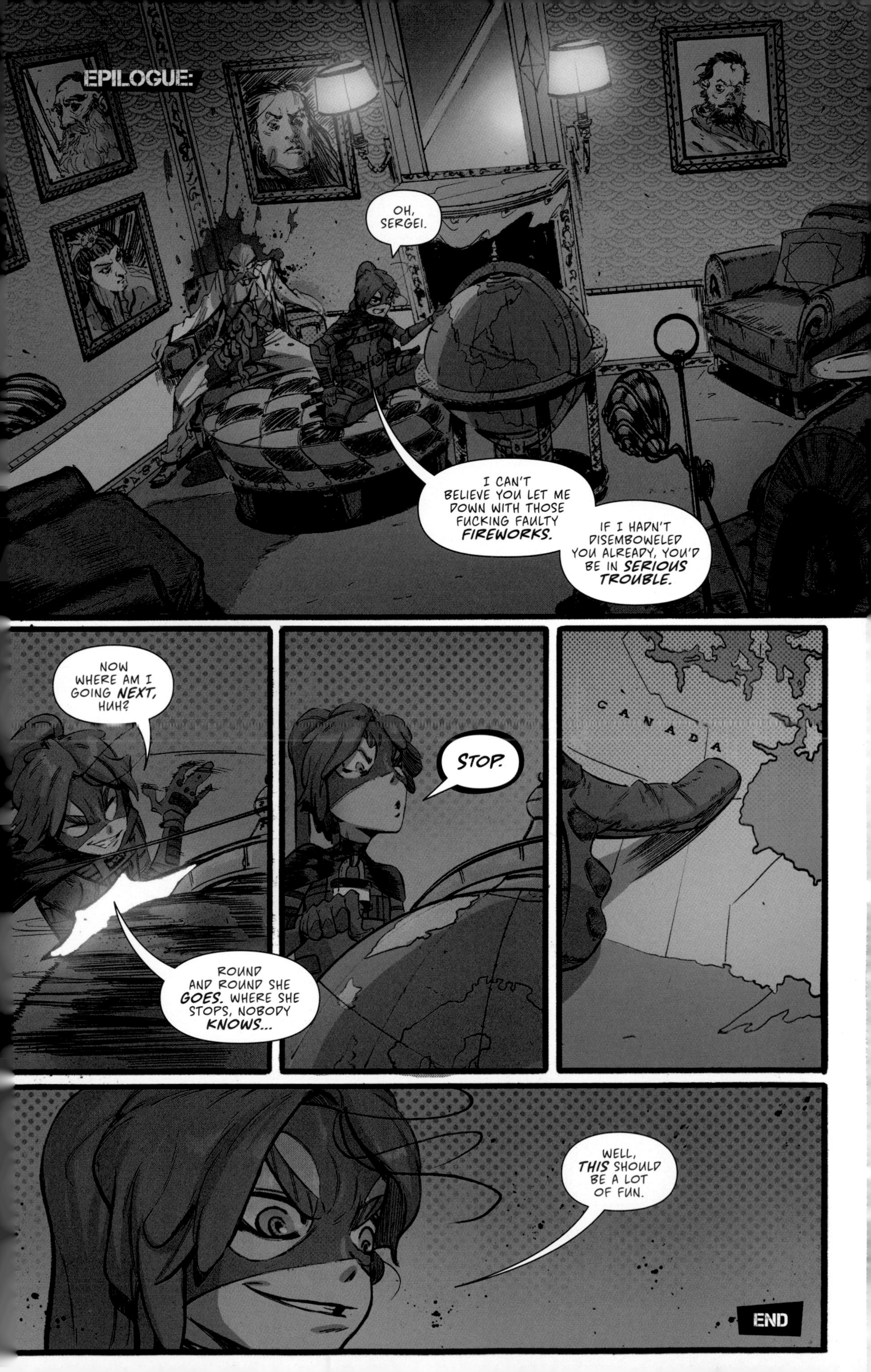
EPILOGUE:
OH, SERGEI.
I CAN'T BELIEVE YOU LET ME DOWN WITH THOSE FUCKING FAULTY FIREWORKS.
IF I HADN'T DISEMBOWELED YOU ALREADY, YOU'D BE IN SERIOUS TROUBLE.
NOW WHERE AM I GOING NEXT, HUH?
ROUND AND ROUND SHE GOES. WHERE SHE STOPS, NOBODY KNOWS...
STOP.
CANADA
WELL, THIS SHOULD BE A LOT OF FUN.
END

RICARDO LOPEZ ORTIZ
CHARACTER DESIGNS

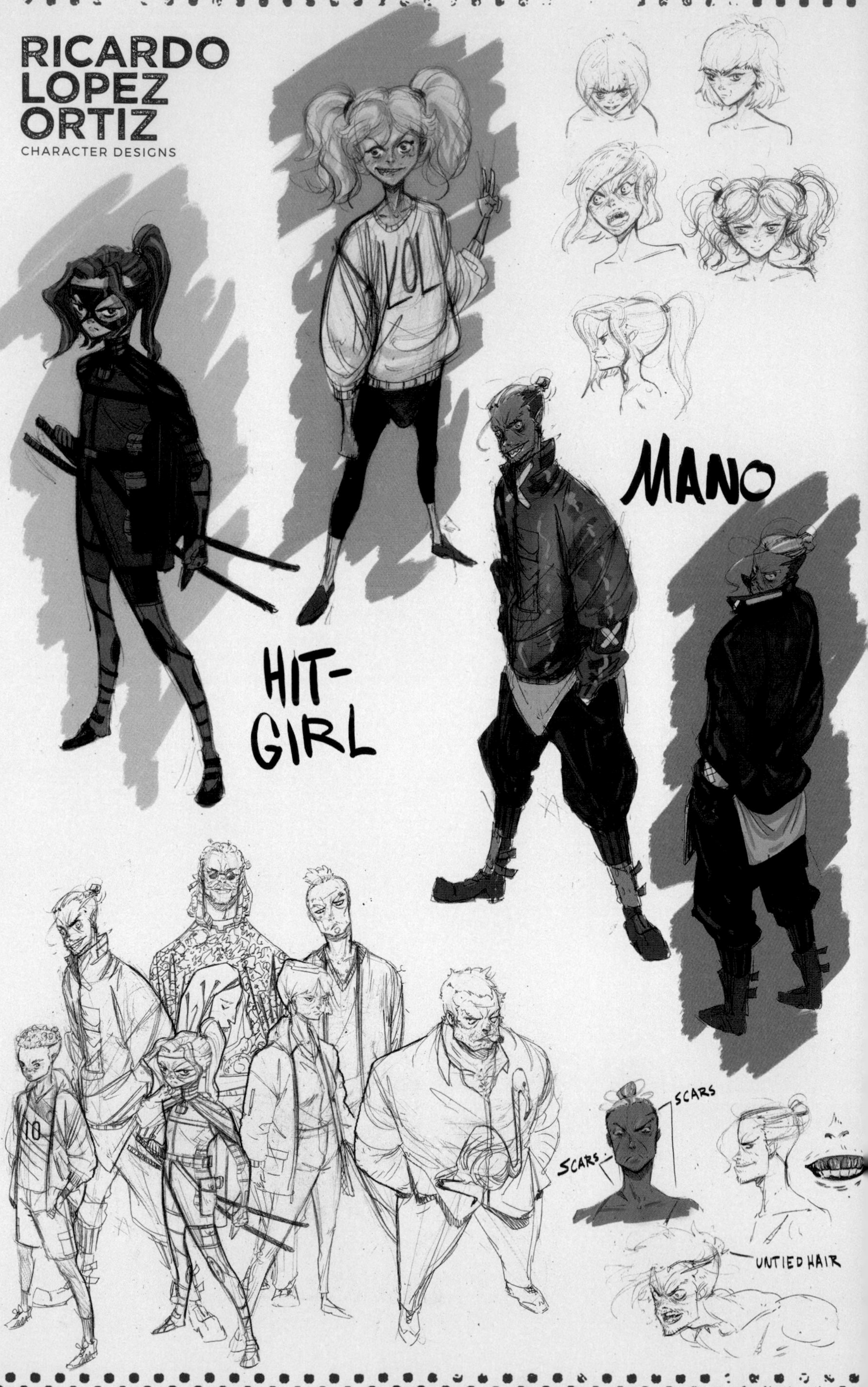
LOL
HIT-GIRL
MANO
SCARS
SCARS
UNTIED HAIR

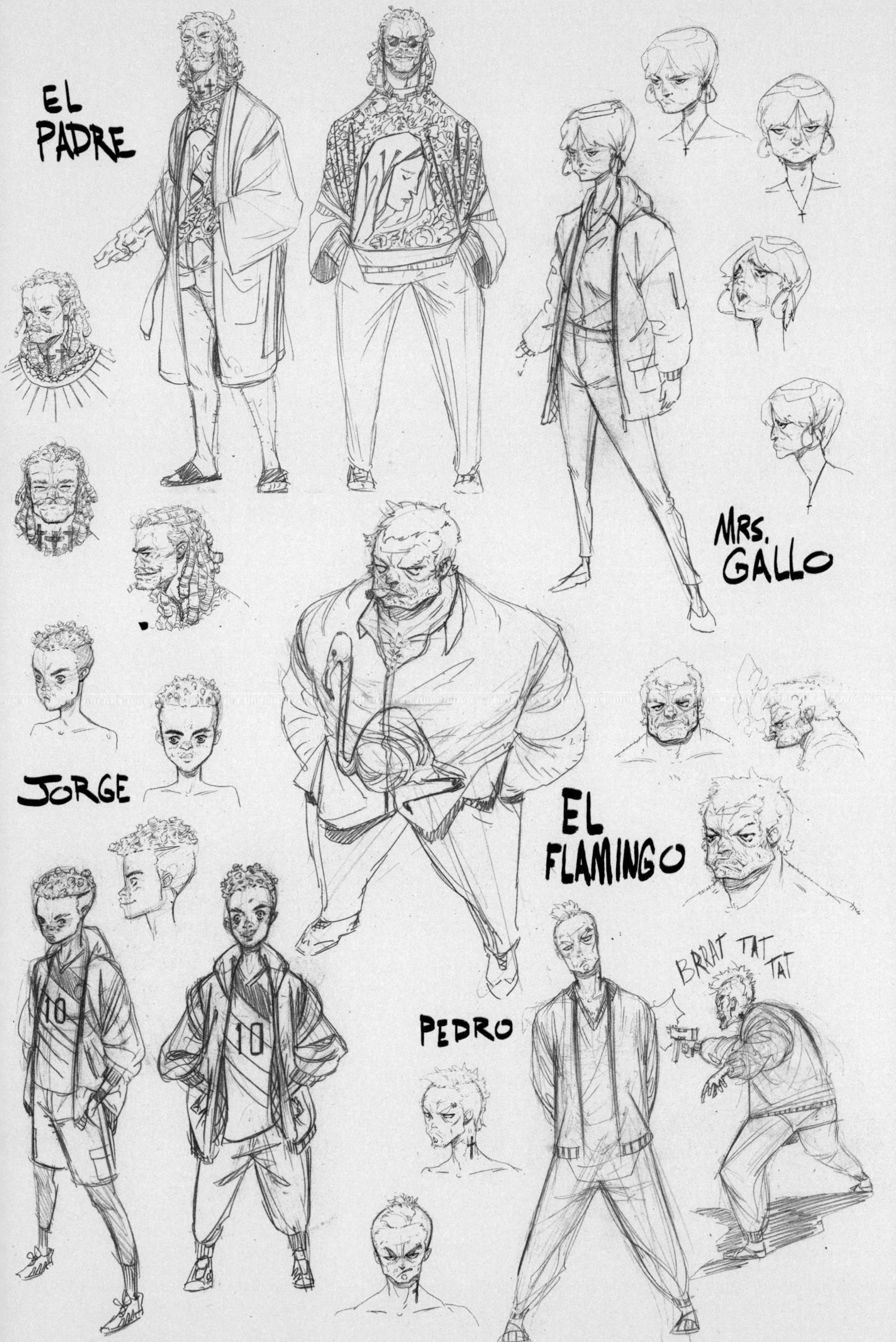
EL PADRE
MRS. GALLO
JORGE
EL FLAMINGO
PEDRO
BRRAT TAT TAT
10
10

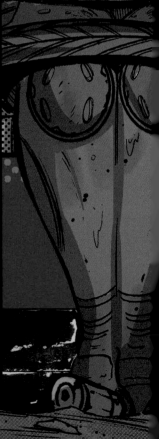

MARK MILLAR

is the New York Times bestselling author of **KICK-ASS**, **WANTED**, and **KINGSMAN: THE SECRET SERVICE**, all of which have been adapted into Hollywood franchises.

His DC Comics work includes the seminal **SUPERMAN: RED SON**. At Marvel Comics he created **THE ULTIMATES**, selected by **TIME** magazine as the comic book of the decade, and described by screenwriter Zak Penn as his major inspiration for **THE AVENGERS** movie. Millar also created **WOLVERINE: OLD MAN LOGAN** and **CIVIL WAR**, Marvel's two biggest-selling graphic novels ever. **CIVIL WAR** was the basis of the **CAPTAIN AMERICA: CIVIL WAR** movie, and **OLD MAN LOGAN** was the inspiration for Fox's **LOGAN** movie in 2017.

Mark has been an executive producer on all his movies, and for four years worked as a creative consultant to Fox Studios on their Marvel slate of movies. In 2017, Netflix bought Millarworld in the company's first ever acquisition, and employed Mark as President to continue creating comics, TV shows, and movies. His much-anticipated autobiography, **I WILL KINK-SHAME YOUR CAT FOR FREE**, will be published next year.

RICARDO LOPEZ ORTIZ

was born and raised in Bayamón, Puerto Rico. After spending his childhood and teenage years binge-watching **GATCHAMAN**, **DRAGON BALL**, **COWBOY BEBOP** and **EVANGELION**, he decided to give this art thing a shot, and after a year of sleeping all over the campus at the University of Puerto Rico, he moved to New York City and studied Illustration at the School of Visual Arts.

His illustration work was recognized by the Society of Illustrators and American Illustration. He first broke into the comic book scene drawing a short story in the **FEARLESS FUTURE** anthology in 2014. Soon after, Ricardo started working on titles for Image Comics and Marvel comics. He's known for his work on **ZERO**, **WOLF**, **CIVIL WAR II: KINGPIN** and **TOTALLY AWESOME HULK**. This all led to some dude called Mark Millar sliding into his DMs and asking him to draw a little thing called **HIT-GIRL**, which, if you're reading this, means you're holding said book in your very own hands. Now walk to the checkout counter and buy this book because it's a damn good time! Currently Ricardo lives in Brooklyn, and spends his days telling his dog Ash that it's not OK to jump on people.

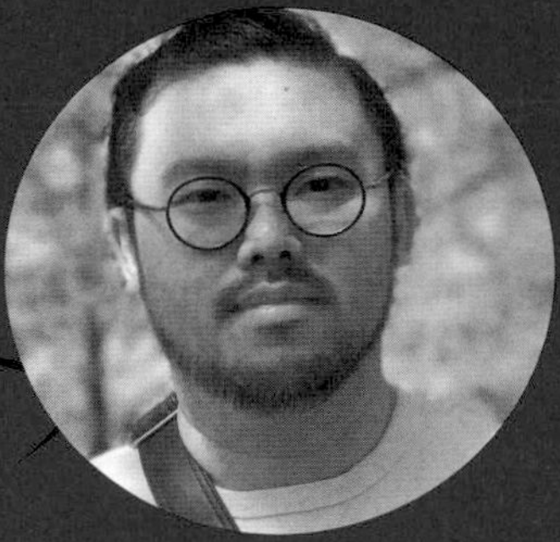

SUNNY GHO

studied Graphic Design at Trisakti University, Indonesia, before going on to work for companies such as Top Cow, Imaginary Friends Studios and GLITCH.

He has colored an impressive array of comic book titles, including Marvel's **CIVIL WAR II**, **THE INDESTRUCTIBLE HULK** and **THE AVENGERS**. For Mark Millar, he has colored **SUPERCROOKS**, **SUPERIOR**, **JUPITER'S LEGACY 2** and **HIT-GIRL**.

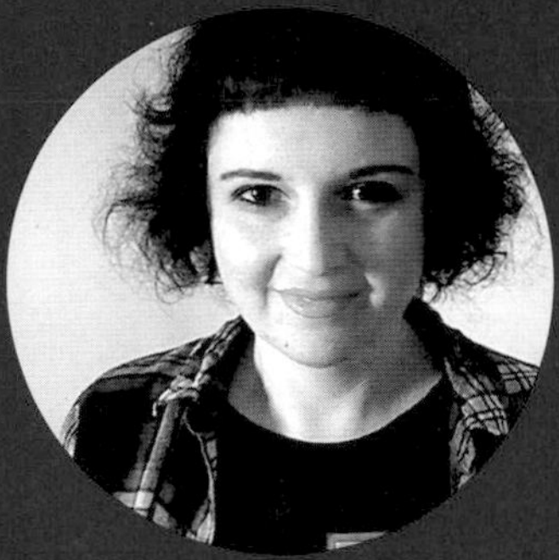

MELINA MIKULIC

hasn't yet won an Eisner Award for Best Publication Design, for one simple reason: she's designed more than a thousand gorgeous comic books (including Fibra's editions of Moebius, and Marjane Satrapi's **PERSEPOLIS** and Tezuka) but all on the wrong continent. That is about to change.

She is a Master of Arts, and graduated from the Faculty of Design in Zagreb, Croatia, where she was born. As a graphic designer, she is primarily engaged in design for print, with a growing interest in illustration and interactive media. She now lives in Rijeka, where despite enjoying the Mediterranean climate, she rarely sees the sun, as she spends her time wandering through shadowy landscapes of fonts and letters.

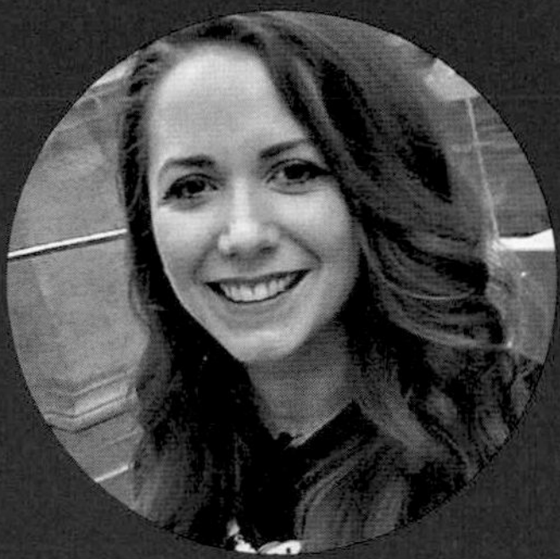

RACHAEL FULTON

is series editor of Mark Millar and John Romita Jr's monthly ongoing **KICK-ASS** series, as well as the monthly ongoing **HIT-GIRL** series, working with talent such as Eduardo Risso, Rafael Albuquerque and Goran Parlov.

She is editor of Netflix's Millarworld division, where she is currently producing **THE MAGIC ORDER** with Mark Millar and Olivier Coipel. Her past credits as series editor include **EMPRESS**, **JUPITER'S LEGACY 2**, **REBORN** and **KINGSMAN: THE RED DIAMOND**.

She is collections editor for the most recent editions of **KINGSMAN: THE SECRET SERVICE** and all volumes of **KICK-ASS: THE DAVE LIZEWSKI YEARS**.

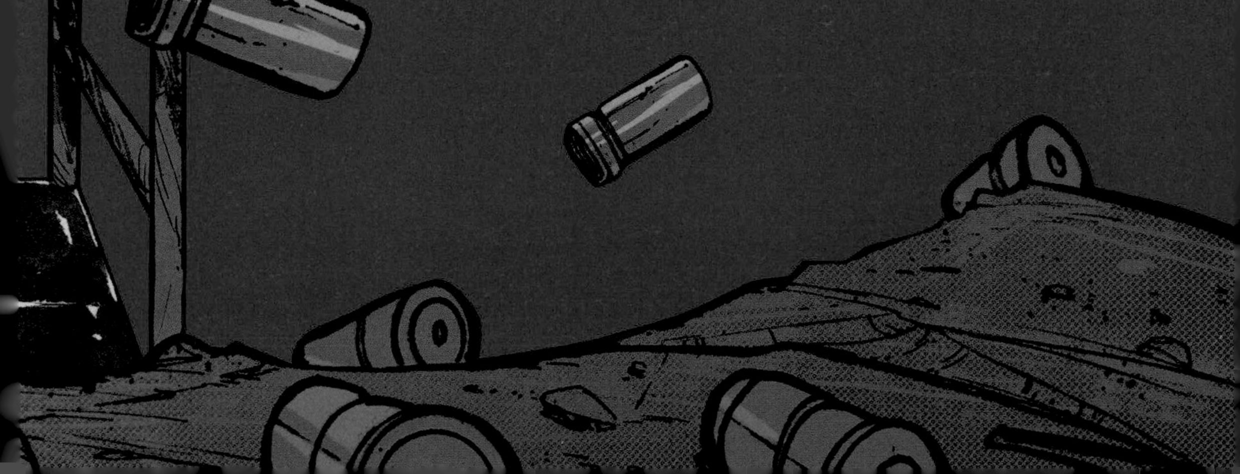

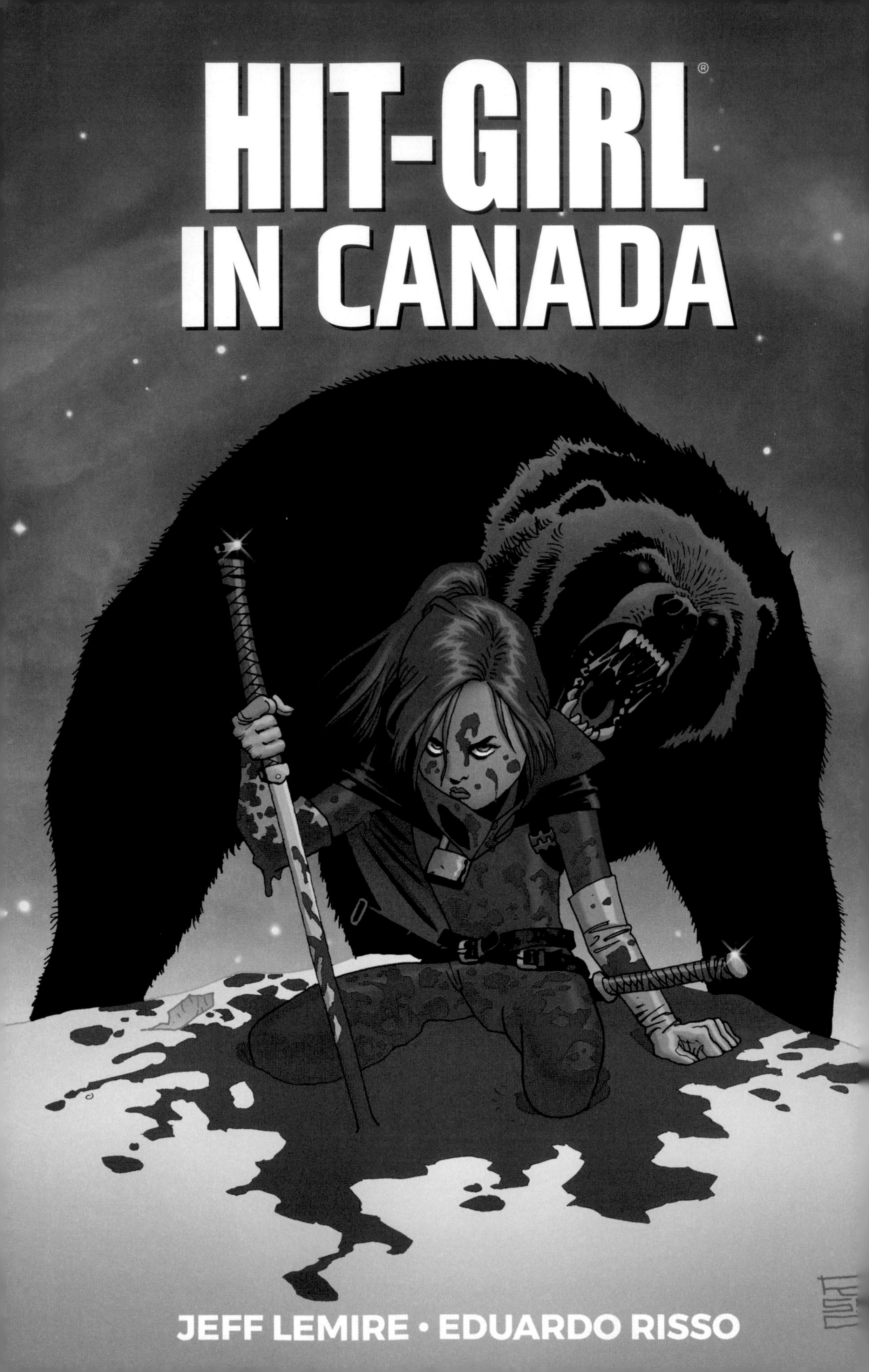
HIT-GIRL®
IN CANADA
JEFF LEMIRE • EDUARDO RISSO

OTHER TITLES IN THIS SERIES

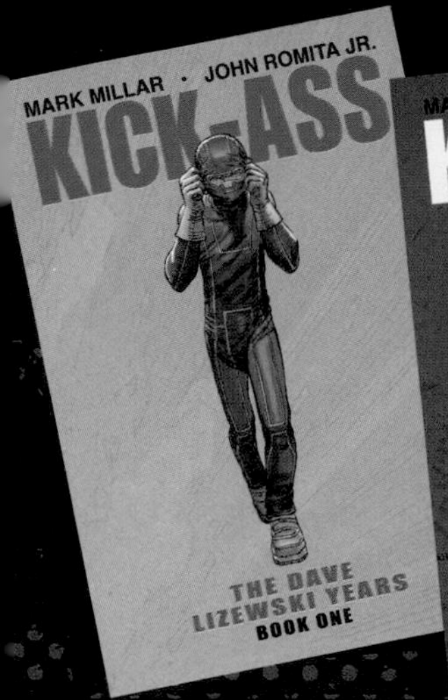
MARK MILLAR • JOHN ROMITA JR.
KICK-ASS
THE DAVE LIZEWSKI YEARS
BOOK ONE

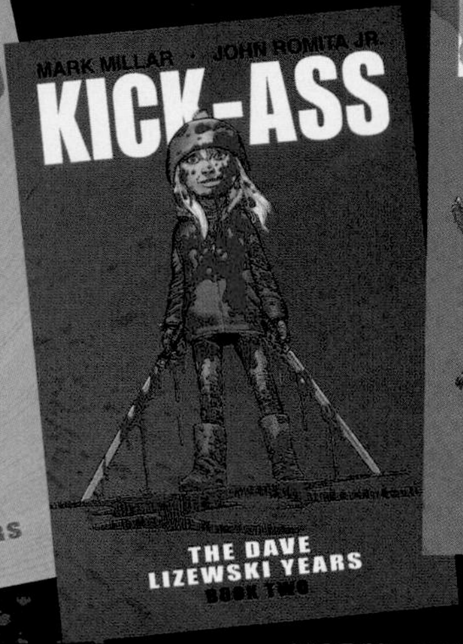
MARK MILLAR • JOHN ROMITA JR.
KICK-ASS
THE DAVE LIZEWSKI YEARS
BOOK TWO

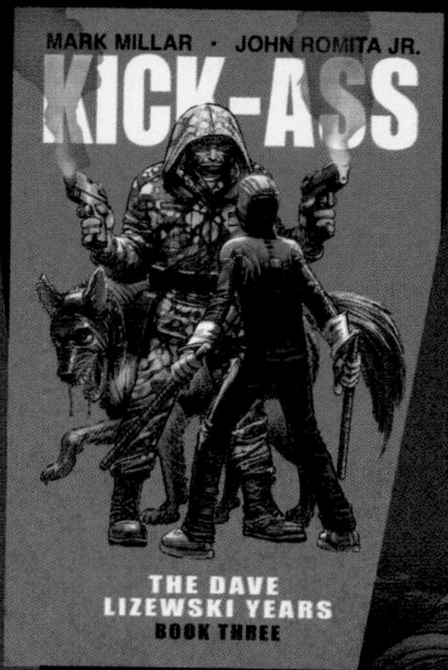
MARK MILLAR • JOHN ROMITA JR.
KICK-ASS
THE DAVE LIZEWSKI YEARS
BOOK THREE

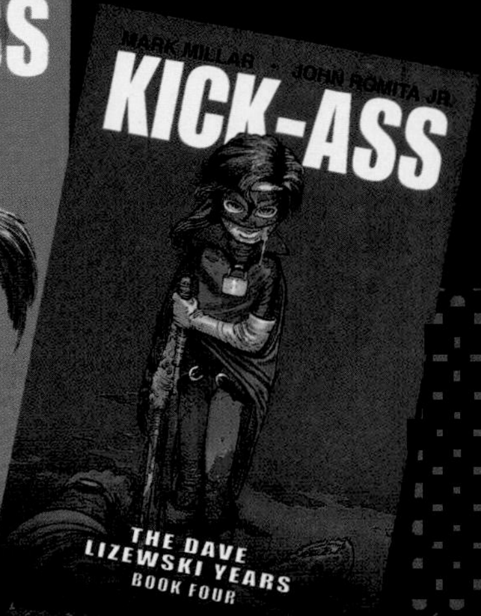
MARK MILLAR • JOHN ROMITA JR.
KICK-ASS
THE DAVE LIZEWSKI YEARS
BOOK FOUR

KICK-ASS: THE DAVE LIZEWSKI YEARS
Vol 1-4

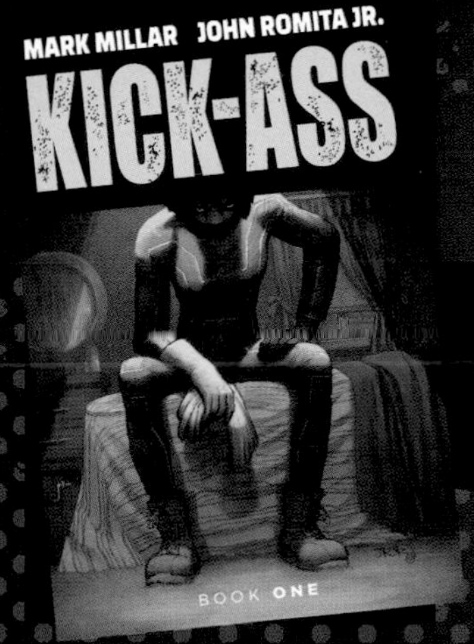
MARK MILLAR JOHN ROMITA JR.
KICK-ASS
BOOK ONE

KICK-ASS: THE NEW GIRL
Vol 1

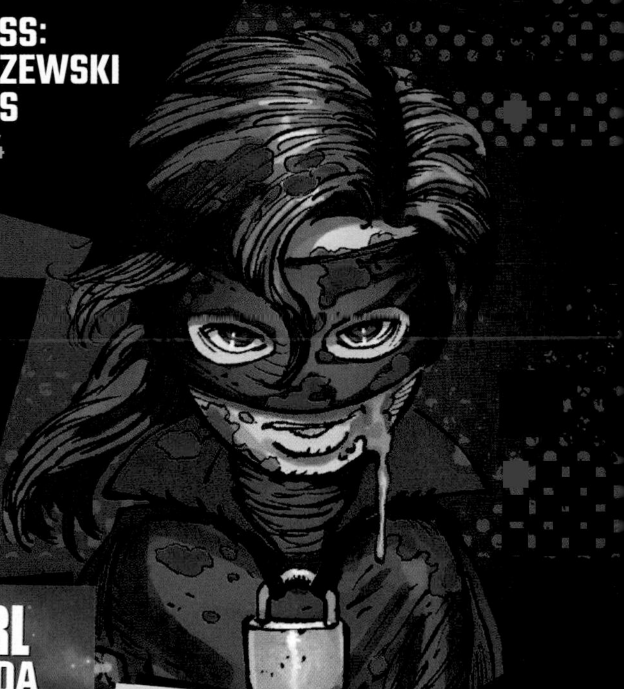

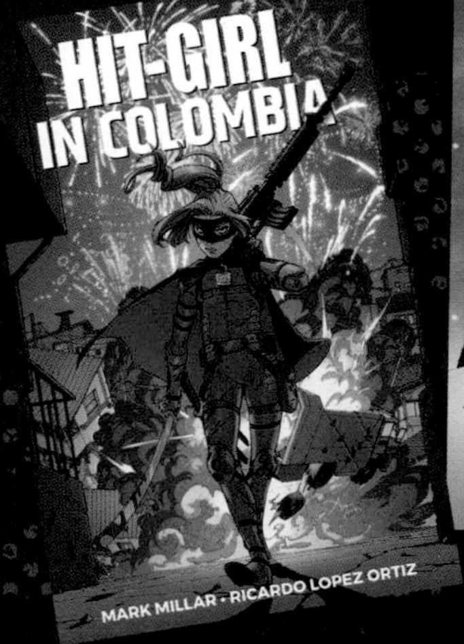
HIT-GIRL
IN COLOMBIA
MARK MILLAR • RICARDO LOPEZ ORTIZ

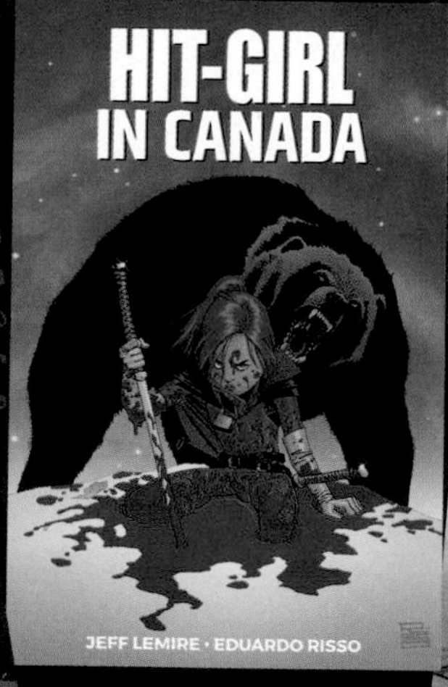
HIT-GIRL
IN CANADA
JEFF LEMIRE • EDUARDO RISSO

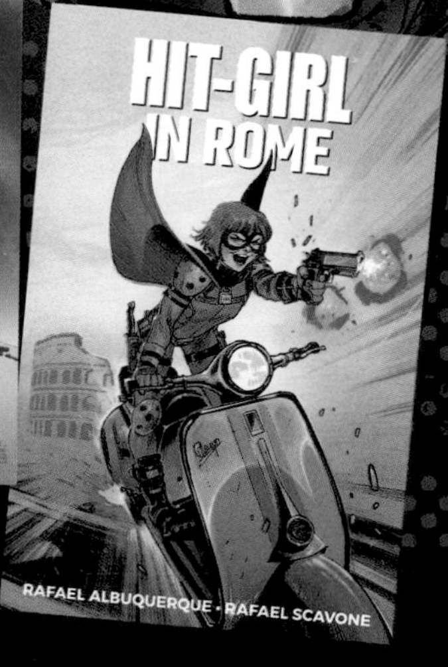
HIT-GIRL
IN ROME
RAFAEL ALBUQUERQUE • RAFAEL SCAVONE

HIT-GIRL
Vol 1-3

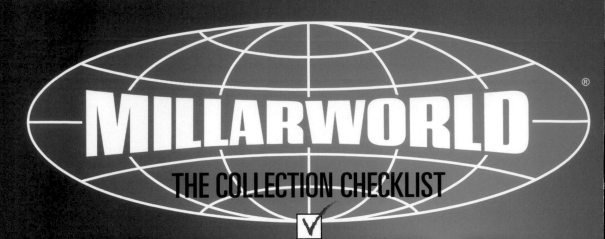

MILLARWORLD®

THE COLLECTION CHECKLIST

EMPRESS
MARK MILLAR
STUART IMMONEN

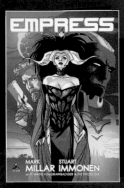

EMPRESS
Art by Stuart Immonen

Huck
MARK MILLAR
RAFAEL ALBUQUERQUE
DAVE McCAIG
BOOK 1
ALL-AMERICAN

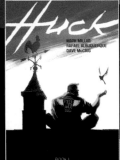

HUCK
Art by Rafael Albuquerque

MILLAR MURPHY
CHRONONAUTS
#1
$3.50

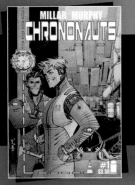

CHRONONAUTS
Art by Sean Gordon Murphy

MARK MILLAR DUNCAN FEGREDO
MPH

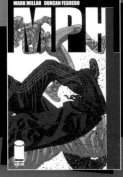

MPH
Art by Duncan Fegredo

MARK MILLAR · GORAN PARLOV
STARLIGHT

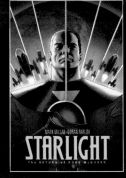

STARLIGHT
Art by Goran Parlov

MILLAR · TORRES · GIANFELICE
JUPITER'S CIRCLE
BOOK ONE

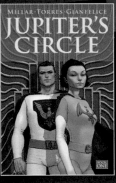

JUPITER'S CIRCLE 1 & 2
Art by Wilfredo Torres

MARK MILLAR · FRANK QUITELY
JUPITER'S LEGACY
BOOK ONE

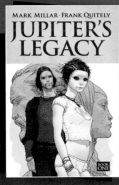

JUPITER'S LEGACY
Art by Frank Quitely

MARK MILLAR LEINIL YU
SUPER CROOKS
THE HEIST

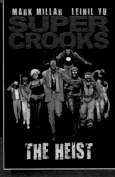

SUPER CROOKS
Art by Leinil Yu

MARK MILLAR & LEINIL YU
SUPERIOR
FROM THE WRITER OF KICK-ASS

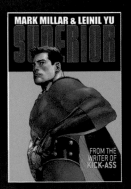

SUPERIOR
Art by Leinil Yu

MILLAR & McNIVEN'S
NEMESIS

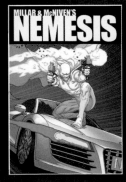

NEMESIS
Art by Steve McNiven

REBORN

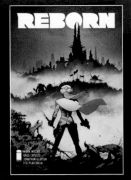

REBORN
Art by Greg Capullo

AMERICAN JESUS
BOOK ONE : CHOSEN
MARK MILLAR ✦ PETER GROSS

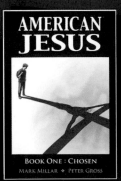

AMERICAN JESUS
Art by Peter Gross

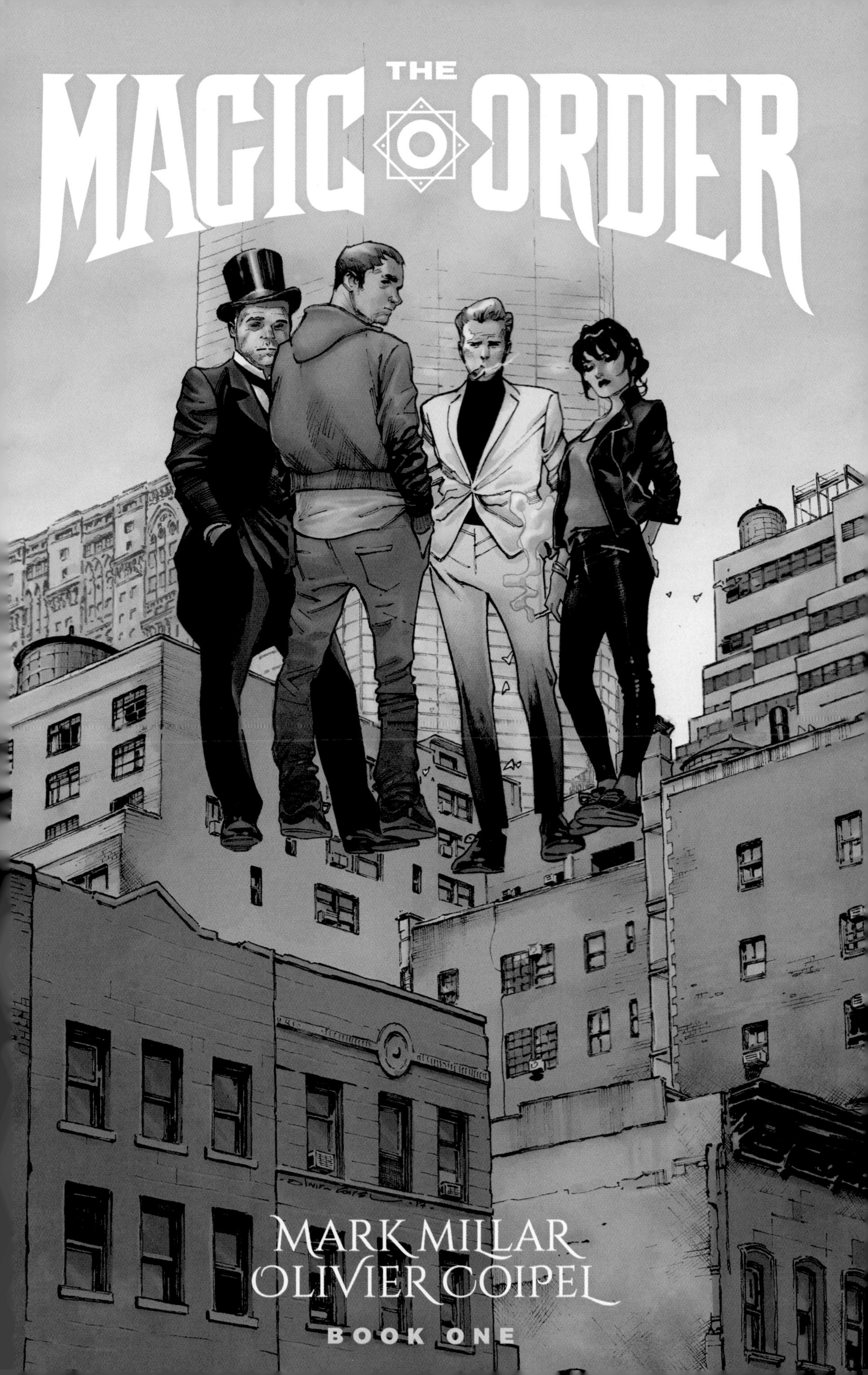
THE
MAGIC ORDER
MARK MILLAR
OLIVIER COIPEL
BOOK ONE

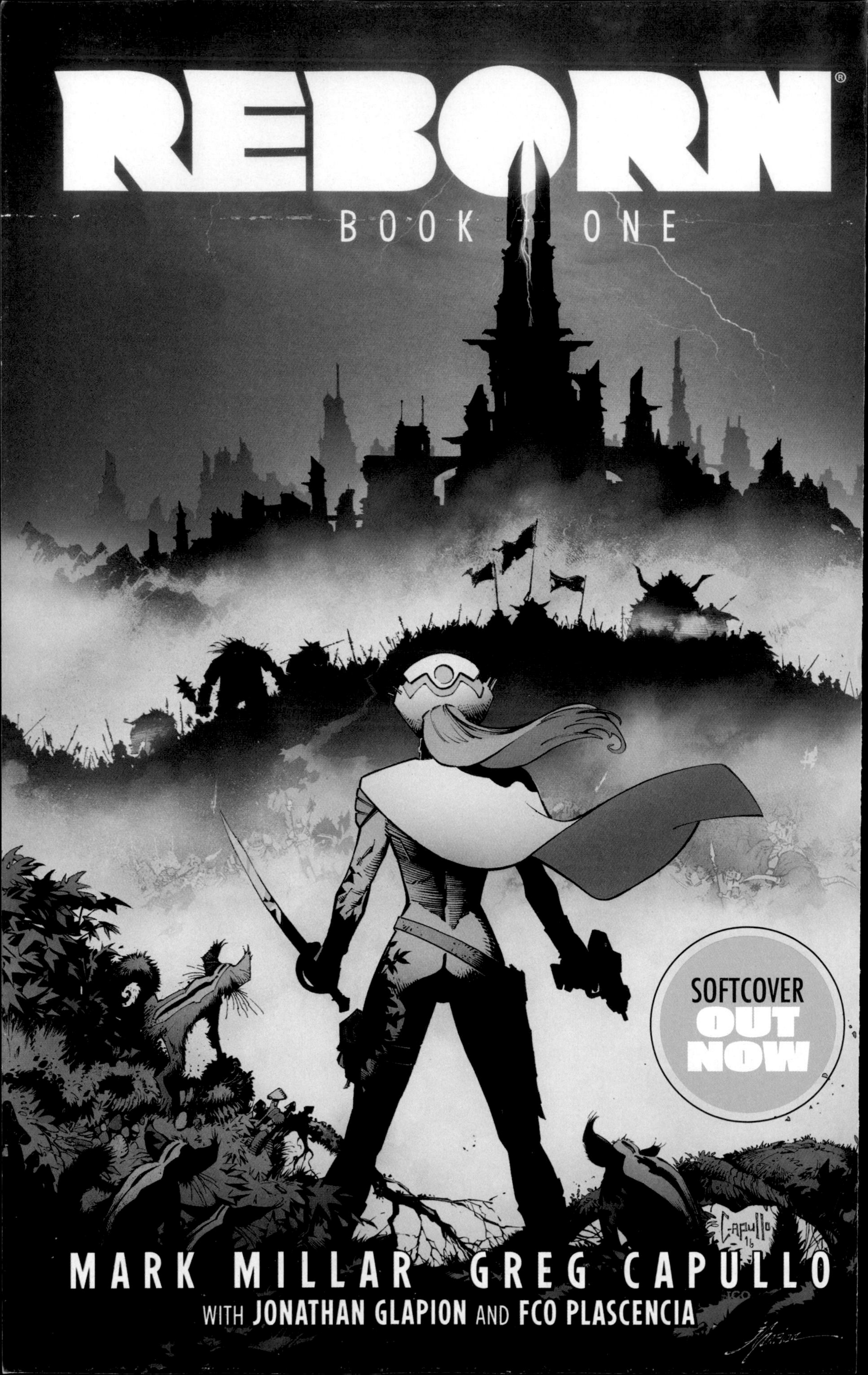

REBORN®
BOOK ONE
SOFTCOVER
OUT NOW
MARK MILLAR GREG CAPULLO
WITH JONATHAN GLAPION AND FCO PLASCENCIA